Interventions is produced on the land of the Wurundjeri people of the Kulin Nation. We acknowledge the Traditional Owners of country throughout Australia and recognise their continuing connection to land, waters and culture. We pay our respects to their Elders past, present and emerging. Their land was stolen, never ceded. It always was and always will be Aboriginal land.

First published 1985 by Stained Wattle Press
2nd edition 2009 by Red Rag Publications
3rd edition 2025 by Interventions Inc

Interventions Inc is a not-for-profit, independent, radical book publisher. For further information:
  www.interventions.org.au
  info@interventions.org.au
  PO Box 24132
  Melbourne VIC 3001

Title: Into the Mainstream: The decline of Australian Communism
Author: Tom O'Lincoln

ISBN: 978-0-6486416-5-0: Paperback
ISBN: 978-0-6486416-6-7: ebook

Cover and interior design and layout of this edition by Stephanie Grigg.

© Tom O'Lincoln 1985

The moral rights of the author have been asserted.
All rights reserved. Except as permitted under the Australian Copyright Act 1968 (for example, a fair dealing for the purposes of study, research, criticism or review), no part of this book may be reproduced, stored in a retrieval system, communicated or transmitted in any form or by any means without prior written permission.

All inquiries should be made to the publisher.

 A catalogue record for this book is available from the National Library of Australia

Into the Mainstream
The Decline of Australian Communism

Tom O'Lincoln

INTERVENTIONS

Dedication

This book is dedicated to the tens of thousands of rank and file members of the Communist Party of Australia who struggled for decades to improve working and living conditions, to resist attacks by the government and employers and to fight for a better world. Despite all the twists and turns of the leadership of the party and its subservience to Moscow, these men and women engaged in strikes and strike support, peace activism, anti-fascist actions and support for Indigenous rights. They marched in the streets and rallied in halls in protest against racism and sexism. They participated in mass movements and small gatherings. In so doing they created a rich history of struggle that activists today continue to rediscover and draw upon.

Tom O'Lincoln interviewed several members of the CPA in writing this book and acknowledged their example in his preface, commenting that many members of the party were among the finest fighters for their class.

Contents

Foreword 2025 Edition	i
Publisher's Preface 2025	ix
Author's Preface	xiii
1 The Fate of a World Movement	1
2 The Rise of Australian Communism	23
3 The Communists on the Offensive	57
4 A Party Besieged	83
5 The Monolith Cracks	113
6 A Revolution in Theory?	143
7 Left Turn, Right Turn: The Party in the 1970s	169
8 Into the Mainstream	209
Abbreviations and Acronyms	231
Endnotes	233
Image Credits	249
Further Reading	253
Index	257
Tom O'Lincoln Legacy Project	263

Foreword 2025 Edition

It is wonderful to see Tom O'Lincoln's *Into the Mainstream* republished 40 years after it first went to print. It is a vitally important book for understanding not only the history of the Communist Party of Australia (CPA) but also the broader labour movement. The CPA developed within this movement, and the party had a strong impact on the trajectory of trade union politics for much of the 20th century. As O'Lincoln's detailed account makes clear, coming to terms with the decline of Australian communism is central for explaining the decline in the power of unions in Australia, a phenomenon far more acutely felt today than it was in 1985.

When O'Lincoln wrote the book, CPA trade union officials were playing a key role in advocating for the Hawke Labor government's Prices and Incomes Accord and organising to bureaucratically enforce the policy on dissenting groups of workers. The Accord was Hawke's grand political strategy to deal with the crisis facing the Australian economy in the early 1980s. While Labor was the main political force driving the strategy, both in the parliament and through the Australian Council of Trade Unions (ACTU), support from the CPA played an important ideological role in selling the Accord and then ensuring that it was not seriously challenged within the union movement. Party leaders could achieve this because of CPA influence in important unions, such as the metal workers, and the loyalty they commanded from a strong network of militant delegates across many industries.

Under the Accord, unions agreed to suspend strike activity in exchange for two presumed benefits: promises of favourable, centrally determined wages and prices; and increases in what they called the 'social wage' through government spending. The implementation of this required ruthless suppression of rank-and-file militancy. In Chapter 8, O'Lincoln called the Accord 'a device to maximise the exploitation of the working-class' and argued that the strategy was already having a disastrous impact on wages and conditions, while the supposed benefits were not materialising. He noted an uncritical CPA conference resolution which indicated that, in September 1982, profits were 11.8 percent of GDP; by December 1983, they were 15.5 percent and were forecast to hit 17 percent by 1984.[1]

In the 40 years since, the share of GDP going to profits has consistently increased. At the time of writing, it is hovering around 30 percent, the highest level in Australia history, while the share going to wages has declined from 58 percent, at the end of the 1970s, to just 44 percent today.[2] O'Lincoln's revolutionary Marxism helps us to understand the key reason for this – a collapse in the self-activity of the working class through its collective organisations. The CPA still had Marxist pretensions at the time they were promoting the Accord. But party leaders had embraced a completely bureaucratic conception of trade unionism and a belief that Australian capitalism could be gradually reformed. They willingly subordinated class struggle to the exigencies of the economy, thereby shackling the capacity of workers to act collectively in their own class interests.

Implementation of the Accord meant demobilising rank-and-file union networks built up over many years and the destruction of a culture of constant activity on the job with which workers could engage to assert their rights. Unsurprisingly, this precipitated a catastrophic decline in union membership. When this book was first published, union membership was just tipping 50 percent of the workforce. It has been in free fall ever since, crashing to close to 12 percent today.[3] The decline that began with the Accord was reinforced by a number of other measures: the destruction of the Builders Labourers' Federation by the Hawke government in 1986; the restrictive industrial regime of Enterprise Bargaining, introduced by the Keating Labor government, also with the support of the ACTU; and further attacks from the Howard Coalition government.

Subsequent Labor governments have perpetuated these attacks, the most recent being placing the construction workers division of the CFMEU under draconian administration in 2024. This is aimed at kneecapping one of the very few unions willing to push at the boundaries of a legal system that now outlaws industrial action outside of a small bargaining window.

Socialists and union activists from my generation have grown up trying to build our campaigns amidst this wreckage. Any serious effort to revive working-class struggle requires an understanding of how things became so dire. The contribution this book makes to this understanding is one reason why it has continuing relevance.

There are other reasons beyond the association between the CPA and the Accord that make *Into the Mainstream* important. The book gives readers like us, who have never experienced a situation when mass politics was a real, consistent feature of working-class life, a window into earlier periods in Australian history when trade unions had a far greater social presence and weight.

In his original preface in 1985, O'Lincoln thanked the activists with long experience in the party interviewed for his book, writing that, while they had been critical of the CPA, 'many pointed out that the party had many achievements to its credit, and that many of its members were among the finest fighters for their class ... I hope that the polemical character of the present work has not obscured this unduly'.

O'Lincoln's critique of the CPA, particularly focused on its leadership, is indeed unrelenting throughout the book. But readers unfamiliar with the history of the important contribution of CPA members to many struggles for justice need to keep in mind that that the polemic is so fierce precisely because the stakes were so high. He was concerned with understanding why the potential embodied in the existence of a mass socialist organisation, claiming the mantle of the Russian Revolution, home for generations to the cream of working-class activists, never fulfilled its revolutionary potential and ended up playing such a rotten role in undermining class power.

We do need to learn from the way CPA members were able to embed themselves in workplaces and communities right across the continent, constantly agitating for and supporting social struggle. Vic Williams, one of the many long-term CPA members interviewed by O'Lincoln, says in the book: 'It didn't matter what happened, if some school committee hit the headlines, you could bet your life there'd be some Communist Party member at the school, and he'd be organising. I used to pick up the paper when I was a Communist Party organiser and I'd be amazed; I'd see all these issues and I knew someone who'd be running them'.

The importance of a serious, outward looking, patient and collaborative practice is emphasised by O'Lincoln in many examples throughout the book. He draws attention to the dangers of sectarianism, with examples of failure to relate to the mass of workers and movement activists who have a reformist consciousness, looking to the Labor party (and, today, some important sections looking to the Greens) as the way to make change.

In his account of the CPA's most militant periods, when the party led unemployed struggles and the Militant Minority Movement (MMM) in the unions the early 1930s, then a serious strike wave in the late 1940s, O'Lincoln demonstrates how unnecessary attacks on sympathetic Labor members and officials aided attempts to isolate the party and undermined the potential to win. And, while O'Lincoln praises the tenacity of Trotskyist groups who 'kept revolutionary Marxism alive during the Stalin period', he also notes that years of isolation had led most to be 'ingrown and sectarian', a danger that still echoes on the left.

At its core, *Into the Mainstream* is a critique of the Stalinist politics that had consolidated within the party leadership by 1930. While CPA cadres did not consciously recognise it, this represented a decisive shift away from revolutionary Marxism, which is grounded in the possibility and necessity of working-class self-emancipation. The party's acceptance of the Stalinist idea that socialism could be delivered 'from above' is central to O'Lincoln's analysis of how the party eventually accommodated completely to Labor and adopted its own brand of reformist politics.

From his arrival in Australia in 1971, O'Lincoln played a crucial role in developing anti-Stalinist Marxist politics, drawing on the tradition of socialism from below associated broadly with the International Socialist tendency.[4] This tendency argues that Stalin's consolidation of bureaucratic power in Russia represented a counter-revolution, ushering in a system of state capitalism. Although the state owned the productive forces, the working class did not control the state; society was subordinated to the logic of capital accumulation and pressure from international competition, leading to alienation and exploitation of workers across the USSR and its satellites.[5]

This clear perspective on the class nature of the Soviet regime, driven by the same imperatives as other capitalist states operating within a global imperialist system, helps O'Lincoln to clearly explain the fortunes of the USSR and the way this impacted on the CPA. After Stalin took power, the Communist International was transformed – from an organisation agitating for worldwide revolution to a network utilised opportunistically by Russia to promote its own foreign policy. Justifying the twists and turns in the Comintern's line required extraordinary political and rhetorical gymnastics from party leaders, transforming Marxism from a tool for serious analysis of reality into a series of phrasebooks that were picked at to justify the latest posture demanded from Moscow. The sophistication of O'Lincoln's own Marxism shines through in his analysis of the way these sharp shifts played out in the particularities of the Australian context, interacting with the ebbs and flows in class conflict and economic development.

Particularly important for O'Lincoln's account is the pressures on the CPA leadership in the post-World War II context, because party members held senior positions in a number of important trade unions. Communist parties in the period immediately following the Russian revolution understood the conservatising tendencies within unionism that develop through holding union office. They knew the need to counter this pressure by ensuring that any Communist officials were subject to the discipline of a democratic revolutionary party driven by a commitment to rank and file initiative as the key transformative force. Stalinism, in contrast, abandoned Marx's central commitment to the self-emancipation of workers for an argument that party leaders in fact embodied the working class; this worked to reinforce inherent tendencies toward bureaucratisation. O'Lincoln convincingly demonstrates the way that Moscow's call to stabilise relations with social democracy in the 1950s consolidated moves already underway in Australia to shore up the CPA's position within the union bureaucracy. It led to an accommodation with Labor and explicit abandonment of a conception of communist organisation aimed at overthrowing state power.

One of the most decisive ways that Stalinism undermined revolutionary politics was the development of the popular front strategy in the mid-1930s. As part of his attempt to form alliances against Nazi Germany, Stalin demanded that Communist Parties across the world cooperate with 'progressive' bourgeois political forces in imperialist heartlands such as Britain, France, the USA and Australia. This saw the Australian party embracing nationalism, mythologising the supposedly democratic popular tendencies of the 'Australian people', rather than opposing Australian nationalism as imperialist, bourgeois ideology. This strategy acted as a conservatising force for the remainder of the party's history. It contained the seeds of the class collaborationist politics that eventually manifested in the Accord, seen by CPA leaders as an attempt to save 'Australian industry' through working-class sacrifice, envisaging a kind of popular front with Australian industrialists against multinational capital.

For much of its history, the CPA's Marxism, while badly distorted, nonetheless did provide basic ideological scaffolding that allowed working-class militants to understand that it was the labour of their class that was the source of all value; that struggle against the boss to gain more of a share was legitimate and necessary; that the courts, police and media served the interests of the capitalist class; and that capitalism as a system led to warfare, colonial oppression and an attempt to use racism to divide workers.

In recent years, there has been a revival of labour history writing focused on recovering some of this militant history, particularly around the important role CPA-led, class-based organisation played in challenging racism, imperialism and colonialism.[6] This has been important in an era of mass Black Lives Matter and Invasion Day marches, the upsurge for Palestinian rights and the context of massive Australian military expansion and deepening integration with US imperialism through the AUKUS partnership. These struggles have posed sharp questions of strategy for many thousands of people; but, in an era of union weakness, the potential power of collective workers' action to offer a real challenge to the system is largely hidden from view.

My own research has focused on the relationship between the trade unions and the movement for Aboriginal and Torres Strait Islander rights in 20th century Australia, where CPA activists played an indispensable role in building solidarity. From its foundations, the party defined itself in opposition to the commitment to White Australia that was hegemonic in the mainstream labour movement. For the next 60 years, party activists played an important role fighting racism in workplaces and communities across the continent. The Darwin CPA branch was formed in 1928 by a group of activists who broke with the ALP specifically over the issue of racism, using early party organisation to challenge the exclusion of Indigenous and other non-European workers from the North Australian Workers' Union.

As the CPA developed a mass base in the unions for the first time in the early 1930s, it used these new networks to wage a mass campaign that stopped a planned massacre in Arnhem Land in September 1933, effectively ending the long period of frontier warfare in Australia.[7] This laid the foundations for a tradition of trade union solidarity with Indigenous struggle that the CPA was vital to maintaining and expanding, contributing in profound ways to all the iconic battles for Indigenous rights, including the Cummeragunja walk-off in 1939, the Pilbara strike in 1946, the battles to break the colour bar across Australia in the 1950s and 60s, the Gurindji walk-off in 1966 and the Black Moratorium and Tent Embassy in 1972.

O'Lincoln does not discuss the CPA's activities against racism in this book in any detail, but it is nonetheless a very important resource for historians seeking to understand the party's broader operations, along with the weaknesses and limitations of its perspective in any given period. The anti-Labor sectarianism of the MMM helps explain why the party's first wave of Black rights campaigning failed to establish deeper roots and grow. And the embrace of Australian nationalism during the Popular Front period contributed to a residual paternalism amongst the party leadership that stifled the full potential of many promising initiatives in the following decades.

Since its original publication, *Into the Mainstream*, with its comprehensive critique of Stalinism in Australia and rich historical detail, has helped educate a generation of socialist activists. This new edition will hopefully bring the book to the attention of many more who are horrified by the carnage of imperialist wars and the way capitalism is causing deep ecological crises and many other injustices, and who are trying to understand how we can make change.

Padraic Gibson
October 2024

Publisher's Preface 2025

Into the Mainstream was first published in 1985. It was Tom O'Lincoln's first book and demonstrates how early he started to think and write about what he saw as gaps in Australian radical history. The final deterioration of the Communist Party of Australia was going on before his eyes. While he was never sympathetic to the Stalinist content of its history, Tom had for some time been fascinated by the important struggles many of its members had engaged in in the 1930s and after World War II. He wrote about several of them, most noticeably a study of the Militant Minority Movement which was published as a pamphlet by Socialist Action in 1986. This piece about Communist work in the trade unions remains an important source for anyone interested in a rank-and-file strategy. This piece is included in the final book by Tom, an anthology of essays published in 2015.[1]

Tom interviewed a number of people in the course of writing the present book, and his comment in the preface to the second edition shows that, despite his criticisms of the party's development, he valued this history. Today, we all continue to draw on the experience of the party and the leading role of many sincere and dedicated members in many struggles over decades.

But is this book, written nearly 40 years ago, still useful today? Given how many books on the topic were already available in 1985 and the number of important new studies that have been published in the interim, is it more than a historical document? Rick Kuhn commented on the importance of *Into the Mainstream* in 2016:

Drawing on primary and secondary sources, in a series of publications culminating in his book *Into the Mainstream*, Tom articulated a systematic historical assessment and critique of the CPA. Its explanations of the Party's character, especially its role in the working class, and course as a Stalinist organisation are superior to others in this comparatively crowded field. Although the CPA implemented the Moscow line from the early 1930s to the 1960s, often to the detriment of workers' interests, it still attracted a layer of impressive militants and led or played a significant role in major industrial and social struggles. The book's account and analysis of the Party as it adopted a conventional social democratic politics, between the mid 1960s and its demise, is easily the best that has been written.[2]

Certainly, *Into the Mainstream* was never short of an audience; it sold steadily over the 20 years after publication of the first edition, and a second edition was published in 2005 with the support of Vulgar Press and the Jeff Goldhar Project.

And now in 2025, another 20 years later, as part of the Tom O'Lincoln Project, we can present a third edition. The present publication is an enhanced version, with a new modern design, using digital technology and print-on-demand so that the book will never go out of print. The new edition follows the previous editions very closely but has been edited to meet Interventions' style guide and includes some minor edits to improve flow and readability. A major enhancement is the inclusion of a selection of images, many of which come from the pages of *Tribune* with the permission of the Search Foundation.

Another significant enhancement is the inclusion of a new Foreword, written by Paddy Gibson, to introduce the book to contemporary readers and comment on its continuing relevance.

With this book having been written originally using 1980s technology (hand-written notes and a typewriter), there are a couple of technical issues that we have been unable to correct. In the earlier editions, most of the references did not include the publisher. The editorial team decided not to spend time rectifying this. In addition, five references had been lost. Suitable substitutes could be found for three, but two references remain missing or incomplete in Chapter 4.

Tom acknowledged many people for advice, criticism and help with the initial writing of the book and the two published editions during his lifetime. More must be added for this third edition. Collectively, they include Megan Conlin, Phil Griffiths, Stephanie Grigg, Eris Harrison, Vik Ivanova, Phil Lee, Tess Lee Ack, Janey Stone, Ian Syson and Vulgar Press, Vic Williams and all who agreed to be interviewed, and Phillip Whitefield.

Let Tom O'Lincoln have the final word for this new edition:

> The Communist Party is long gone, yet *Into the Mainstream* retains a following. I think that's because left activists feel a need to know how to avoid the mistakes that wrecked this important political movement, as a starting point for discussing how to build something new. The Communists set out to create a better world; and today, we need that as much as ever.

Author's Preface

This essay is about the fate of the Communist Party of Australia.[1]

Still a monolithic Stalinist party of some strength in the late 1940s, it was transformed by the postwar decades. It rejected Stalinism but was unable to replace it with a coherent political alternative. By 1985, it had declined into a confused and demoralised rump.

Most commentators welcomed the political changes when they occurred, arguing that the CPA's break with Stalinism was a historic step forward. A minority deplored them, contending that the party was abandoning a socialist vision in favour of trendyism, opportunism and reformism. By and large, the debate over the party's postwar development was conducted between these two poles.

I argued for a third perspective. Stalinism was an odious political tradition and had also become unviable in the postwar era. Its claims to embody a socialist vision were a sham. However, in turning away from Stalinism, the CPA had embraced liberal and reformist ideas that were no real improvement. Few among its members were interested in a revival of the revolutionary traditions of Marx, Lenin or Trotsky. Fewer still were attracted by the revolutionary socialist strategies that far-left activists like me offered as a road forward in contemporary Australia.

Yet, without a return to revolutionary Marxism, the Communist Party could only end up liquidating itself into mainstream capitalist politics. This book traces the complex process by which it moved toward that end.

By the time *Into the Mainstream* first appeared in 1985, the party had taken steps that effectively sealed its fate.

A majority of the Victorian branch had formed a new group called Socialist Forum, most of whose members eventually (as I foreshadowed) joined the Labor Party. The majority nationally was already looking to form a broader New Left Party, but this lasted only a few years (1989 to 1993). The party itself survived on paper until 1995, by which time it had transferred its resources to the Search Foundation, which continues to support left-of-centre endeavours. For practical purposes, the party's life ended in 1991 – around the same time that Mikhail Gorbachev presided over the collapse of the Soviet Union.

In keeping with my basic thesis, the treatment of the process in this book is often quite polemical. The first two chapters are brief sketches, providing essential international and historical background. The main argument begins in Chapter 3, which considers the Communists' attempt to take the offensive in the late 1940s. They soon found themselves on the defensive in the 1950s, an experience discussed in Chapter 4, and then entered a period of fragmentation and confusion in the 1960s (Chapter 5). The 1960s were also a time of attempted theoretical renewal, and Chapter 6 considers this process. Chapter 7 looks at the party's short-lived lurch to the left in the early 1970s and its subsequent drift back to the right over the remainder of the decade. Finally, in Chapter 8, we see the party move towards its final resting place in the political mainstream.

I will always be grateful to those who consented to be interviewed. Many of them stressed that, in doing so, they didn't wish to be thought to have rejected the entire CPA experience. Vic Williams particularly emphasised this. They pointed out that the party had many achievements to its credit and that many of its members were among the finest working class fighters. It is a sentiment with which I sympathise, and I hope that the book's polemical nature hasn't obscured it unduly.

The Communist Party is long gone, yet *Into the Mainstream* retains a following. I think that's because left activists feel a need to know how to avoid the mistakes that wrecked this important political movement, as a starting point for discussing how to build something new. The Communists set out to create a better world; and today, we need that as much as ever.

Tom O'Lincoln,
April 1985 and March 2009

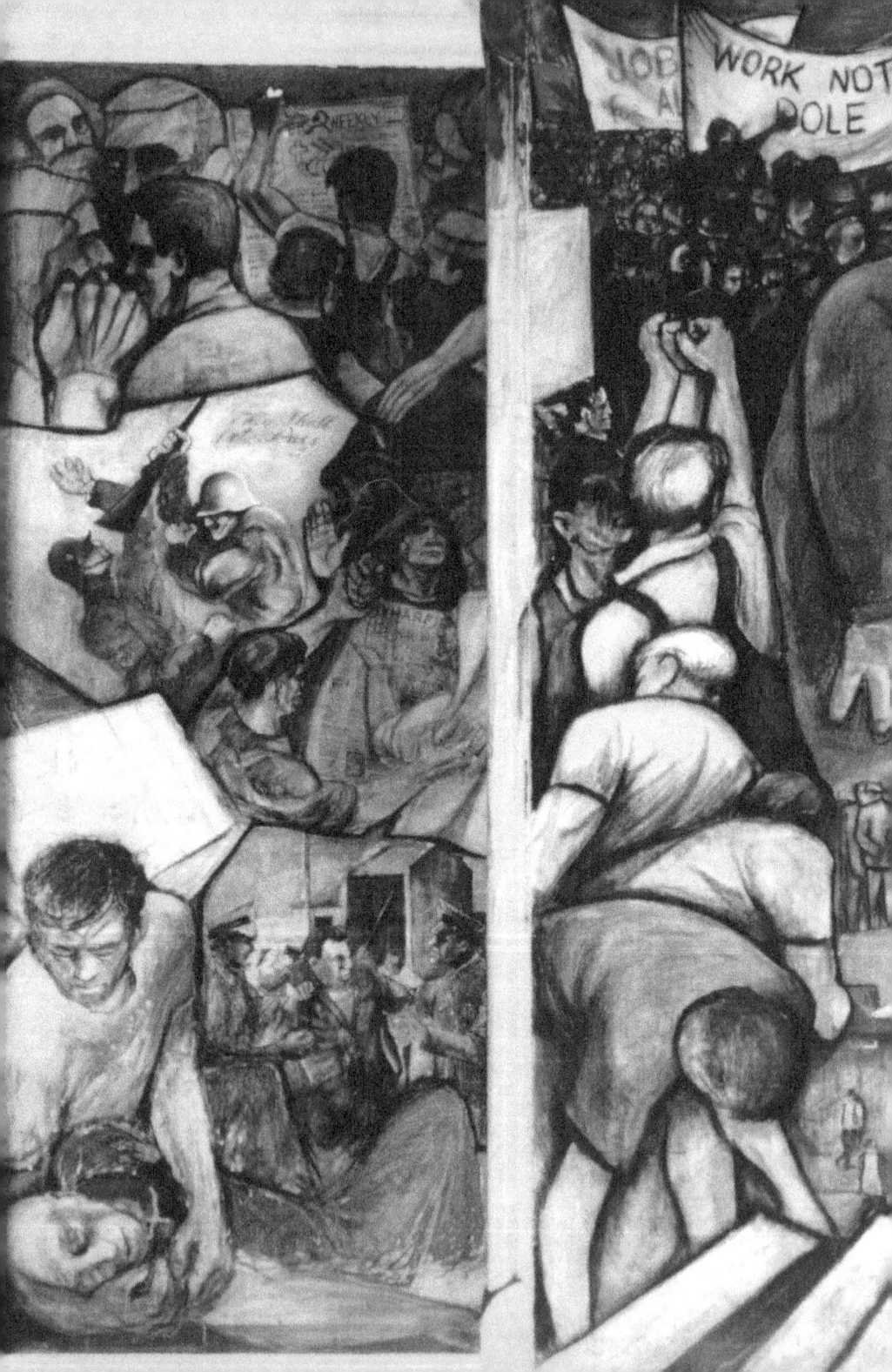

Previous page: Mural of waterside and labour history from the Waterside Workers' Federation's headquarters Sydney. Displayed are police confrontations on the wharves, Henry Lawson, wharfies' leader Jim Healy, Newcastle coal union leader Peter Bowling, the eight hour day struggle, the dole queue, conscription, both world wars, the Communist Party, Spanish Civil War and the fight against fascism. Many of the artists worked as wharfies; they include Rod Shaw, Sonny Glynn, Vi Collings, Clem Millward, Ralph Sawyer, Pat Graham and Evelyn Healy. Now at the Australian National Maritime Museum, Sydney.

1
The Fate of a World Movement

> Lenin's internationalism is not a formula for harmonising national and international interests in empty verbiage. It is a guide to revolutionary action embracing all nations. Our planet, inhabited by so-called civilised humanity, is considered as one single battle-field where various nations and social classes contend.
>
> *Leon Trotsky*[1]

Communists have always called upon the workers of the world to unite. It is undoubtedly the most famous thing Karl Marx ever said, and few who claimed to stand in his tradition have failed to repeat it.

Still, slogans are one thing, practice another. Marx himself lived in a time when capitalism was still a young and expanding system, achieving economic and social progress in one country after another. And it was doing so on a national basis. Industrial economies arose, agriculture was modernised, political democracy triumphed in much of Europe, and the key social and political structure associated with these changes was the nation state. The labour movement grew up on a national basis as well.

Marx sought to unify the workers across national barriers, with episodic success, but he was unable to build an ongoing mass movement which did so. The International Workingmen's Association, or 'First International', was a step towards such a thing, but it was never much more than a ramshackle federation of national organisations – ranging from the conservative British trade unions to the anarchists of southern Europe.

2 INTO THE MAINSTREAM

Founding conference of the International Workingmen's Association (First International) 1864.

The Second International, in its turn, grew up as a federation of national parties. It was capable of passing grand resolutions about fraternal unity; but, when World War I put it to the test, all its national sections endorsed the war effort of their own bourgeoisie. The workers were sent by their leaders to slaughter each other on the battlefield. The international solidarity of the proletariat was exposed as something of a myth.

It might have seemed audacious indeed, then, for Lenin and the Russian Bolsheviks to attempt to launch a Third, or Communist, International on 4 March 1919. Yet, the new movement's founders were convinced that, for the first time, the workers of the world might truly be united in struggle. The project was not based on abstract sentiment but on the analysis Lenin and his followers made of their own revolution, its international significance and the development of capitalism in their own time.

By the turn of the century, the prospects for any more nations to achieve industrial development were becoming increasingly poor. The industrial powers that already existed were carving up the world and sewing up the world market. They could so dominate the terms of trade that it was more and more difficult for new nations to join the industrial 'club'. Japan and Germany had just managed to do so, but only with extensive government intervention in their economies. In much of the world, moreover, direct colonial rule choked off any chance of independent economic development.

Further, by the turn of the century, capitalism as a whole was reaching the limits of a historic period of expansion. A tendency for profit rates to fall, which Marx had pointed to as a feature of capitalist crisis, was making itself felt throughout the world system in the first two decades of the new century. Expansion to new markets and sources of labour, which had staved off the problem for a time, was becoming more and more difficult once the great powers had completed their division of the world at the turn of the century.

Lenin concluded that solutions to the major problems confronting humanity – class oppression in the West, national and class oppression in the rest of the world – could not be achieved within individual nations, nor within a capitalist framework. The path forward for humanity was social transformation on a world scale, and the agency was the revolutionary proletariat.

In 1914, when he first addressed this message to any listeners among a labour movement disoriented by the World War, only a handful of revolutionaries supported him. Yet, by 1919, he had an audience of millions. Nationalism had been discredited by the war, as had the old, nationally limited socialist parties who had led the working class into the slaughter. And the war had led to revolution in Russia, making the Russian Bolsheviks an attractive model for militant workers everywhere.

Lenin, May, 1920. Note Trotsky standing at the foot of the podium on the right.

4 INTO THE MAINSTREAM

Founding conference of the Communist International (Comintern), March 1919.

The possibility existed of building a world movement based on the politics of Bolshevism. Lenin considered this not only important but absolutely necessary. Although the Bolsheviks held state power within the borders of a single nation, they did not believe that they could maintain that power, let alone solve the terrible economic and social problems of Russia, within those national limits. Lenin argued that only an international revolution could save the Bolshevik regime from eventual collapse.

He was adamant on this point. Eight months before the revolution, he had written: 'the Russian proletariat cannot by its own forces victoriously complete the socialist revolution'. Four months after it, he said: 'the absolute truth is that without a revolution in Germany, we shall perish'. A year later, he wrote: 'the existence of the Soviet republic side by side with imperialist powers for any length of time is inconceivable'.[2]

The formation of the Communist International was thus a matter of urgency. At the beginning, its prospects looked hopeful, because it was formed amid a wave of revolutionary struggles across Europe which reached insurrectionary proportions in centres such as Berlin, Munich and Budapest. Important sections of the European labour parties came over to the new movement, and the 'Comintern' bound them together into a single world party with a centralist structure.

The centralism was not, in those days, an obstacle to democracy. Extensive debates on major issues – union work, parliamentarism, relations with non-communist workers, national liberation struggles – took place, where Bolshevik views were openly challenged by leaders of such stature as Sylvia Pankhurst, Anton Pannekoek and Amadeo Bordiga.

The Stalinisation of the International

This wave of working-class radicalism declined by 1921, and the last serious attempt at a revolution in Germany was defeated in 1923, leaving only a single revolutionary party in power: the Bolsheviks. It was a situation that Lenin, who expected the leading role of the Russians in the Comintern to be temporary, had not anticipated:

> Leadership in the revolutionary proletarian International has passed for a time – for a short time it goes without saying – to the Russians.[3]

> It would ... be erroneous to lose sight of the fact that, soon after the victory of the proletarian revolution in at least one of the advanced countries, a sharp change will probably come about: Russia will cease to be the model and will once again become a backward country[4]

But, with the ebb of the European revolution, Bolshevik leadership within the world movement became permanent and entrenched. This brought with it grave problems.

The Bolsheviks were struggling to hold together an embattled workers' state at home, to cope with the ravages of civil war. They had few resources to devote to leading the vast international movement they had created. Moreover, Russia was a backward country, its working class small and further reduced by civil war. How could it lead a movement based on the large and culturally advanced working classes of Western Europe? Lenin noted the problem as early as 1921. Discussing a Comintern resolution, he wrote:

> The resolution is an excellent one, but it is almost entirely Russian, that is to say, everything in it is based on Russian

conditions. This is its good point but it is also its failing. It is its failing because I am sure that no foreigner can read it ... and ... if by way of exception some foreigner does understand it, he cannot carry it out ... we have not learnt how to present our Russian experience to foreigners.[5]

Russian leadership was, therefore, a distortion from the start; but, while the Soviet regime continued to place world revolution at the centre of its perspective, it was not a fatal one. In the mid-1920s, however, the internationalist perspective was gradually abandoned.

With the ebb of revolution in Europe, the prospects for salvation from the West for the embattled Soviets appeared increasingly doubtful. Within Russia, the state bureaucracy under Stalin's leadership gradually strengthened its grip on society. This bureaucracy was interested in its own power and privileges, which could only be jeopardised by new workers' revolutions abroad. Stalin began to develop a new theory, according to which Russia could build 'socialism in a single country'.

What did 'socialism in a single country' mean in practice? In Russia, which had not even completed the capitalist stage of economic development, it meant the ruthless accumulation of capital by the state and the ruthless exploitation of the workers and peasants in the interest of industrial development. To achieve these ends, a powerful repressive apparatus emerged.

Trotsky charged that the revolution had been 'betrayed': more accurately, it had been transformed into its opposite by the pressures of political and economic reality. Lenin had been proved both right and wrong. Right, in saying that the revolution could not survive unless it spread to the West; wrong, in saying that no country could achieve an industrial transformation on a national basis in the age of imperialism. The Russian workers' state gave way to a dynamic state capitalism, which industrialised the society at the workers' expense.

Abroad, 'socialism in a single country' meant the subordination of the Communist Parties (CP) to the national interest of the Soviet bureaucracy. The Chinese party was instructed to place its faith in Chiang Kai-shek because Chiang was Stalin's ally. It did so, agreeing even to disarm itself after seizing the city of Shanghai on his behalf, only to have Chiang turn on the Communists and massacre them. The British party was tied to the left wing of the trade union

The Communist, May Day edition, 27 April, 1923

bureaucracy, because Moscow wanted to use the 'Anglo-Soviet Trade Union Committee' to pursue its own diplomatic ends. The consequence was to give the more left-wing officials a radical image they did not really deserve and to build illusions in the Trades Union Congress as a whole (the Communist Party of Great Britain (CPGB) slogan was 'all power to the General Council'). In the 1926 General Strike, these illusions were to be cruelly shattered; worse, because they half shared them, the Communists were unable to provide a coherent revolutionary alternative to the official leadership of the struggle.

When Stalin made an all-out attempt to industrialise Russia in the period from 1928 to 1934, the CPs were instructed to launch a frontal offensive against the bourgeoisie and also against the social democrats, who were denounced as tools of the bourgeoisie. Within the International, Stalin had to carry out a purge to ensure subservience to this radical turn in policy:

> Of the 275 persons at various times elected to leading bodies of the International, not a single one was elected at all seven Congresses held between 1919 and 1935, nor even at six out of the seven. Of the five members of the 'small bureau' elected by the

Executive Committee after the Second Congress in 1920, only one – Alfred Rosmer, pioneer Trotskyist – physically survived the purges of the thirties.[6]

The sudden left turn involved a number of suicidal actions – most disastrously, the theory of 'social fascism', according to which the social democratic and labour parties were the left wing of fascism itself. Such an orientation made unity against the real fascist threat impossible, paving the way for Hitler to take power over the bodies of a divided labour movement.

The German debacle led to a major new stage in Comintern policy. Georgii Dimitrov elaborated the so-called 'United Front Against Fascism', soon to become the Popular Front, which called for an alliance with the 'democratic' or 'patriotic' bourgeoisie – i.e., that section of the capitalist class that was prepared to oppose fascism, at least for the moment. The aims of the alliance were to fight fascism and defend bourgeois democracy, and the struggle for socialism was separate from these aims and explicitly postponed to a later stage.

To a *tactical* alliance against the common foe, no reasonable person could object. However, the Popular Front quickly emerged as a policy of subordinating the class struggle to what became a long-term alliance. In their efforts to woo the bourgeoisie, the one-time internationalists of the CPs indulged in enthusiastic patriotism: in France, they sang the *Marseillaise* and waved the tricolour; in the USA, they carried pictures of Lenin and George Washington side by side. Even more seriously: they began to oppose strikes, and working-class militancy generally, for fear of upsetting the alliance with sections of the bourgeoisie.

In France, the Popular Front formed a government, supported by a coalition of the Socialists, the CP, the Radicals and even the association of 'Masonic Employers'. It was quickly put to the test by a massive strike wave. The new government opposed the strikes. The CP, which had put forward the accurate slogan, 'the Popular Front is not the revolution', told the strikers: 'The present situation ... cannot be protracted without danger to the security of the people of France.'

Looking back with pride on this dismal episode, CP leader Thorez later commented: 'The Communist Party had the courage to proclaim: it is necessary to know how to end a strike.'[7]

In the same year, the Spanish Popular Front swept to power on the crest of a wave of grassroots struggle. A fascist revolt led by Francisco Franco set out to crush this upheaval but was thrown back in sections of the country by a virtual insurrection of the workers and peasants. The country was plunged into a civil war, in which the USSR supplied aid to the anti-fascist forces – but at a price. The Spanish CP, originally a very small organisation, was able to use its Soviet connections to transform itself into a major force. Aided by the Russian secret police, it led moves to liquidate workers' organisations which refused to subordinate the class struggle to the alliance with pro-Republican sections of the bourgeoisie. Countless revolutionaries were killed and organisations to the left of the CP eventually smashed. The result was a fatal weakening of the one force that could have defeated Franco: the independent struggles of the working class.[8]

The Popular Front was suspended in 1939–40, when Stalin concluded his non-aggression pact with Hitler. For a brief interlude, the CPs were instructed to wage struggles of every sort, and British and French preparations for war were vigorously denounced. However, the strategy was renewed with a vengeance once Germany invaded the USSR; Stalin once again sought an alliance with the Western powers.

During World War II, the CPs everywhere restrained workers' struggles. The war was the most extreme form of the Popular Front – an explicit alliance with the Western ruling classes against Hitler – and therefore demanded the most severe dampening of the class struggle, through no-strike pledges and the like. The CPs defended this policy on the grounds that stopping fascism was an overriding priority, and many workers supported them in this view. Yet, *after* the war, with fascism totally defeated, every effort was still made to continue the wartime collaboration with the bourgeoisie. In 1945, when Churchill proposed a postwar coalition with Labour, the British Communist press headlined the story: *'All-Party National Government is Essential After the Election.'*[9]

The French party raised the slogan, 'One State, one Army, one Police Force',[10] and CP deputies in the Assembly voted for a resolution praising the role of French forces in Indochina.[11]

The basis of Stalinist mass support

The role of the CPs in the period from the late 1920s through to the postwar period, the years 1928–34 apart, was designed first and foremost to effect an alliance between Moscow and the CPs, on the one hand, and the social democrats and sections of the bourgeoisie on the other. The independent struggles of the working class were subordinated to that end. The CPs had become faithful agents of Soviet foreign policy. Why?

It is not hard to see why Moscow wanted foreign agents. But why should mass workers' parties, embodying a fair proportion of the working class vanguard, be content to play this role for an entire historical period? Most writers on this question suggests that the millions of Communists, many of them working-class leaders, were essentially morons who could be manipulated by any clever commissar. It is important to dispel this elitist myth.

The strong attraction that so many workers – not only Communists – felt for Russia had a sound basis at first. Russia, as the home of the first workers' revolution, was subject to the most vicious attacks from capitalist governments and newspapers. Militant workers naturally learned to rally to the defence of the Soviet regime and to reject horror stories about it circulated by establishment sources.

With the rise of Stalin, the revolution was lost, and a regime of terror was imposed. But reports about this terror were, quite understandably, seen by militants as a mere continuation of the same old slanders. Communists in most countries now had over a decade's experience of being lied about by the same sources. Why believe what they said about Russia now?

In the 1940s, wide sections of Western society were enthusiastic about the role played by the Soviet Union in the war, and the CPs recruited massively on this basis. In the postwar period, Communist governments came to power in one-third of the world, replacing fascist and other vile regimes and beginning reconstruction.

If the Western daily press published horror stories about the new societies, it made little impact on many militant workers. They only concluded that the bosses were up to their usual lying tricks and that defence of the 'socialist bloc' was an urgent priority.

As for the policies that emanated from Moscow, they all seemed to have a certain logic. This even applies, up to a point, to the insane ultraleftism of the period 1928–34. As part of his policy of frontal offensive for the CPs, Stalin announced that the labour and social democratic parties were 'social fascist', to be attacked like the bourgeoisie. This approach was exceptionally destructive, and many militants knew it. But the reason that it could be sold at all to the rank and file of the CPs was that, to some extent, it reflected real experience.

The CPs had been formed through splits in the social democratic parties, and Communist militants retained feelings of hostility to social democracy. It was the social democratic parties who had led the workers into World War I, it was they who had stifled the revolutionary upheavals that followed the war, and it was they who had murdered Rosa Luxemburg and Karl Liebknecht. To Communists who knew of all that, the description 'social fascist' could have a certain appeal.

The strategies that went with it divided the German working class and led to the triumph of Hitler, so Communists everywhere began to question it. But, right at this point, the Comintern itself took a new turn to the Popular Front.

The Popular Front meant collaboration with a section of the capitalist class, but that did not seem entirely unreasonable to the many militants for whom Hitlerite fascism appeared as a terrible danger, overriding other considerations. In the aftermath of Hitler's defeat, the rise to power of Communist regimes in a dozen countries seemed a triumphant vindication of the policy.

It is true that various twists and turns of Soviet policy over the years caused unease among the rank and file. Partly, the unease was contained within bureaucratic structures, which we will examine in another chapter. It was also partly contained by a sophisticated ideological smokescreen. This, too, will be examined later. But there was another important factor. Workers felt a strong loyalty to their party, even if they were uneasy about its policies. This is often dismissed by writers as a blind faith, but the reality is more complex.

Intellectuals (including many writers of Communist history) are generally trained to think in individual terms; moreover, society gives them the opportunity to make good on the basis of their individual achievement. Workers, by contrast, must more often rely on solidarity to accomplish their goals. This solidarity tends to take an organisational form, often that of a political party. Building a party demands struggle and sacrifice; so, once it is built, workers are reluctant to abandon it. James Cannon, a US Communist leader who did abandon his party to support Trotsky, explained workers' party loyalty:

> An intellectual dilettante is capable of joining a party without attaching any great significance to such an action, and of leaving it at the first disagreement ... The worker, on the other hand, who as a rule will not join a party unless he means business, will not leave it at the first disappointment or when the first doubt enters his mind. No, the worker clings to his party and supports it until all his confidence and hopes in it are exhausted. This is the great factor which underlies the extraordinary tenacity with which thousands of militant workers stick to the Communist Party. Superficial intellectuals are inclined to regard these workers as incurable idiots. Not so. This sentiment of seriousness, devotion, sacrifice, tenacity – horribly abused and betrayed by the Stalinist fakers – is a sentiment that in its essence is profoundly revolutionary.[12]

The dedication of the CP rank and file was also strengthened by the conditions that workers faced. They had been battered by repeated defeats, and they faced devastating levels of unemployment during the 1930s. From the vantage point of the crisis-ridden capitalist West, the successes of Soviet industry seemed impressive. And, to workers who felt rather powerless in the face of very difficult economic conditions, Stalinist dogma offered some of the consolations of religion. Religion, Marx had once commented, was the 'sigh of the oppressed creature'. To workers who lacked confidence in their own ability to change the world, Stalinism played that role. Rank-and-file Communists came to believe that their parties were the anointed agents of history, as Arthur Koestler explained:

> You could resign from a club and from the ordinary sort of party if its policy no longer suited you; but the Communist Party was something entirely different; it was the vanguard of the Proletariat, the incarnation of the will of History itself. Once you stepped out of it you were *extra muros* and nothing which you said or did had the slightest chance of influencing its course.[13]

Postwar militancy

Such a triumphant view of the party's historic role appeared tenable for a short time after World War II. Hadn't Communism triumphed in a dozen countries? Wasn't the Soviet Union becoming a major world power? Weren't the parties in the West growing in strength?

But the immediate postwar period was a historic high point of the world movement. From that point, it began to fragment. The parties began a historic decline in some countries but retained their mass character in others. But, all over the Western world, they began to be transformed politically and organisationally.

The war was followed by a short, balmy period of East–West détente, during which neither Russia nor the USA wished to start hostilities. Russia was recovering from the effects of the war, while the USA was busily engaged in extending its economic penetration throughout the West. During this period, the wartime Popular Front was maintained. The CPs were able to enter coalition governments in France, Austria, Belgium, Iceland, Italy, Chile and Finland. Wherever they were in government, they maintained a pattern of support for more production and opposition to strikes.

Yet it was a time of ferment among the working class. After the sacrifice of the war period, workers everywhere waged intense class struggles, most notably in Italy, where the end of the war led to the seizure of Milan and Turin by organised workers. The CPs, however, helped the bourgeoisie to ride out the storm. The Italian CP leader Togliatti collaborated with the allies in disarming the workers; in France, Thorez lectured workers on labour discipline; and in Britain, when troops were used to break a go-slow on the Surrey docks, the *Daily Worker* simply reported the events without comment. The détente between Russia and the West was the central concern of the parties; the class struggle would have to wait.

But the uneasy international peace could not last. Notwithstanding Cold War rhetoric, neither side had actually set itself the goal of world conquest; but neither Russia nor the USA was satisfied with the way the world had been divided up at Yalta and Tehran. In 1947, President Truman announced the 'Truman Doctrine', aimed at containment of Communism. In the same year, the Marshall Plan was announced. The USA would pump economic aid into Europe, but it would do so at the price of political subservience. As part of the deal, CP ministers were to be ejected from European governments.

Stalin responded vigorously, moving firstly to tighten up Soviet control in Eastern Europe.

Throughout Eastern Europe, the CPs had remained in coalition with social democrats and others, and much of industry had remained in private hands. Now, industry was nationalised, and the CPs tightened their grip on state power. In Czechoslovakia, a carefully controlled mobilisation of the workers was used to force the non-Communists out of government. Elsewhere, the mere presence of Soviet troops was enough to discourage resistance.[14]

The Comintern had been dissolved in 1943 as a goodwill gesture to the West, but it was now partially revived. The Communist Information Bureau (Cominform) was established in October 1947, consisting of nine parties: Russia, Hungary, Poland, Romania, Bulgaria, Czechoslovakia, Yugoslavia, France and Italy. Other parties in the West got their 'information' indirectly, through the French and Italians or from Soviet propaganda organs.

The main aim of the Cominform was to tighten up discipline, especially among the Western parties, who were to turn sharply left and cease cooperation with their local bourgeoisie. They were also to be more critical of the social democrats.

One party refused to fall into line. The Tito regime in Yugoslavia rebelled against attempts to subordinate its economic development to Soviet needs. It saw its future instead in continued cooperation with the West. In fact, the International Monetary Fund was invited in to play a major role in Yugoslav development.

The Cominform hurriedly moved its headquarters from Belgrade to Bucharest and denounced the Yugoslav 'nationalists'. By late 1949, it was calling them fascists. In the rest of Eastern Europe, a series of trials and purges of 'Titoists' tore through the ruling parties, leading to the jailing and execution of many top leaders. The fear haunting the Kremlin was that Tito's example might prove infectious. Other Eastern Bloc states might attempt to become independent of Moscow, and other parties, especially the big ones in France and Italy, might attempt to steer an independent course. This, at the beginning of the Cold War, was to be avoided at all costs.

In the short term, the purges and vilification worked, and all the parties denounced Titoism. But, in the long term, the example of Tito was to prove more and more attractive.

Meanwhile, in the West, the parties moved into a phase of militant struggle. In France, they launched an intense campaign against the Indochina War. In Italy, an attempted assassination of Togliatti was answered by a three-day general strike which reached insurrectionary proportions in some places. These struggles in the industrialised countries occurred against the background of Communist-led armed struggle in Asia: in China and Vietnam, where it was victorious, and in the Philippines and Malaysia, where it was eventually suppressed. The victory in China was followed by the events in Korea, where the Cold War became a hot war.

For a brief moment, it seemed that the final turning point in the international class struggle was at hand. Strike levels were high, and Communism seemed to be everywhere on the march. The Western ruling classes appeared to be on the defensive. Even the growing repression by governments and the growth of right-wing extremist organisations could be perceived as part of the class polarisation typical of a revolutionary period.

Leading Soviet economists predicted that the postwar boom would soon give way to a new depression, and not many of their Western colleagues were prepared to dispute the prediction. The final crisis of capitalism seemed near, and the general offensive ordered by Moscow might appear justified.

In reality, the offensive had come two years too late. The strikes of the late 1940s were militant enough, but they were the tail end of the postwar strike wave. The victory in China proved to be the end of the main wave of Communist territorial expansion. The Western economies were about to enter a prolonged boom; together with a sustained anti-communist drive by employers, governments and media, it would lay the basis for a conservatisation of the working classes and a sharp decline in Communist influence.

Moreover, the Communist offensive itself had a built-in limitation: it took on sectarian and sometimes overambitious features. The parties stressed the politicisation of strikes, in a period when most workers were largely concerned with immediate economic issues. In Australia, the CPA attempted to challenge the Labor Party in an all-out assault, at a point where its strength did not justify the move.

Finally, the CPs paid the price of their own previous class collaboration. For several years, they had discouraged strikes and preached class peace. Now, with no warning, the militants were flung into intense, sometimes suicidal struggles. The political grounds for the sudden shift were far from clear to the rank and file.

By the early 1950s, the offensive was grinding to a halt. Government repression and right-wing extremist groups combined to take a heavy toll on party members and supporters, and some places attempted to outlaw the CPs altogether. Membership fell off, sometimes drastically, and those Communists who did not leave the party bore permanent scars from the bitter isolation that followed.

Towards 'polycentrism'

The first Soviet hydrogen bomb was exploded in 1953. It was to prove a turning point:

> the development of a situation of – more or less – nuclear stalemate between Russia and the West means that the international communist movement no longer plays any significant role in the defence of Russia. Of course the parties still play a useful public relations role, but they are not needed to lead struggles or even to contain them. A power that relies on the threat of mass destruction has no interest in the politics of mass mobilisation.[15]

The worldwide 'balance of terror' ran parallel to a final recognition on all sides that the balance of power in Europe had been consolidated. The division of the continent between the two great power blocs was final, and neither side would challenge it. The CPs were no longer needed by the Russians as a Trojan horse within the opposing camp; indeed, overly aggressive behaviour on their part might jeopardise the emerging relationship of 'peaceful coexistence' which the nuclear parity between Moscow and Washington had made both possible and necessary. Consequently, the Soviet Union called on the CPs to move away from their frontal attacks on the bourgeoisie and from their hostility to pro-Western social democratic parties; they were to move closer to the latter and to 'heal the split in the working class'.[16] If this were done, Khrushchev told them in 1956, they could attain their aims through parliament:

The parliamentary means of achieving socialism are now possible. The right wing bourgeois parties are more often suffering setbacks. It is possible therefore for the working class and its allies, the real majority of the population, to take possession of parliament and transform it from an instrument of capitalist rule into an instrument of the working class and its allies.[17]

There is no doubt that the mass of Communists in the West accepted this new course with relief, after the failure of the previous offensive. Even so, the new policies were not easy to put into practice. The previous period of frontal assaults had left the parties very isolated indeed; certainly, the bourgeoisie did not trust them for a minute. The social democratic parties, attacked only yesterday by the Communists as class traitors, were also naturally suspicious of new CP offers of collaboration.

It would be a slow and difficult task, not made any easier by the events of 1956.

Early in 1956, Nikita Khrushchev delivered a 'secret speech' to the Twentieth Congress of the Communist Party of the Soviet Union (CPSU). The speech, which soon became public knowledge around the world, told the truth about the horrors of the Stalin regime. Khrushchev did not make these revelations out of moral outrage; those who felt moral outrage had been purged years before. The totalitarian style of government associated with Stalin had to be modified for purely *practical* reasons: it was unsuited to the modern, sophisticated economy that Russia was now developing. You can force people to do manual labour by terror tactics, but you cannot use the same methods to improve productivity in a technologically advanced enterprise.

Khrushchev also used his speech as a factional weapon. To secure his position as Stalin's heir, he wished to mobilise the lower levels of the bureaucracy against his rivals at the top. The lower levels had been kept in a continual state of fear under Stalin and were happy to support the man who promised a liberalisation.

But, while de-Stalinisation was necessary, it also brought with it serious dangers. Stalin had been a symbol of the monolithic quality of the world movement, so attacks on him could get out of hand, as indeed they did. As early as 1953, the year of Stalin's death, building workers in East Berlin had sparked a substantial

A model of the Monument to the Third International, by the Russian artist and architect Vladimir Tatlin. This design inspired Interventions' logo.

rebellion in East Germany, and there had been strikes in Czechoslovakia, Hungary and Romania. However, coming at a point where the Cold War was still very intense, these events had little impact on the parties in the West.

In 1956, the lid blew off. Strike struggles forced a change of leadership in Poland. In October, mass strikes followed student demonstrations in Hungary. The Hungarian strikes became an insurrection, with workers' councils established in the major enterprises. A brutal armed intervention by Soviet forces was required to restore order.

The events of 1956 caused grave unrest in and around the Western CPs. They had received no advance warning of Khrushchev's secret speech, being left to read the news in the gloating establishment press. Apparently, now that the Russians had the bomb, they did not much care how their actions affected the parties in the West. It was galling for the CPs, especially those like the French and Italians – who commanded millions of votes – to be treated in such a fashion.

Injury was added to insult with the Soviet invasion of Hungary. An uproar resulted among Communists and their supporters. Intellectual and artistic figures, such as Picasso in France, protested against the invasion. More significantly, the French party could not carry the pro-Soviet line in the trade unions under its control. The British Communist paper found its Budapest correspondent, Peter Fryer, sending reports that sympathised with the Hungarian rebels. Even in the USA, denunciations of the invasion appeared in the CP press, and it took a year before orthodoxy was restored.

In the aftermath of these events, the parties began to take a hard look at their position. As early as the immediate postwar period, the Italians had begun to think in terms of an independent course; now, all the bigger CPs began to chafe at the bit. The 'Russian connection', which had not been an asset for some years, had now become a massive liability.

The parties began to take to its logical conclusion the Soviet suggestion to heal the rift with the social democrats and the local bourgeoisie. To ingratiate themselves, they began to distance themselves from the USSR. The example of Tito assumed a sudden appeal, and Italian Communist leader Togliatti declared:

> There is coming into being ... a polycentric system, corresponding to the new situation ... The solution that today probably most

nearly corresponds to this new situation may be that of the full autonomy of the individual movements and Communist Parties.[18]

At the same time, the CPs were loosening up the old authoritarian internal regime. There had already been a *tendency* in this direction since the end of the war, as the tight organisational forms required for underground resistance activity gave way to more relaxed structures suited to broadening the parties' membership base. But 1956 gave a great impetus to the process. The crises of that year raised issues. Debate could not be easily suppressed, but, if the CPs were to improve their 'democratic image' in the eyes of Western public opinion, these debates had to be survived without massive purges. Limits on internal discussion were eased. At a Central Committee meeting of the Italian Communist Party in November 1961, there were calls for restoring factional rights. These calls were resisted; but, in the same month, the party's youth newspaper published a reference to Leon Trotsky as 'one of the most original figures of the October revolution', leading to considerable controversy.[19]

In order to make themselves acceptable to the bourgeoisie in each country, the parties began to indulge in fervent nationalism. As usual, the Italians took the lead, declaring:

> Italy's national independence is something extremely precious for all Italians. And we Communists ... are convinced that we are among the most stubborn and inflexible supporters of national independence.[20]

The nationalism is partly genuine but partly a cover for something even more remarkable: a shift from the former pro-Sovietism to acceptance of the NATO alliance. The Spanish party stated:

> In accordance with the realities of the present international situation, we are prepared to accept the presence of US bases until an international agreement is reached to remove all foreign bases from all countries without exception.[21]

Twice in the 1960s, world events accelerated the polycentric tendency. In the early years of the decade, Beijing split openly and decisively with Moscow.

China rejected the Soviet proposals for peaceful coexistence with the West, fearing that a deal between the two superpowers would leave Beijing out in the cold. The Chinese especially feared that nuclear détente would prevent China from developing an independent nuclear weapons program. They also believed that the Russians were attempting to use aid programs to reduce them to satellite status. The real issues were, therefore, those of Chinese national interest; but they were translated into different terms within the world movement. China denounced Khrushchev's theory of a peaceful transition to socialism and his belief in the possibility of removing the threat of war without removing imperialism. The appeal was to the most left-wing elements in the CPs. There was also an appeal to those of the older cadres who thought that Stalin had been badly done by in 1956.

Some exceptions (including Australia) notwithstanding, the numbers of cadres that China could win to its breakaway splinter groups were small. The main importance of the Sino-Soviet split for the Western CPs was the shattering of Russia's position as unquestioned leader of the world movement. Yugoslavia's defection in the 1950s had been a problem, but Yugoslavia was a small country. Now, the Communist leaders of the world's most populous nation were defying Moscow. In the aftermath, major parties like the Japanese moved to a neutral position in the Sino-Soviet dispute, and even ruling parties like the Romanians began to distance themselves from the USSR.

The final blow, however, was delivered by the events in Czechoslovakia in 1968. In that country, the Dubček government had pursued both polycentrism and liberalisation. Alarmed, the Soviets firstly tried indirect pressure, then sent in the tanks. The CPs in the West hastened to denounce the Russian action. The Italians expressed strong disapproval, the French criticised the invasion, and the Australian CPA held public meetings to campaign against the Soviet intervention.

Not all the membership of the CPs was in favour of this sort of public criticism. Some workers and particularly some union officials were uneasy. They – quite rightly – drew the connection between the anti-Sovietism and the accommodation to the bourgeoisie they saw taking place in their own countries and were open to the alternative argument that linked pro-Sovietism with a working-class stand. Minority currents emerged, often encouraged by Moscow, and a number of splits took place – one of the more substantial being in Australia.

The parties were undeterred. The trend away from Russia, towards accommodation to the bourgeoisie, was pursued with renewed vigour. By the 1970s, it was finding a fairly finished theoretical expression in the ideas of 'Eurocommunism', which will be discussed in the Australian context below.

In this chapter, I have sought to sketch the development of the world Communist movement through three periods: firstly, its revolutionary period under Lenin; secondly, the transformation of the CPs into instruments of the Soviet bureaucracy under Stalin; thirdly, the break-up of the Stalinist monolith in the postwar period. In what follows, I'll trace the same general development within the Australian party, concentrating on the fragmentation and decline of the CPA after World War II.

2
The Rise of Australian Communism

'There's going to be a meeting in Perth about Russia,' Feathers said ... 'I think I'll go and hear what they have to say.' He paused and ran his hand through his hair. 'You never know. It might be the start of something new. We need a new start.'

Judah Waten, The Unbending[1]

Australian socialism has always reflected the weaknesses of the labour movement more than its strengths.

To be sure, the Labor Party was 'socialist' – but what did that mean? For William Lane, 'we are all socialist only some of us don't know it'.[2] Cardinal Moran suggested how seriously ALP socialism might be taken when he remarked: 'If men in the advancement of their political interests chose the name Socialists, I say again what's in a name ... ?'[3]

For the mainstream Labor supporters, socialism meant little more than state intervention in the economy, to ensure a more rational capitalism and a society in which the unfair advantage enjoyed by the employers on the industrial battlefield would be neutralised. At the same time, it was closely tied to the role of the state in promoting tariff protection and White Australia.

The only real socialists were isolated in small sects and, for a time, in the Industrial Workers of the World (IWW). While the IWW was largely smashed by repression during World War I, the small sects survived, but only in greater or lesser isolation from the big battalions of the working class. And even *their* socialism was confused; certainly, it was only tenuously Marxist.

Marx's works were ill digested. The young socialist Harry Holland had complained that, to read Marx, you needed 'a hard seat, a bare table, and a head swathed in wet ... ice cold towels'.[4] But, if the Australian socialists were backward, they were still frustrated by the even greater political backwardness of the labour movement. They tended to respond to it in a didactic and sectarian manner, dwelling on the stubborn stupidity of the masses and hoping to overcome it with lectures.

Harry Holland complained that, while socialists were the sculptors of the new society, they were working on the 'man with the stone head'.[5] The Australian Socialist Party (ASP) described the horrors of capitalism and then abused its own audience, the very victims of these horrors:

> Yet you have bitterly cursed those who would teach you to understand these things, and chased after every will-o'-the-wisp that came from our common oppressors.

The ASP went on, however, to place its hope for converting the heathen in education: 'Lose no time joining the campaign to capture your brother's brain.'[6]

The first socialist organisation was the Socialist League, founded in 1887 and uniting all those interested in socialism. But differences of opinion soon arose, particularly over how to relate to the Labor Party. One point of view argued for 'boring from within' the ALP, to transform it into a genuine socialist party or at least to reach militant workers inside it. In Victoria, this current found its expression in the Victorian Socialist Party, which achieved a short-lived mass presence under the leadership of Tom Mann. In NSW, the left inside the ALP was less coherent but more influential, counting among its ranks people like Jock Garden, leader of the Trades and Labour Council (TLC).

Standing proudly outside the ALP were the socialist sects, most prominent among them the ASP and the Socialist Labor Party (SLP). Then, as now, Sydney was the home of the sectarians. The SLP were the followers of Daniel De Leon and considered that De Leon had perfected the blueprint for socialism; hence, by definition, the SLP was the only true socialist party. The ASP was less self-important, but they also refused to go anywhere near the Labor Party, not only on tactical or strategic grounds but as a matter of absolute principle:

The Labor Party does not clearly and unambiguously avow Socialism, nor does it teach it; it is unlike any other working-class creation in the world in that it builds no socialist movement, issues no socialist books, debates no socialist problems. It is not international, it is not Marxian. In politics and practice it is liberalism under a new name; in utterance and ideal it is bourgeois.[7]

To create a CP in Australia, it would be necessary to somehow resolve this historic divide between those operating within the ALP and those opposed on principle to doing so. This was difficult indeed, and it would perhaps have been impossible without the impact of both a major upsurge in the class struggle in Australia and a revolution in Russia.

In Australia, as in so many places, the latter stages of World War I brought a dramatic escalation of the class struggle; then, after about 1920, militancy declined. The strike figures tell some of the story:

Strike Days Lost (thousands)[8]

Year	Days Lost	Year	Days Lost
1914	1,090	1919	4,304
1915	583	1920	3,587
1916	1,679	1921	1,286
1917	4,500	1922	859
1918	581	1923	1,146

Strike levels began to rise significantly in 1916, the year that a historic struggle began over Billy Hughes' unsuccessful attempts to introduce conscription. In the following year, they reached spectacular proportions, as workers in NSW waged a near-general strike over speed-up in the railways. Although the strike was crushed, militancy had bounced right back within a year in a series of economic struggles. To get an appreciation of the scale of these events, one need only multiply the statistics to bring them into line with the size of today's trade union movement, whose membership is three times larger. In 1974, the high point of latter-day industrial militancy, about six million strike days were lost

– a level of struggle high enough to help destabilise the Whitlam government. Suppose the figure had been more like 12 million!

The failure of the 'Great Strike' of 1917 led to a discussion of strategy, and many gravitated towards a project of union reform: the idea of 'One Big Union'. This won support from many official union bodies and fired the imagination of activists at a time when there was a radicalisation of the left wing of the ALP.

An All-Australian Trade Union Congress was held in Melbourne in 1921, providing 'a microcosm of the ideas and influences at work in the labour movement'.[9] Chair E. J. Holloway, Melbourne Trades Hall Council president, called for a program that would 'make the next decade the transition period from Capitalism to Socialism'.[10] In order to make such a prospect possible, the Congress set up a Council of Action of labour and union leaders. Clearly, Australian labour was moving rapidly leftward.

In addition to the obvious Australian factors in this radicalisation, we must also consider the impact of the Russian revolution. This took some time to make itself felt, both because of Australia's geographical isolation and because local events – like the conscription struggle of 1916–17 – were foremost in people's minds. At first, there was only a vague sympathy with the revolution; when Archbishop Mannix greeted it as 'the end of an age old tyranny',[11] he clearly did not understand its significance. Then came a slow process of clarification which the young war hero turned socialist, Hugo Throssel, summarised as follows:

> With the arrival in Australia of Lenin's classic, 'State and Revolution', clarity was definitely stimulated. It was the first clear Marxist exposition of the role of the State ... Other works of Lenin followed in quick succession. They were augmented by eye witness accounts such as John Reed's thrilling book, 'Ten Days that Shook the World'; then followed rapidly reports by Arthur Ransome, Professor Goode, Rhys Williams and Colonel Robins. They were all snapped up by workers and political activists.[12]

If clarity was stimulated, however, it was by no means rapidly achieved. The SLP claimed Lenin for its own; the ASP declared itself 'communist' and published a manifesto restating its traditional politics; Jock Garden declared Bolshevism to be the basis for building the 'One Big Union'. However, one idea of the Bolsheviks penetrated in some quarters: a belief in the immediacy of revolution. Australia had seen a massive split in the ALP over conscription and a gigantic political struggle over the issue, followed by two major strike waves. Unemployment rose sharply to 11 percent in 1921, while the Melbourne Union Congress called for socialism within a decade. To some Australian leftists, the Communist International's declaration that 'the epoch of final decisive struggle ... has arrived'[13] seemed a reasonable proposition. Accordingly, 26 people representing various radical socialist currents met in Sydney in late 1920 to found the Communist Party of Australia.

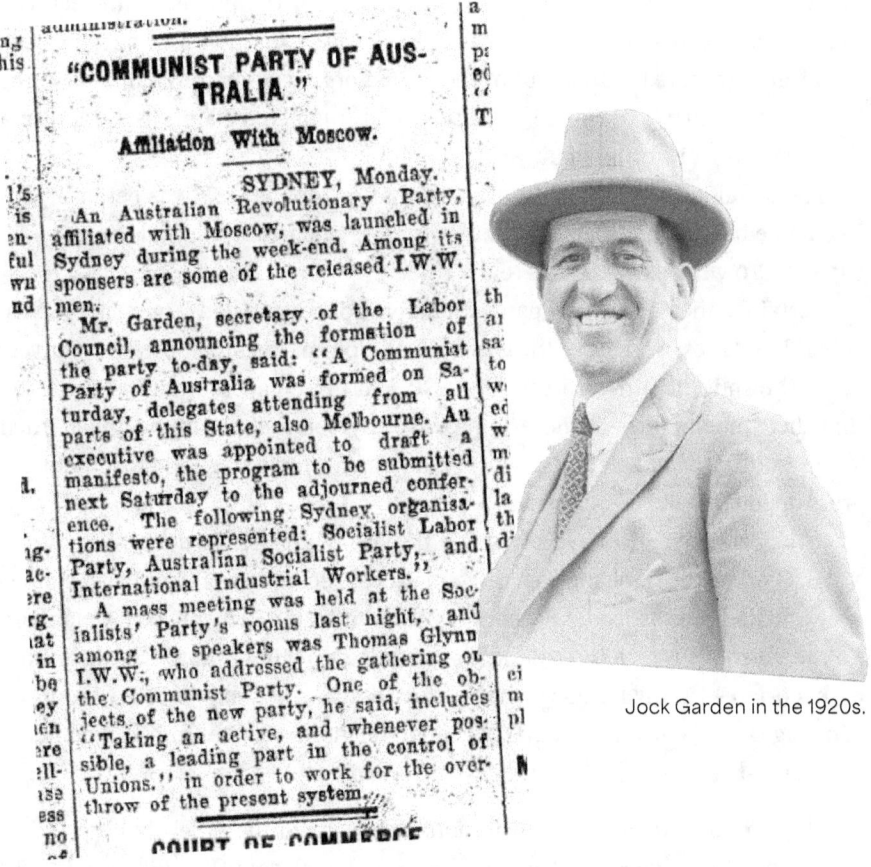

Jock Garden in the 1920s.

The formation of the CPA announced in Murwillumbah, New South Wales, 2 November, 1920.

A decade in the wilderness

The new party led a chequered existence. Among its founders were the 'Trades Hall Reds', led by Jock Garden, who were active inside the ALP; the remnants of the IWW, who hoped to win the new party to revolutionary syndicalism; and the ASP, for whom both these approaches were anathema. However, the ASP, which possessed the largest cadre force and a coherent political line, expected to be able to dominate the new organisation. They were to be disappointed.

Jock Garden, who made up in tactical agility what he lacked in numbers, blocked with the IWW elements to gain control of the provisional executive, then postponed elections to the permanent executive for months. The ASP, finding itself outflanked, pulled out of the united organisation to rename itself the 'Communist Party', and there were two rival fragments claiming to represent the Communist International.

The usual judgement of historians is that, while the ASP was better organised and educated, the Garden group was more practical – and thus, in the end, superior. To what extent is this really true?

Certainly, the ASP were organisationally stronger and had larger paper sales. When J. B. Miles, a leader of the Queensland Communists, came down to investigate the split, he reported that the ASP sold more papers than its rivals and that their meetings were more impressive. By contrast, he found the Garden group confused and demoralised – but, much worse, he indicted them for gross opportunism.

'"Tactics" seems to have become a disease' with the Garden group, wrote Miles. Garden had published a totally uncritical account of a Labor Party conference and had put the leader of the New Zealand Labor Party on a CPA platform (to the horror of the New Zealand Communists).[14] Miles' impression is backed by historian Miriam Dixson, who records that Garden supported a proposed 'One Big Union' constitution that excluded Asians and quotes him as advancing a gradualist conception of the road to socialism:

> No one can make a revolution. It is something which is born by things developed under the capitalist system. It will come. It is coming. Everyone knows that. When the system of its own weight starts to collapse, then it is for a movement like this one

to take directing authority in Parliament and everywhere else, so that the whole machinery will act at the one time.

When an Australian Workers' Union (AWU) leader retorted that 'That is purely evolution', Garden did not demur.[15]

Similarly, veteran Communist Richard Dixon later described Garden as 'something of a demagogue'.[16] Yet, his victory was sealed by the sectarianism of his rivals.

According to the ASP's own correspondence, some of the better members of the Garden group came to the ASP's conference to beg them to unite, 'in order to assist in expelling an admittedly bad element';[17] they spurned the approach. Such intransigence was not designed to win the favour of the Comintern, which, according to the party's own representatives in Moscow at the time, would 'listen to nothing but unity'.[18] The Comintern demanded a unity conference on very fair terms, but the ASP refused, and Garden won recognition as the official representative of the Communist movement. The bulk of the ASP rank and file now defected to the new organisation, which was known for a time as the United Communist Party of Australia.

Garden's approach thus became the dominant line in the CPA for some years, and the party sought affiliation to the ALP. In NSW, this was successful for a time – a success that was of international significance, given the failure of the British party to achieve the same thing. However, it seems clear that the entry work was conducted on an opportunist basis consistent with Garden's previous track record. Historian Frank Farrell, who can hardly be accused of criticising the CPA from the left, records:

> In [1921] Garden made overtures to the AWU – long the bête noir of the IWW ... and he came to an arrangement whereby the much vaunted One Big Union became acceptable to the AWU. Garden's flirtation with the AWU was not only significant in union affairs generally ... but was also aimed at ingratiating Communists directly into the ALP. The AWU virtually ran the ALP in Queensland, and held precarious control of it in New South Wales through the Party's State executive. This plan to enter the Labor Party aroused deep hostility among many rank and file Communists.[19]

While the party might be united, it was far from politically coherent. Farrell describes it as having been 'a curious mixture of groupings' in which the Garden leadership was 'closely adapted to the industrial environment and the prevailing mood of important elements of the labour movement', but recruits from the socialist sects 'kept alive a sense of party identity, and a certain sectarianism and spirit of criticism of the existing labour movement'.[20] In Melbourne, the small and struggling CPA branch was a 'congerie of groups either new to the labour movement and ignorant of its affairs, or doctrinaire and sectarian'. When the Adelaide branch collapsed, 'its place was taken by several organisations'.[21]

Such an organisation was likely to be torn apart by outside pressures. If the party could claim a sizeable membership at first, up to 1,500 according to *Pravda*,[22] it could not hold it together. The more militant and/or sectarian elements alienated the friends Garden was trying to make with his opportunist alliances. These friends then denounced the party or attacked it and stole away the right wing of its rank and file.

In 1923, the more militant sections of the party, whose views found regular expression in the CPA newspaper *Workers' Weekly*, antagonised the leaderships of two key unions. Firstly, in the early part of the year, they criticised the management of a maritime strike in North Queensland and made an enemy of Tom Walsh, the Seamen's Union leader, who had supported the party and was still a leftist. Later in the year, the *Workers' Weekly* carried on a ferocious polemic against the Miners' leader, A. C. Willis, who had been important in securing Communist affiliation to the ALP.

In the course of a dispute in Maitland, the CPA had called for a general strike of all miners. For this, they were accused of playing into the hands of the coal owners, and Willis told the establishment press that both the coal owners and the Communists wanted a general strike. During a long and heated series of exchanges, the party was able to demolish the latter contention[23] but not to keep Willis from moving to isolate the CPA in the union and the ALP.

By the end of the year, the Communists had been expelled from the Labor Party. Despite an impressive defence campaign among rank-and-file ALP supporters, the expulsion was final. A large section of the CPA membership, who had held dual memberships with the ALP, elected to stay in the Labor Party and ceased to be Communists.

The party now turned to rank-and-file union work, which will be discussed below, and to electoral activity. Jock Garden stood for the NSW State Parliament and is said to have been bitterly disappointed by receiving only a few hundred votes. Certainly, the electoral initiative must be judged a failure: all six candidates, standing in working-class electorates, lost their deposits.

The result should not have been a surprise, because the party was now operating in a very difficult social environment. The CPA had been formed on the expectation of the final crisis of capitalism, but it was now clear that it had been founded at the tail end of the postwar radicalisation, after 1920 strike levels fell. The 'One Big Union' movement fell prey to bureaucratic delays, AWU obstruction and declining interest on the part of union members. The ALP left, after the high point of 1921, became increasingly isolated.

Guido Baracchi, 1917.

The CPA seemed to be confronted with an indefinite period in which it would be confined to passive propaganda. Because this prospect was rather less inviting than the grand hopes of a few years past, defections continued. Guido Baracchi, a leading intellectual, called for liquidating the organisation into the ALP and, when he was defeated, resigned and went overseas. A year later, Garden himself departed, taking with him his fellow union officials on the TLC.

Those who remained pursued propaganda from 1926 to 1928 under the leadership of a Canadian immigrant named Jack Kavanagh, fighting a determined struggle to hold the party together. Kavanagh himself probably deserves more credit for sustaining the party than he is usually given. He firstly carried out a systematic debate with Garden to defeat those who sought to liquidate the party, then tried to introduce a more centralised and organised regime. It was the Kavanagh leadership who first called for a 'Bolshevisation' of the party. Unfortunately, he was up against immense odds. After a year of supposed 'Bolshevisation', Norman Jeffery complained of a 'lack of co-ordination and a systematic method' as well as the 'indifference of nucleus leaders'.[24] Kavanagh's political method has been called sectarian and doctrinaire, but it is not clear what options were open to the party at this time except propaganda and holding

32   INTO THE MAINSTREAM

Unemployed march to the Treasury Buildings, Perth, March 1931.

firm to what organisation it possessed; to later generations, working in a more fruitful environment, this may appear sectarian in retrospect – even if it was unavoidable at the time.

And Kavanagh never got an opportunity to show what he could do in changed circumstances, because he was pushed from power just as the party's fortunes began to pick up.

Around 1927, the economy began to slide towards depression, and unemployment began to rise. From 1928, there began a series of major industrial confrontations, involving firstly the waterside workers, whose prolonged unofficial strike was broken, leaving them weakened for years and forced to work with non-unionists. The defeat of the timber workers followed – a struggle that led to a lengthening of working hours, not only in that industry but in many other places. Finally, in the latter half of 1929, there was a lockout on the northern coalfields of NSW. Here, too, the union was defeated, and rank and file bitterness found its most spectacular expression in a riot at Rothbury.

These struggles, although defeated, marked a permanent change in the political climate which was to benefit the Communists enormously. Militant workers were disillusioned with traditional trade unionism, especially with the timidity shown by many union officials. They were disillusioned, too, with the response of Labor governments, which presided over the same sort of union bashing as the conservatives. Meanwhile, unemployment was reaching astronomical proportions. Only a small minority of workers were led by these events to turn towards Communism, but that minority was enough to turn the CPA from a sect into a small mass party.

As it became clear that a new crisis was beginning, debates began within the CPA about how to respond. Kavanagh had opposed dissolving the party into the ALP, but he did not believe that the CPA had the resources to challenge Labor for the allegiance of any significant section of the working class. After the electoral fiasco of 1925, he was dubious about standing candidates against the ALP. Instead, he called for a policy of critical support for Labor candidates: support for their election, but criticism of their policies, combined with a call for the workers to rally to a revolutionary program. The transformation of the workers to revolutionary consciousness 'is not effected through political miracles', said the CPA policy adopted at the end of 1928, 'nor will we accomplish it through virtuous isolation of the C.P. from the masses, but it is a long and difficult process whose various phases we must help in speeding up'.[25]

In retrospect, this attitude appears somewhat overconservative, although we must remember that the party did not know how vast the coming crisis was going to be. There was soon to be a considerable radicalisation; there were those who predicted new opportunities opening up for the CPA and called for a more aggressive and left-wing approach to meet them. Moscow increasingly backed them. Stalin had heralded the advent of a new 'Third Period', to be filled with wars and revolutions. Capitalism would face deep crisis, and reforms would be impossible; hence, the bourgeoisie would turn to fascism, and the reformists would become mere tools of the bourgeoisie. The reformists were 'social fascists'. The Communists must strike out boldly and independently, calling on the workers to rally around them against 'social fascism'. In electoral terms, this meant standing Communist candidates.

Early in 1928, Norman Jeffery and Jack Ryan brought back from Moscow the so-called 'Queensland Resolution', calling on the party to stand candidates against the Queensland Labor government. This the party did, with some modest success, and a faction based primarily on Queensland called for the policy to be implemented nationally. Kavanagh resisted, but his opponents secured explicit support from the Kremlin in the form of a cable, followed by a letter that accused Kavanagh of a 'grave Right deviation':

> Apparently, the party regards itself as being merely a propaganda body and as a sort of adjunct to the Left Wing of the Labor Party, whereas our conception of the role and functions of the Communist Party is that it should be the leader of the working class and the driving force in its political and economic struggles.[26]

The faction, led by Lance Sharkey and J. B. Miles, was now emboldened to take the offensive. In discussions preceding the 1929 Congress, they accused the leadership of 'treachery to the working class':

> The independent leadership of the Communist Party is the biggest question facing communists today. The workers are given two alternatives: organise under an independent leadership and fight, or capitulate to capitalism and its reformist allies.

Kavanagh's protests that the party was too small and isolated to carry out this perspective were brushed aside: 'It is a definite lie to say we can do nothing because we are only a small propaganda sect, *we are a party*.'[27]

With Soviet backing, the faction's victory was assured. With the help of Comintern agent Harry Wicks ('Herbert Moore'), the Sharkey–Miles grouping consolidated a new leadership and began to reshape the party. This was the *Stalinisation* of the CPA.

From the 'Third Period' to the Popular Front

Stalinisation meant two things: the disciplined implementation by the Australian party of a new international line 'which takes its place *everywhere*'[28] and a determined attempt to organise the party along the lines demanded by the Comintern. This involved building factory cells, careful planning and reporting 'upwards and downwards'. It also meant authoritarian control, for which purpose a new constitution was introduced. The key ruling body on paper was the

Central Committee; in reality, the Secretariat ran things because it was the transmission belt for Comintern policy, to which the whole party was subordinate.

However, the tightening up was only relative, if only because it could not keep pace with the growth of the organisation. The Depression, which threw nearly 30 percent of trade unionists onto the dole queues, brought a stream of recruits: at one stage, workers in Melbourne were literally queuing up outside the CPA offices to join. Rapid growth also brought high turnover, especially because the party was recruiting among the unemployed. In Victoria, for example, membership stood at 287 in 1933, but many of them were paper members; at the start of 1935, the figure stood at 683, but there were still 'abnormally high fluctuation' and 'less members in the Party now than we recruited to the Party in the past two years'.[29] In the early years of Stalinism, the CPA was by no means the well-oiled machine it is sometimes imagined to have been.

In immediate political terms, Stalinism meant the theory of 'social fascism', with its attendant tactical stupidities. When Labor Premier Jack Lang was dismissed from office in 1932 for defying British banks, and a vast crowd of people who perceived Lang's defiance as an anti-establishment stance rallied in his support, the Communists could only denounce him as a traitor. And the ALP Socialisation Units, which managed to temporarily commit the NSW ALP to socialism, were treated as 'left social fascists'. In Victoria, the CPA prevented the units from forming for several years; when they tried to organise in industry in NSW, this was denounced by the party as a conspiracy against the Communist-led Minority Movement.

Yet, in a sense, it was also the great heroic period of the party. These were the days of free speech fights, when Noel Counihan spoke to a crowd from a steel cage atop a truck while police frantically tried to cut him out. They were the days of eviction struggles, when destitute families were defended, sometimes violently, against attempts to put them out into the streets, and of clashes with the fascist New Guard. Above all, they were the days of unemployed struggles, in which the party was immersed for the simple reason that its membership was largely unemployed. The CPA's jobless followers were even able to dominate the Melbourne May Day of 1932, rallying 2,500 people – as against 500 led by Trades Hall – and ultimately storming the official platform.

No wonder that Sharkey said of these years that, despite all the sectarian errors:

there was a great deal of energy and enthusiasm, and it would not be all a bad a thing if we were able to recapture some of the energy and enthusiasm, perhaps 'fanaticism' of that period.[30]

The cohering of a Stalinist leadership and cadre at this particular time is of some interest. In most countries, it was accomplished in the late 1920s against the backdrop of a rightward drift in society and a commensurate rightward trend in the CPs themselves. For most parties, the 'Third Period' was a time of defeats. By contrast, in Australia, the new leadership established itself in the context of the left turn of the 'Third Period', a turn that was associated with a dramatic growth of the party. Does this, perhaps, provide some hint as to the origins of the much-remarked 'leftism' displayed by the Miles–Sharkey leadership in later years?

Lance Sharkey, 1931.

The worst excesses of the 'Third Period' began to come to an end in 1934, partly because the CPA was becoming something of a force and, therefore, had responsibilities. Wild-eyed rhetoric and ultraleft confrontations might successfully regroup a thousand activists; but, as the party grew, the task was to win broader layers of people. For this, a marginally saner approach was advisable. The Comintern began to provide it. After Hitler's triumph in Germany, signals began to come out of Moscow that the left turn was to be reversed. Its abandonment in favour of the 'United Front Against Fascism' was decided by 1934 and fully elaborated in Georgii Dimitrov's famous speech at the Seventh Congress of the Comintern in 1935.

At first glance, the new strategy appeared not only sensible, but also to be a return to the united front strategy of the early 1920s. The unity of all working-class organisations against fascism was only logical, and even the 'Popular Front' which soon replaced it made sense if it only meant a tactical alliance among all groups who opposed the common enemy. As we have seen, it soon became something more than that: the subordination of the working class to the liberal bourgeoisie. This did not become obvious in practice in Australia very quickly, for the simple reason that the CPA did not have a mass worker base to deliver to the bourgeoisie. Nevertheless, we can see some of the same logic at work in the party's campaigns against war and fascism.

A 'Movement Against War' was set up in the early 1930s and achieved some notable initial support – the secretary of the League of Nations Unions in Australia noted that, within months, it had won more support than had the League Unions in 12 years.[31] Peace activists had become disillusioned with moderate tactics and were prepared to be associated with radicals and Communists. The growth ceased around the end of 1934, but interest was revived by the visit of Egon Kisch, the European anti-fascist campaigner whom the government unsuccessfully tried to keep out of Australia. Later, the renamed Movement Against War and Fascism was able to build an 'International Peace Campaign' which held a Congress of 4,000 in Melbourne in 1937. The movement was deeply rent by the Stalin–Hitler pact, and its demise was naturally sealed by the beginning of World War II.

The political line of the anti-war movement was determined by the CPA, so its political evolution gives a good indication of what Popular Front policies

Egon Kisch, Sydney Domain, 1935.

Mineworkers from Wongawilli, New South Wales, carry CPA popular front banner, 1930s.

meant in practice. In the early days, the Communist approach had been simple: war was caused by capitalism, and only a fool would fight for King and Country. At the end of 1929, as the Sharkey–Miles leadership assumed control of the party, *Workers' Weekly* declared that '"The spirit of Eureka still lives" is a meaningless bleat'.[32] In 1933, Ralph Gibson told a Melbourne audience: 'When we are called on to fight for King and Country we are called on to follow our enemies and shoot our friends'.[33]

The new policies took the party in quite a new direction. The main enemy was now fascism, and all other questions became secondary. To be sure, there was still a struggle for peace, but the main threat to peace was fascism. Dimitrov made the implications quite clear:

> In the present concrete international situation, the instigator of the approaching war is *Fascism*, this mailed fist of the most aggressive forces of imperialism ... It is ... completely wrong

to predict *all* countries as aggressors at present.³⁴ [Emphasis in original]

This opened the way for national defence. And, given that there was to be a multi-class alliance to boot, it paved the way for the party's turn to Australian nationalism. Thus, by September 1936, the CPA had become an:

> Australian Party par excellence ... the real inheritor of the true Australianism of the spirit of the fathers of democracy, of the Dunmore Langs, Parkeses and Wentworths, of the heroic fighters of the Eureka stockade, of the gallant anti-conscription army.³⁵

The anti-war movement soon became the 'Australian League for Peace and Democracy', and its desire for respectability was reflected in the name of its journal: the old *War – What For?* with its IWW associations gave way to the new *World Peace*.

The drift to nationalism and national defence was reflected in the refusal of Port Kembla wharfies to load pig iron bound for Japan, a struggle strongly supported by the CPA, which had recently captured both the national and local leadership of the Waterside Workers.

The wharfies were implementing Australian Council of Trade Unions (ACTU) policy and had already placed bans in other cities, only to back off when threatened with the licensing provisions of the *Transport Workers' Act*. This Act allowed the government to insist that each wharfie who wanted to work take out a license; once licensed, they had no right to strike. The Port Kembla wharfies refused to bow to this sort of intimidation and were only forced to compromise, in the end, by a total lockout of their fellow workers at the BHP steel mills.

To a great degree, the wharfies were motivated by internationalist sentiments. The ACTU policy had been adopted as a

CPA popular front pamphlet, 1938.

protest against Japan's invasion of China, and the wharfies saw themselves as acting in solidarity with the oppressed peoples of Asia. The strikers treated the Indian crew of the banned ship to shore outings, and some of the crew spoke at public meetings in support. When the ship sailed, at least nine of them remained behind rather than transport the pig iron. Chinese people in Australia also rallied behind the watersiders. At one meeting, the local press reported that 'Black, yellow and white men and women' had joined in a show of solidarity.[36]

At the same time, the intervention by BHP gave the struggle a cutting edge directed against Australian capital. But, if internationalism and class politics were part of the picture, they were not all of it. In condemning the Japanese invasion of China, watersiders' leader Jim Healy went on to warn that 'fascism is within striking distance of our shores',[37] and it is noteworthy that large sections of the bourgeoisie supported the wharfies' stand, openly or covertly.

The *Sydney Morning Herald* expressed sympathy for the strikers, as did Sir Isaac Isaacs. More covert support was forthcoming from none other than Billy Hughes, then minister for external affairs – who, not long before the outbreak of the dispute, had privately urged the union to 'stand solid'.[38]

At a mass meeting at the height of the dispute, two major resolutions were carried, one condemning Japanese imperialism in China and the other condemning the government for being remiss in maintaining Australia's defences.

So, despite the many progressive sentiments, the struggle helped pave the way for an alliance with the Australian bourgeoisie on a nationalist basis, for national defence. This was soon to reach its fruition in World War II, but not before a strange interlude occurred which seemed to move the CPA dramatically in the opposite direction.

In 1939, the Soviet Union signed a peace pact with Nazi Germany. It came as something of a jolt to Communists who had been making anti-fascism the centre of their politics; still, the Communists could defend it after a fashion. They could point out that Western governments had refused to ally themselves with the USSR, and Russia had to look to its own survival. This was not a totally unreasonable argument. *Tactical* alliances with even the most reactionary forces had been accepted by Lenin and Trotsky when they led the Soviet state. But they had always subordinated these alliances to a basic orientation to the *class struggle* as the central means for defeating reaction. Stalin, by contrast, had for some time been subordinating the international class struggle to the needs of Soviet diplomacy. Now, the CPs in the West paid the price: their respectable allies turned away from them, and their working-class supporters were bewildered. Soon, the CPA was outlawed. It was not to be formally legal again until well into the war.

Still, the party survived. This was largely because, among the more militant sections of the working class, there was a great scepticism about the war. Government austerity measures in 1940 met a hostile reception in wide sections of the population, and many workers felt that the fighting was both geographically remote and irrelevant to working-class concerns. Even in 1942, when there was fighting in the Pacific, and Russia was involved, the most advanced workers were not enthusiastic. A survey in the coal mining centre of Cessnock (NSW), for example, showed that the local citizens felt that 'the war, as a war [did] not concern them.'[39]

Before looking at World War II itself, we must make two digressions. The summary of events and political trends thus far has necessarily been very sketchy. To provide a bit more depth, we shall look at two specific aspects of CPA work in more detail, tracing the party's political evolution as reflected in each. One is trade union work; the other is work among women.

Organising the 'Militant Minority'

By mid-1923, when it had become clear that the Labor Party was not to be a happy hunting ground for the Communists, they turned their attentions towards the unions. For the small parties in the Anglo-Saxon countries, the Communist International recommended the creation of a militant rank-and-file movement in the unions to oppose the reformist officials – a specific application of the united front. In 1924, the CPA called rank and file conferences in NSW to launch a 'Left Wing Movement'. But, despite a 'grand meeting' which saw the 'Communist Hall ... crowded with militants',[40] the party was soon forced to face the fact that it lacked the resources to build an ongoing movement. Nothing daunted, the CPA launched a 'Militant Minority Movement' (MMM) a few years later and, by 1929, was able to hold another major rank and file conference. The conference was told that the MMM had no base outside Sydney, apart from the mining centres, which provided some strength. In Queensland, the movement was 'not of a very strong nature', but it had carried out a successful intervention in the waterside strike of the previous year.⁴¹ Although this conference did not succeed in laying the basis for a broader movement, the MMM did play an important role in the coal lockout of 1929.

The MMM had groups in all the major mining centres. At the 1928 convention of the Miners' Federation, MMM members had been able to win support for the formation of pit committees. During the lockout of 1929, its call for a general strike of all members won increasing support as the struggle dragged on and discontent grew among the rank and file.

The Miles–Sharkey group later charged Kavanagh with a lack of dynamic leadership in this struggle,⁴² but Jack Blake has argued convincingly that the charges are unfair.⁴³ What *is* clear is that the industrial struggles of this period opened up increasing opportunities for Communists; under the new Miles–Sharkey leadership, they were able to seize on them.

In three major battles – the timber, maritime and mining struggles – the unions were utterly defeated at the end of the 1920s. This was followed in the early 1930s by a general collapse of union militancy, as officials became increasingly timid, and unions found their bargaining power eroded by soaring unemployment. When the Arbitration Court imposed a 10 percent wage cut across industry in 1931, the ACTU Congress voted to do nothing. Into this vacuum stepped the Communists, who appealed to the minority of workers who were militant, moving to the left and wanted to fight.

A revamped rank-and-file movement with the shorter title of Minority Movement (MM) was launched in 1931. By mid-year, the MM was the Australian section of the Red International of Labor Unions (replacing the NSW Trades and Labor Council, which was now considered 'social fascist') and had an eight-page weekly paper, the *Red Leader*.

The MM organised workers on relief projects – and, astonishingly enough, won major wage rises for them. It won control of the Pastoral Workers' Union, a small breakaway from the AWU. It intervened from outside in areas where it had no base, such as the important textile strike in Victorian spinning mills in 1932.

Above all, it built a sizeable base in the big battalions of the union movement, to the point where, at the end of 1932, the Red International of Labour Unions congratulated the MM on its:

recruitment of nearly 3000 members ... the building of 60 job groups and the organising of eight shop committees; the winning of affiliation from reformist union branches

and even the temporary affiliation of the Australian Railways Union.[44]

The strongest base was among the miners, where MM Secretary Bill Orr was elected General Secretary at the end of 1933. Soon after, the miners won a major victory at Wonthaggi in a strike that was a model of rank-and-file organisation. The key to the strike's success was the previous year's organising by the MM, which went into the strike with a membership of 140 in Wonthaggi and recruited another 130 in the course of the dispute.

In the same year, the movement began to hold rank and file conferences among the sugar workers of North Queensland, and it was the MM's rank-and-file organising that laid the basis for the unofficial strikes against Weil's Disease, chronicled in Jean Devanny's novel *Sugar Heaven*.[45] Meanwhile, the Minority Movement was intensely involved in building shop committees. In fact, outside the NSW railways, where the shop committee movement got its start, it was largely the MM who built it. J. J. Brown and Ted Rowe, later to be prominent CPA union leaders, got their start by organising shop committees in Victorian railway workshops.

By the end of 1933, the MM was a mass movement of sorts, and its national Congress registered delegates accredited by 20 trade union branches as well as Ballarat Trades Hall. But, not long after this, the CPA's industrial policy began to change.

The 'Third Period' was coming to an end, and with it the worst sectarian excesses. The ALP was no longer 'social fascist', and Communists could hope to influence its supporters more readily. Unfortunately, as in other areas of work, the party moved from an ultraleft stance to the opposite extreme and began to accommodate itself to the conservatising pressures of the trade union officialdom. Ironically, the seeds of this shift were even contained within the apparently super-militant ideas of the 'Third Period' itself. This was quite clear in the CPA's analysis of the problem of union bureaucracy, perceived during the 'Third Period' and decried along with its sell-outs, but understood in terms of moral failings and wrong attitudes. For example, in 1932, the *Red Leader* offered the following definition of bureaucracy:

> A bureaucracy is a group of officials who take dictatorial powers to themselves and issue commanding orders without consulting those who may be affected by those orders.
>
> When we speak of 'trade union bureaucracy' we refer to those trade union officials who have entrenched themselves behind rules and constitutions and by these means assume unlimited power without consulting the rank and file.[46]

Here, we find no grasp of the material roots of bureaucracy, only a purely moral approach that could be easily turned around as the party began to move to the right. If the problem is the *attitudes* of the officials, then cannot these attitudes be changed? If the problem is *moral*, then isn't it simply a matter of replacing bad officials with good ones? By 1935, the CPA had reduced the problem to just that:

> The Communists must learn to be more flexible, to adopt better tactics ... and to exert every effort to win to our side the union officials who are honest and sincere, but who, maybe [!] are still steeped in a whole series of reformist illusions, habits and customs.[47]

This was no longer a concept of building new forms of struggle from below, but rather of reforming the existing structures from the top. Certainly, all the later writings by CPA leaders on the unions see Communist trade union work as aimed at improving existing union structures. In Sharkey's later historical writings, too, the role of the MM in building the CPA's first mass industrial base is downplayed.[48]

As the party moved back towards mainstream trade unionism, as a consequence of the turn towards the Popular Front, the MM as a national organisation across union lines was allowed to fade away. Organisation within individual industries remained, but was, even here, more and more subordinated to the task of winning and holding office.

When Bill Orr had won office in the Miners' Federation in 1933, the *Red Leader* had emphasised the power of the rank-and-file organisation that put him there. By contrast, when later union offices were won, the Communist press emphasised the personal qualities that had won them support.

THE RISE OF AUSTRALIAN COMMUNISM   45

Right: 'Pig Iron Bob' (Menzies) at Port Kembla strike, 1938.
Below: Port Kembla strikers.

And the first signs of conservatism were definitely beginning to emerge among Communist officials by the time of the pig iron struggle. Well before the Port Kembla events, Jim Healy had said privately that 'to avoid the Government taking action we will have to agree to some compromises'.[49] This might have appeared as simple realism at a time when some branches of the union had appeared reluctant to take firm action over the issue. But, when the Port Kembla wharfies made it clear that they were ready to fight, the union leadership's attitude did not change. In early negotiations over the strike, union leaders were mainly concerned to get the *Transport Workers' Act* lifted, only to find that 'in concentrating on the *Transport Workers' Act* (they) had misinterpreted the mood of the strikers'.[50] A peace settlement, argued for on 17 January by all the members of the Disputes Committee, including Healy and the local CPA official Roach, was rejected by 100 votes to 30 at the mass meeting and was only accepted two days later on the insistence of the leadership. The Communist officials were, perhaps, feeling the pressure from more conservative sections of the union in other centres. But, for Communists in the past, the main thing had been to base themselves first and foremost on the militants. Now, they were beginning to lag behind them.

As yet, this was only a tendency. A more dramatic shift to wholesale bureaucratism and class collaboration took place during the war, as we shall see.

Work among women

From the beginning, the CPA was far in advance of the society around it on the 'woman question'. At the time of its foundation, it even seems to have been in advance of the rest of the socialist left.

A layer of feminists from the peace movement had been won to socialism towards the end of World War I. The best known was Adela Pankhurst, who joined the Victorian Socialist Party. Many of these women, including Pankhurst, were won to Communism in the early 1920s, with both rival CPA factions making conscious efforts to attract them. Other women came over from the Socialist Labor Party, motivated by a rejection of both SLP sectarianism and its internal sexism – these women 'often emerged within the Communist Party as champions of women's rights'.[51] In 1925, a report from the hapless Melbourne branch noted:

> the only section with any fight in them is the women. They beat the men in Melbourne by miles. One of these women is worth a hundred of these arm-chair philosophers.[52]

The first successful attempt at building a separate women's organisation was in 1928, when Militant Women's Groups were established to parallel the MMM; the Groups published the duplicated *Woman Worker* in Sydney. The *Woman Worker* gave way in the early 1930s to the *Working Woman*, a printed monthly newspaper, and the party turned to organising women more directly through its own structures.

In the 1920s, the party was motivated by a desire to build a women's movement 'not based on sex antagonism, but on the class struggle'.[53] If women:

> show their resentment at their repression by men it will only set the clock back ... They will only bring disruption, strife, bitterness and misunderstanding by carrying their sex war into the class war.[54]

In the 'Third Period', this rather one-dimensional orientation became even more dogged. Women were just another group fighting to build the party. The MM, which believed in setting up women's groups in industry, nevertheless

THE RISE OF AUSTRALIAN COMMUNISM

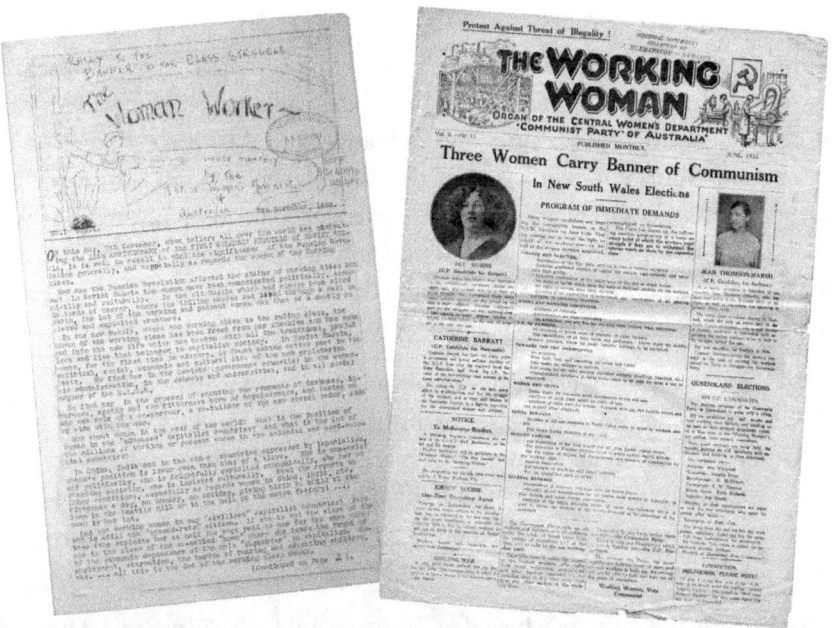

Left: *The Woman Worker*, publication of the Militant Women's Group, 1927.
Right: *The Working Woman*, CPA women's publication, 1932.

insisted that their task was simply to 'draw the masses of the workers into the MM'.[55]

On the other hand, the Communists paid much more attention to women than is commonly supposed – or, at least, the central leadership devoted much ink to trying to make the membership do so. The Militant Women's Groups published a major pamphlet, *Woman's Road to Freedom*. In 1932, the Central Women's Department of the CPA published another: *Women in Australia, From Factory, Farm and Kitchen*. The MM published an ambitious eight-point women's program and held several women's conferences. But, in the MM as elsewhere, there was a great shortage of women cadre:

> Although it is essential that a woman comrade should take up work among women, the National Committee finds itself without any assistance from a woman comrade. This appears to be an indication that women comrades regard the MM as purely a man's organisation.[56]

It was a dismal fact that only about 10 percent of the party membership in the deep Depression years were women, reflecting perhaps the low involvement of women in the unemployed movement. The great strength of the CPA's work before 1935 was its class politics and militancy, and this came through in the work among women. An early issue of the *Working Woman* took obvious delight in reporting the actions of a woman picketer engaged in 'jumping on the back' of a scab and 'bearing him to the ground, scratching and screaming'.⁵⁷ But perhaps the spirit of the Communist women of the time is best expressed in their explanation for why they refused to publish 'household hints' in their paper:

> The 'Working Woman' exists for the purpose of helping all working women to see the necessity to fight for the improvement of their conditions – not to help the boss to further lower their standards and increase his profits. The workers have always *been forced* to economise, but there is no need for them to do it voluntarily and take pride in it.⁵⁸

To be sure, the militancy included the usual wild attacks on 'social fascism', a category that included feminists such as Muriel Heagney. This sectarianism but – alas – also the fighting spirit began to fade as the decade advanced. The *Working Woman* became a magazine from 1934 and showed the first signs of wishing to model itself on establishment women's publications – including the once-shunned 'household hints'. Then, with the advent of the Popular Front after 1935, it gave way altogether to a new magazine, *Woman Today*. Nor was the name randomly chosen. The class politics had to be removed, because its founders were 'influenced by the great need to unite all classes of women to meet the growing threat of fascism'.⁵⁹

The new magazine was supposedly 'without party political ties'⁶⁰ and clearly reflected the desire of the CPA to win over the middle class. Class struggles assumed a secondary importance in the articles; for many issues, the front cover was ornamented by a sizeable advertisement featuring 'Beautiful Film Stars Who Use Mercolized Wax'.⁶¹ The same pattern emerged in actual organising work; for example, in North Queensland, the Women's Progress Club of Townsville, whose membership consisted mostly of Communists or their wives or daughters, nevertheless declared in its constitution that 'neither religion or politics shall be discussed at its meetings'.⁶²

It is not clear that such measures could be justified even on the narrowest grounds of expediency, because the continual watering down of the party's politics in the latter half of the 1930s did not produce a significantly higher rate of membership growth. In fact, one writer has suggested that the party's growth after 1935 was more the consolidation of the periphery established in the first part of the decade than any major new gain in support.[63]

The 'Patriotic War'

Once Russia entered World War II, so did the Communist Party of Australia. The fighting was no longer considered an imperialist conflict. It was a democratic struggle, and workers were called on to participate in it, both on the battlefield and on the home front.

Most Australians, and many of my readers, probably feel that the party was right to do so. Was it not, after all, a war for democracy against fascism? The alternative viewpoint, represented at the time by the Trotskyists, was that the war remained an imperialist war; that, at any time, the Western powers might still line up with Hitler against Russia, and the bombs produced by Western workers might rain down on Moscow; that Britain and the USA were fighting to retain imperialist possessions (within which they did not uphold democracy at all); and that Australian workers had no interest in dying for such things. They might also have added that the CPA itself had joined the war not to fight fascism (Germany had also been fascist during the Stalin–Hitler pact) but to advance the foreign policy of the USSR.

I agree with the argument; but, because the debate posed in this fashion rests on a discussion of international questions which would take us far afield, I do not intend to pursue it further here. What matters for this discussion is the war's impact on the postwar CPA. In that regard, a slightly different question is more relevant: even if it were correct to support the war, the test of *how* the war was fought by Communists remained crucial. The CPA's response was portentous for the future.

It must be stressed at the outset that the Australian party's performance was, in some ways, superior to that of other CPs. It was certainly much more internationalist and anti-racist than any other mass force in Australian society. The party campaigned against the racism of the US army and led strikes

CPA 13th National Congress, 1943.

among Australian soldiers to win better conditions – actions which the North American party considered 'traitorous'. A well-known CPA member published a pamphlet on self-determination for New Guinea, and it was partly to the CPA's credit that Australian troops were considered too 'unreliable' for use in ferrying Dutch colonialists to Indonesia at the end of the war. These experiences helped to lay the basis for Australian trade unionists' support for the Indonesian independence struggles a few years later.[64]

On the other hand, when it came to forms of national chauvinism that suited Soviet foreign policy, the Australian Communists were not so well behaved. *'Rumanians Must Pay for Crimes'* thundered the Melbourne *Guardian* in 1944, and apparently the entire Romanian working class were among the criminals.[65] The Germans, too, were expected to pay, although in this case Lance Sharkey was generous: 'This does not mean the destruction of the German people, nor their outlawry for all time'.[66] It did, however, mean the payment of reparations to the USSR, which is what the whole discussion was really about.

Finally, there was the use of caricatures of Japanese leaders – which even the most generous interpretation must concede were racist.[67] But the worst features of the CPA's war effort were at home, where the class struggle was totally subordinated to the wartime alliance with the bourgeoisie.

Craig Johnston has described the party's industrial policy as 'collaborationist', by which he means the following:

> endeavouring to maintain a truce between the two main classes: attacking capitalists for misusing the situation and offering advice to the state on how to solve production problems, and exhorting workers to greater efforts and yet still leading them in unavoidable disputes in order to find solutions as quickly as possible.[68]

This may be a fair summary of how the party leadership perceived the situation; in reality, class collaboration was not, and could not be, so neatly balanced. After all, solving 'production problems' necessarily means, in Marxist terms, raising the rate of exploitation, an issue around which there can be no class alliance except at workers' expense. In fact, the CPA was working towards the increased exploitation of the working class. Further, the party did rather more than just 'exhort' workers to toe the line, and the category of 'unavoidable' disputes meant those which the CPA could not suppress.

The shop committee movement, once a means of strengthening the independent organisation of the workers, was now consciously used as an integrating mechanism. The bourgeois historian Orwell Foenander has noted that, during the early years of World War II:

> Australian employers were disposed to look with some favour on multi-union shop committees ... and encourage their operation in their establishments. They indulged the hope that these bodies had a contribution to offer to promotion and maintenance of industrial peace in the community.[69]

We will see a bit later what price the party was to pay for this after the war.

> **Metal union will support strike by women**
>
> Any stoppage or strike by women metal workers to enforce payment of award rates will be backed by the Sheet Metal Workers' Union.
>
> This assurance was given by union secretary Tom Wright yesterday to a meeting of women union members.
>
> Another development among discontented women warworkers yesterday was the cessation of work in all Sydney woollen, worsted, and cotton textile mills—affecting about 8000 employees.
>
> About 50 Sydney factories, which employ 1500 women sheet metal workers, were represented at an all-day conference of women members of the Sheet Metal Workers' Union.
>
> It was the first time in the history of Australian metal trades that women shop delegates had held a conference.
>
> Commenting on a refusal by some employers to pay women workers 90 per cent. of the male wage, as ruled by the Women's Employment Board, Union Secretary Wright said that about 20 factories had not yet adopted the board's decision.
>
> "These 20 factories are still trying to find legal loopholes in the board's ruling in order to withhold higher wages," he said.
>
> "Our union dislikes hold-ups in any factory, but where an employer opposes the board's decisions, direct action is the only solution."
>
> The union would support any direct action the girls decided to take, he added.
>
> A union decision, as the result of which all employees in Sydney woollen, worsted, and cotton textile mills stopped work at 7.30 a.m. yesterday when night workers finished their shift.
>
> These mills normally employ 8000 hands. Most of the strikers are involved because key women workers walked out last week.
>
> Stopwork meetings to deal with a strike involving 5600 workers (mostly women) have been arranged by the Textile Workers' Union at Leichhardt, Liverpool, and Parramatta at 10 a.m. tomorrow.
>
> Meetings will also be held at Lithgow, Orange, Albury, and Goulburn. Mills in these centres employ about 1000 hands and are not so far involved in the strike.
>
> The strikers claim that the Arbitration Court has unduly delayed delivery of a judgment concerning claims for higher wages.
>
> Union officials hope that at tomorrow's meetings strikers will decide to resume work immediately.
>
> **Lockers, Footbaths**
>
> Union women's organiser, Miss Doris Beeby, outlined the new Federal Industrial Code, drafted by the Women's Employment Board.
>
> The code's "minimum standard" re-

Women metal workers strike over pay rates, Sydney, February, 1943.

The attitude to strikes was generally hostile, even where demands were obviously justified, and the CPA began to get used to the experience of suppressing the rank and file.

At Austral Bronze in Sydney in 1943, management tried to introduce a speed-up scheme. When the Ironworkers went on strike, their CPA union officials led strikebreakers onto the job. Fortunately, the engineers refused to work with the scabs, and the strikebreaking move collapsed.[70]

Some of the most impressive industrial militancy during the war was shown by women, whose very lack of long-term union tradition made it difficult for union officials to control them. And they had plenty to fight about. In the metal trades, the Women's Employment Board (WEB) had mostly awarded them 90 percent of the male rate of pay, but the employers used countless legal tricks to avoid paying it. Their concern was not so much immediate profitability, which was guaranteed by war contracts, as with trying not to set a precedent for the postwar years. In other words, what was at stake was women's legal rights at the time and their right to equality for long into the future. The CPA, however, was not as farsighted as the employers.

At the Richard Hughes factory in Sydney, when management refused to pay the WEB rates, the Communist-led union spent six months going through the courts, until the women forced the issue with a strike which brought quick results. And Jessie Street described the role of the Ironworkers' leadership in a Melbourne munitions factory, where women called a meeting to discuss action to get the WEB rate. The union secretary urged them to return to work 'as the boys in the trenches...'. At this the women became even angrier and shouted, 'We know all about our boys in the trenches ... they're our husbands and sons'. A strike followed which forced the government to ensure payment.[71]

Perhaps the most striking, as well as famous, events were those on the Balmain docks, where Trotskyists and other militants held the shop floor leadership at Mort's Dock. After a minor stoppage, the CPA officials of the Federated Ironworkers Association (FIA) decided to act against the well-known Trotskyist Nick Origlass and seven of his fellow militants. They laid charges against him for his conduct of the dispute and rammed them through a sparsely attended branch meeting, then imposed new job delegates on the rank and file.

They soon found themselves confronted with an unofficial strike that spread to 23 waterfront workshops and about 2,900 workers. This strike not only won the reinstatement of Origlass; it created a new, independent branch of the FIA, led by Trotskyists and other militants, which lasted for some time after the war.[72]

So if, by the late 1930s, the Communist officials had found themselves lagging behind the militancy of their rank and file, they had now had numerous experiences of head-on collisions with it. The seeds of a long-term contradiction in CPA practice had been sown.

Meanwhile, to be sure, the party membership was growing apace. Once the CPA had swung around to support the war, the numbers began to rise steeply even before the party was restored to legality. At the height of the Russian offensive, membership had risen to about 20,000. But what sort of people were being recruited, and on what basis?

Up to 1943, it appears that recruitment was heavily proletarian and was the pay-off for years of competent trade union administration and anti-fascist work. From 1943, however, when the party could operate legally, there was an increasing influx of middle-class recruits, estimated by estimated by scholar Alistair Davidson as about half of new members.[73] And, increasingly, the recruits were responding to the CPA's role as the 'leading war party'. Communists threw their energies into the war effort on every part of the home front, from sending comfort parcels to the armed forces to campaigning for immunisation against diphtheria; from rural fire brigades to mobilising labour for fruit canning. Diane Menghetti wrote:

one would have needed to be suspicious to the point of paranoia to perceive that a sinister foreign plot was being hatched by the compulsive organisers of street stalls, dances and bazaars who contributed so substantially to the relief of distress in the community ... they were, to use the terminology of the popular front, 'the useful people'.[74]

Unfortunately, if no one could discern in this activity a foreign plot, neither was there much sign of revolutionary work. The danger was that, in the postwar period, such recruits might carry the party further to the right – or, when bitter class struggle was eventually thrust upon the CPA, that they might be ill suited to it.

The CPA at the end of the war

At the end of World War II, Australia had a very different Communist Party than before it. While some of the wartime recruitment melted away fairly quickly, membership was still around 16,000. Another few thousand left in the following two years, but, with 12,000-odd members in 1947, the party was still several times larger than before the war.

It was also much changed by the wartime experiences. Certainly, the advent of the Cold War was to show that it had not lost its capacity for militancy. But it had gained a variety of other traditions: the acceptability of wholesale class collaboration, the pleasures of respectability and bureaucratic trade union work. Moreover, it went into the postwar years with a fantastically over-optimistic view of the future, although with some apparent excuse.

Russia was still in alliance with the USA for a time, and the United Nations was seen as offering hope for a world of peace and security. Colonies were moving towards independence; there were pro-Communist 'people's governments' in Eastern Europe – without any violent revolution; and Communist ministers were entering governments in the West.

In 1947, the CPA published a pamphlet called *Women In Our New World*, and the 'new world' was a socialist Australia. 'When Socialism began to get underway,' said the pamphlet, discussing the career of its imaginary heroine, 'Margaret went to work'. But about just *how* socialism was to 'get underway', the pamphlet and the party remained studiedly vague.[75] It seemed that it would somehow just come naturally.

It was, of course, a false dawn. Communists were about to face a much rougher world than they imagined. Far from the CPA transforming that world, the party itself would be further transformed by the confrontation.

3
The Communists on the Offensive

At the end of World War II, there was an explosion of industrial struggle. As early as 1944, a journalist had written:

> New South Wales, during the 20 months ending August 31, had 1,432 industrial disputes [depriving] the neutral citizen of meat, bread, laundry, newspapers, tyres, theatrical entertainment, hospital attention, buses and trams, coke for stoves, potatoes, restaurants, hot baths, country and inter-state travel and other amenities.[1]

In the three years 1945–47, nearly 5.5 million working days were lost in strikes. By comparison, only about 2.5 million days had been lost in the three last pre-war years of peace. The general ferment was so intense that, in September 1946, the Communist newspaper *Tribune* could report that the Leichhardt Boy Scouts' Band in Sydney was on strike and had black-banned its scout hall.[2]

After years of wartime sacrifice, workers felt that it was time for some reward. They were in a strong bargaining position. Industry was booming as it rushed to meet a sudden demand for consumer goods, and the unions felt an immense determination to hammer home this advantage:

> All members of the work force retained vivid, and usually bitter, memories of the depression years. This meant not only that the victims of that economic disaster were determined that it should never happen again, but also that the attitude of organised labour was coloured by a desire for something akin to revenge, for a

squaring of those industrial and social accounts left suspended with the outbreak of war. This time, it was felt, the bosses, the financiers, or however 'they' might be described, were not going to get away with it.[3]

At the start, the CPA was not behind the unrest. Indeed, it was not doing much to encourage it. Until 1947, the CPA considered itself to be in a united front with the ruling Labor government and was unlikely to foment industrial unrest for its own sake. On the other hand, the CPA, unlike some CPs in Europe – or even the British CP which was working hard to elect Attlee – made no particular effort to restrain strikes either. Communist union officials more or less followed the tide of events; just how militantly they performed depended on the particular situation, as we will see.

The central issues were wages and hours. The ACTU was pressing for a 40-hour week, and individual unions and workplaces were fighting for shorter hours and substantial wage rises. The federal Labor government, backed by the mostly Labor state governments, tenaciously resisted the union pressure on both fronts. Arbitration and conciliation proved a tortuously slow means to winning claims. Workers thus turned to strike action on a massive scale. The first major battle occurred in the Victorian metal trades.

The metal employers locked out 20,000 engineers and ironworkers at the end of 1946, in a dispute over wages. Within two months, the lockout was abandoned, but the unions now pressed home their advantage, turning the lockout into a strike. At the end of five months, the unions had won a major victory. They won wage gains that flowed on to other sections of industry, and the outcome undoubtedly hastened the granting of the 40-hour week in 1947.

The behaviour of Communist union officials varied. The leading Communist in the Amalgamated Engineering Union (AEU), 'Red Ted' Rowe, took a militant line throughout. He fought against other, more conservative, members of the AEU Commonwealth Council to ensure continuing support for the Victorian strikers. In this, he was in complete agreement with Joe Cranwell, an ALP member who was also on the Commonwealth Council.

By contrast, Ernie Thornton, Communist leader of the FIA, took a less aggressive stance. At the national conference of his union, Thornton:

seemed to imply that the Victorian dispute had gone on too long, that union tactics had failed and that the strike should be brought to a speedy end. He referred to the disheartening effect such a long drawn out dispute had on the rank and file, to the weakening of union organisation and to a backlash effect against communists.[4]

Thornton was hardly a more fainthearted person than Rowe. The different stances arose out of the different positions of their two unions. The AEU possessed large financial resources. It spent well over £100,000 from its supplementary fund, as well as selling and spending £120,000 of Commonwealth Bonds. At the end of the dispute, it was about to begin drawing on a £9 million fund held by its parent organisation in Britain. Moreover, it was comparatively easy for the skilled engineers to find other work during the stoppage, and most of them seem to have done so.

By contrast, the FIA was a poor union, its members without the easily saleable skills of the engineers. Its industrial militancy was correspondingly fragile in a dispute that lasted five months. In the Victorian metal dispute, Communist officials were clearly more influenced by their immediate environment than by an official party policy.

By the following year, that was beginning to change. In 1948, a second important dispute occurred in Queensland in the railways, and the CPA intervened in a much more coherent way.[5]

At the start of February 1947, 3,000 railway employees, together with tradesmen and their assistants, came out on strike demanding rates of pay equal to their equivalents in other states. The strike occurred against the background of great bitterness among Queensland workers. Both in agriculture and in industry, the economy was depressed, and half of Australia's unemployment was in Queensland. Railway workers were also particularly angry over poor safety conditions, which the government seemed reluctant to do anything about.

The rail strike met severe repression by the Hanlon Labor government. Other railway employees were stood down in an attempt to create divisions among the workforce. Legislation was rushed through to give the police authority to enter homes and eject any non-resident; to arrest without warrant; and to act against anyone suspected of aiding strikers. Picketing was banned. On St. Patrick's Day, a small demonstration was violently dispersed, police taking the opportunity to

Trade Hall staff and men released from jail for breaching Hanlon's Anti-Picketing Laws, 1948.

strike down Communist MLA Fred Paterson, who was watching the demonstration from across the road.

This latter incident brought a wave of revulsion against the police, with even the conservative *Daily Telegraph* being moved to criticise them. The unions responded with a demonstration of 8,000–10,000 people in King George Square.

The police violence hardened the strikers' determination. New groups of workers were drawn into the dispute. Waterside workers struck in all Queensland ports, seamen banned shipping, and all interstate rail shipments to the state were banned. It was widely considered that this blockade was the turning point in the dispute. After two months, the workers accepted terms in early April that represented a significant victory.

The CPA played a more prominent and more concerted role in this dispute than in the Victorian metal trades struggle. Ted Rowe came to Queensland to lead the strike, along with Alex Macdonald, the Communist Queensland branch secretary of the FIA. They brought a high level of organisation to the strike. Still, it was the strong CPA influence among seamen and wharfies that made it possible to organise support from these unions in such an effective manner.

The state government paid its own tribute to the importance of the Communists by singling them out for repression. Everyone injured in the attack on the St. Patrick's Day demonstration was a Communist.

Almost simultaneously with the battle in Queensland, there was another major clash in Victoria. The new Liberal–Country Party government there had seized on a transport strike as a pretext to introduce an *Essential Services Act*. This Act declared strikes illegal unless they were authorised by a secret ballot conducted by the Chief Electoral Officer. Even if a secret ballot had been held, the government still had powers of direction, and anyone failing to obey a direction could be prosecuted.

Several militant unions threatened industrial action if the Act were proclaimed or operated. When the government did proclaim it, the unions called a stoppage and a rally at Yarra Bank, which some 10,000 people attended.

The influence of the CPA was evident in the coordination of action by different unions and in the publicity campaign. The Engine Drivers and Firemen threatened to withdraw key workers from the Latrobe Valley power stations, and the Seamen's Union threatened to cut off coal supplies. Meanwhile, a massive publicity push was organised, with frequent leaflets and a newspaper called *Trade Union News*. Ted Hill reported that the first eight-page edition began distribution at 7:30am, and 75,000 copies had been distributed within an hour.[6]

The union paper enraged the employers and government by the unforgiveable act of publishing the *Essential Services Act* word for word. The press had suppressed the details; now, the government was forced to admit that there were objectionable clauses in it.

The strength of the union response produced a split in the government. The Liberals came under pressure from retailers who feared a long disruption of trade, while the Country Party was free from such direct pressure. The balance was probably tipped in favour of conciliation by unrest in the police force, who were angered by changes in regulations. Premier Hollway approached Trades Hall, which conveyed the government's terms to the transport unions. Summonses against unionists would be adjourned, with an undertaking that they would be permanently shelved. Proposed amendments to strengthen the Act would be dropped. The Act was a dead letter from that day onwards.

In the period that followed the war, the unions had so far won every major strike. There were also many minor victories. At the same time, and no doubt owing in large part to the industrial militancy, the Federal Arbitration Court granted the 40-hour week in 1947. To Communists and industrial militants generally, the picture was one of continual success, achieved through militant action – usually in opposition to Labor governments. And, increasingly, it was the Communists who appeared in the leadership.

As the confidence of the militants grew, the hostility of governments and employers hardened. As the CPA became more prominent in the struggles, the party was more and more singled out for attacks by governments, employers and media. An all-out confrontation seemed increasingly likely and, indeed, took place in 1949. Before looking at the events of that year, however, we will look at the evolution of CPA political and industrial policy after 1947.

The Cold War and the left turn

As the class struggle was reaching its height in Australia, the Cold War was beginning between Russia and the West. Stalin summoned the CPs to a new militant opposition to Western governments. Labor governments were not exempt.

The new turn was welcomed with enthusiasm by the Australian party leadership. Even before the shift in Soviet policy, the CPA leaders had been under pressure to adopt a more militant stance. Jack Blake, Victorian secretary, had called as early as 1945 for a 'consistent campaign of enlightenment on the essence of the class collaborationist views of the Labor Party leadership'.[7] The following year, Blake led his home state into virtual opposition to the Central Committee, as Ralph Gibson relates:

> In 1946 we had got out of step with the Central Committee of the Party. In preparing the draft resolution for the State Conference of that year, we took the stand that in the new circumstances of the Cold War the united front of the working class could be built only from below and only against the Labor Party leaders ... The Central Committee called for a change in our draft but we then circularised it unchanged in a clear breach of discipline.[8]

Richard Dixon intervened in the Victorian conference to reassert the official line of unity with the ALP leadership. But his words must have rung hollow in the following period, because Labor governments attacked every major union campaign. In the course of 1947, the party began to reconsider its position. Dixon told the Central Committee in February that 'we must present the Party as the alternative ... in order to establish socialism we must defeat reformism'.[9] By May, Lance Sharkey was taking a harder line at the Congress:

> when the Labor Party tends ever more in the direction of the camp of the imperialists and ever more clearly embraces the sabotaging role of social democracy, it is clear that we cannot pursue a policy that strengthens the reformist grip over the trade union masses. On the contrary, we must work to separate the masses from the right wing leaders in the trade unions and elsewhere.[10]

The CPA therefore anticipated the official declaration of the new Soviet policy, which was elaborated in September 1947, when the founding conference of the Communist Information Bureau announced that the world was being divided into two camps. One was the 'imperialist and anti-democratic camp' led by Washington, and the other was an 'anti-imperialist and democratic camp' led by the Soviet Union. A major attack was made on the 'right wing socialists' – meaning the social democratic and labour parties. The CPs were to adopt a more independent posture, to 'take the lead of all forces that are ready to fight for honour and national independence'. There was to be a new militancy on all fronts:

> The principal danger for the working class today lies in underestimating their strength and overestimating the strength of the imperialist camp.[11]

There was now an interaction of domestic experience and Kremlin directives, which led to an acceleration of the CPA's militant turn. The ALP began to be criticised in sharper and sharper terms. Queensland party leader Jack Henry announced that 'conditions are maturing for a very big break with reformism'. The Central Committee reported that the 'Federal and State Labor Governments [were] pursuing a bourgeois-liberal policy' and had 'allied themselves with the employers'.[12]

The Queensland rail strike provided much of the justification for the new policy. The strikebreaking tactics of the Hanlon government were held up as proof of the bankruptcy of Laborism; at the same time, the success of the strike was considered proof of the potential of militant policies. Jack Henry said that it showed 'the tendency of the reformist union officials and reformist workers to come over and fight very unitedly side by side with the Communists' in the face of attacks by press and government.[13] Dixon hailed the strike as a:

> classic example of what Marx and Lenin described as the intertwining of the economic and political struggle, of the raising of the economic struggle to the level of the political struggle against capitalism. We must aim in strike struggles not only to achieve economic gains, but also to draw the masses into the fight against reaction and to the side of the Communist Party.[14]

The urgency of stepping up the struggle arose, in the Communist view, from the imminence of a new economic depression. This new depression had been predicted by the Soviet economist Eugen Varga, but it was not only Communists who believed that it was coming. The Melbourne Chamber of Commerce thought in March 1948 that there was 'no dispute ... that the well-being of the economy is in jeopardy', and an ALP newspaper said 'all kinds of people – workers, businessmen and university professors – are talking about another depression'.[15]

The CPA expected the coming depression to bring with it a political radicalisation, leading masses of workers to support its policies. The Communist treasurer of the Sydney waterside union warned that 'there is no fury like the lash of dying capitalism' but predicted that 'the working class will move to the left, to communism; there is nowhere else for them to go'.[16] The party leaders announced hopefully:

> if we warn of the perspectives ahead, if we lay down the measures to meet it, then when that perspective develops, as we

Arrest of Bob Myles during the Queensland rail strike, March, 1948.

know it must, it will be to the Communist Party that the workers are saying in their tens of thousands: 'You were right. And from now on it is the Communist Party who leads our union'.[17]

One consequence of the new orientation was a turn to aggressively independent electoral campaigns. The party announced that Communists would give second preferences to the ALP, and, where no CPA candidate was standing, would give first preferences to Labor *where their opinion was sought* (emphasis added).[18] The party was no longer campaigning for the return of an ALP government.

Another interesting, if unsuccessful, CPA move was a bid to win trade union financial support. Taking to heart a declaration by Sharkey that 'to affiliate the trade unions to the reformist party strengthens reformist ideology',[19] Ernie Thornton moved to put the sentiment into practice in the FIA. In 1949, the FIA decided to alter the terms of its affiliation to the Labor Party. Individual members would pay a political levy, to go either to the ALP or CPA as they indicated. Where no indication was made, the levy would be used as decided by the FIA National Council. Branches of the union would affiliate to the ALP on the basis of the proportion of their membership which had directed their levy to that party.

The Labor Party refused to allow affiliation on this basis, and the scheme also ran into trouble in the Arbitration Court, so it was ultimately abandoned. It remains interesting as a kind of high-water mark in the tide of worker and Communist militancy in industry after the war.

The new left-wing orientation also found its reflection in the work among women, which was centred among housewives. Runaway inflation, lack of child care and the lack of even minimal amenities in some of the new working-class suburbs had produced a considerable ferment among housewives after the war, and the Communists had initially worked to build influence within the established Housewives' Association. Later, they formed their own breakaway New Housewives' Association (NHA). Some indication of the scope of the party's work can be gained from the NHA's claimed 50 branches in NSW with 3,000 members.[20] In Melbourne, a leader of the original Housewives' Association conceded that the breakaway group had branches in 32 suburbs.[21]

Whether working through one of these two organisations or directly, the CPA women showed a notable militancy in this period. NHA members

Left: The New Housewife features Daphne Gollan, delegate to Paris Peace Congress, 1949. *Right:* NHA march down Russell Street, Melbourne, 1949, Alma Morton in the lead. Slogans attacking Premier Thomas Hollway were painted on aprons due to the ban on political placards. Participants had to remove the aprons before being allowed into Parliament House.

addressed factory meetings on issues concerning women and on general political questions. In Sydney, a group of women stormed into the gas company to protest against rising gas prices and were able to force the manager to see them. In Melbourne, 100 wives stormed the Prices Branch office demanding controls on meat prices. And the agitation around rising prices reached higher levels in a mass demonstration in Sydney in 1948, which *Tribune* claimed numbered 10,000 and which won support as far away as Melbourne, where building workers in Moorabbin held a one-hour stoppage to coincide with it.[22]

Finally, the radicalism of the period found a remarkable kind of documentation in a heated exchange of polemics with the CPGB. In the postwar years, the British party had first called for an all-party 'national government' at a time when the workers were preparing to sweep Labour into power. Then, when forced by events to modify their approach, they moved to a position of virtually uncritical support of the new Labour government. To this, the Australian party took exception. In 1948, they wrote a letter to say so.

The Australians claimed that the CPGB had stated that Britain under Labour was in 'transition to socialism', had backed the government's attempts to boost exports to the point of raising the slogan 'Produce or Perish' and had 'consistently opposed the strikes of the workers':

> Their own documents relate that, in the big dock strike, in which they came out in opposition to the striking workers, Party speakers were in danger of being lynched by the workers, and that the strike ended in the hands of the Trotskyists and other rotten elements.
>
> The same applies to the opposition of the Party to a number of strikes in the coal industry.

Finally, the CPGB was guilty of:

> referring to the British Empire in the past tense, insufficient struggle on behalf of the independence of the colonies; and worse still, the example of the British comrades which led to opportunism and confusion in a number of the colonial Communist Parties.[23]

The British party denied the substance of the charges, and the Australians wrote back with extensive documentation. However, what matters here is not so much who was right and who was wrong, but the spectacle of the Australians delivering the British a lecture on militancy and class struggle (a lecture at which they are said to have been not a little annoyed). Not only was the CPA turning to the left; it was obviously prepared to go farther than some of its fellows abroad.

A kind of conventional wisdom has grown up about the militancy of the late 1940s and especially about the defeat of the coal strike of 1949. There is a three-stage argument which goes roughly:

1. The Communist Party was in continual decline from the end of the war onwards.

2. The Communist Party adopted an ultraleft policy, overestimating its influence and being sectarian towards the ALP. Such a policy is always wrong, but was particularly wrong in a time when the party was in decline.
3. This ultraleft policy was the cause of defeat in the coal strike.

Undoubtedly, there is some truth in each point. But they are certainly not the whole truth. The conventional wisdom stresses the dangers of ultraleftism and sectarianism towards the ALP. But it omits or underplays other problems, both in the strike and in Communist practice in the postwar period, particularly the problem of bureaucratic and manipulative practices by the CPA union officials.

The coal strike will be dealt with shortly, as will the problems of union bureaucracy. For now, let us consider two questions. Was the CPA in *continual* decline from 1945; and was the left policy of the party as entirely mistaken as most writers contend?

The state of the party

Alistair Davidson writes that 'the party declined in strength between 1945 and 1956', implying a steady decline, and notes:

> In 1945 there were 16,280 members; in 1946, 13,450; in 1947, 12,108. The heavy government onslaught on the party in 1948–52 further reduced the party to about 6,000 members.[24]

Other writers point out that the CPA was up to 23,000 members during the war and went downhill from there. Historians have, therefore, drawn the conclusion that the coal strike of 1949 was 'an act of bravado and adventurism when the party was in decline', as Robin Gollan puts it.[25] But a closer examination reveals a more complex picture.

The massive wartime recruitment was artificial and took place largely among the middle class. Eric Aarons commented in 1946: 'Many members recruited during the People's War had a rather one-sided view of Party traditions'.[26] They had joined a party associated with the glorious Russian ally and, equally significantly, they had joined a party that was discouraging strikes because of the war effort. It was not likely that all of them would be suited to a party caught up in fierce class struggles, and the departure of some of them was probably not a great loss.

By contrast, the end of the war brought the return of numerous war veterans to the party, a (literally) battle-tested cadre.

Most importantly of all, the party held its numbers after 1947 and consolidated its membership, at least in Sydney, where the number of new members was higher for 1948 than for 1947 or 1946 – suggesting an upswing in the party's fortunes. And fluctuation (turnover) of membership fell from 23 percent in 1946 to 19 percent in 1947 and 11 percent in 1948.[27]

The financial base of the CPA allowed *Tribune* to move from weekly to twice-weekly production. No doubt, this had a lot to do with the easing of wartime shortages of newsprint. Even so, there is no sign of *decline* here.

The real mass character of the CPA of the time is illustrated by the Sydney branch structure. There were five branches at the Chullora railway workshops alone in 1948.[28] The East Sydney area boasted eight branches with a total of 200 members.[29] A Sydney district conference held in 1947 was attended by 136 delegates representing 113 branches.[30]

Historians also suggest that the CPA's trade union base eroded steadily from the end of the war, and Gollan argues that the 1949 ACTU Congress 'provided the clearest evidence' of this decline.[31] Before considering Gollan's claim, let's look at the trends from 1946. Davidson, who accepts the thesis of continual decline, nevertheless records the following:

> It was symptomatic of worker support for communist policies that, until the 1947 Congress, communists continued to strengthen their positions in the very unions that were striking, while losing support in the ACTU itself and in the Trades Halls.

He then goes on to devote considerable space to the ACTU and Trades Halls, where the party's influence certainly began to wane as soon as the wartime honeymoon with the bourgeoisie came to an end. In these bodies, the high temples of class collaboration, that was to be expected. But what ought to be central for Communists is strength among the rank and file. And this strength was by no means quickly eroded after 1947. Indeed, Davidson must note one page later that 'quick gains were made' in industrial struggle in 1948. One page after that, he says that, despite a determined offensive by the Industrial Groups, 'the

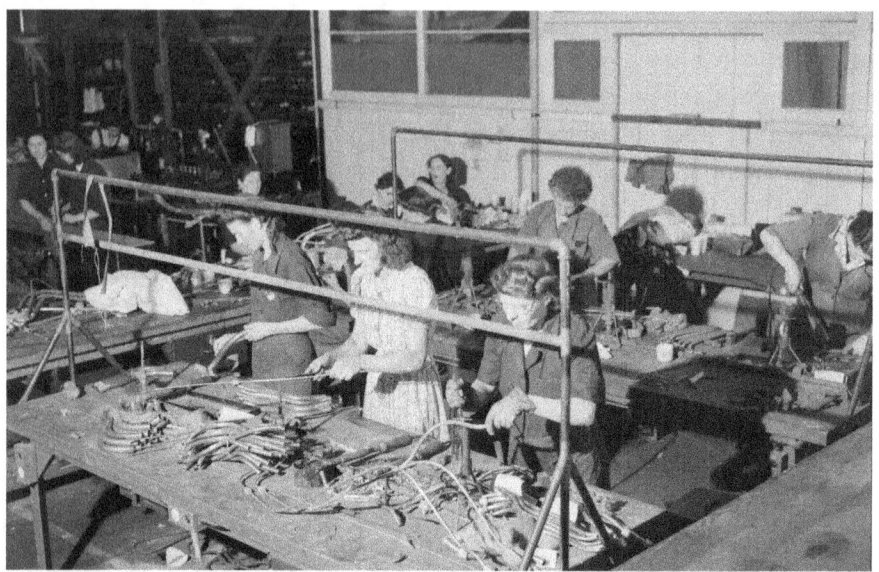

Women workers at Chullora, New South Wales, 1942.

communists continued to hold their own for a while. Groupers were beaten in elections for low level positions in some unions'.[32]

Now, what of the 1949 Congress? Gollan himself quotes Tom Wright of the Sheetmetal Workers, a Communist official:

> At the two preceding Congresses, the left wing succeeded in leading the discussions and carrying the day on all vital questions of policy. At the 1949 Congress the left wing had approximately the same number of delegates as in 1947, but there was a large increase in delegations under right wing leadership.[33]

This assessment, which Gollan does not challenge, suggests that the Congress results reflected more a mobilisation of the right than an erosion of the CPA's own base. The two are not the same.

The general picture is of a party which, between 1947 and 1949, was holding its position, both in numbers and in influence, among rank-and-file workers. To be sure, it was soon to suffer massive setbacks in both areas; but the party cannot be faulted for not having a crystal ball.

The charge of ultraleftism

There remains the charge that the CPA badly misread the political situation and adopted an ultraleft and sectarian political line. Looking back at the defeat in the coal strike, CPA leaders have assigned much of the blame to the 'Left line' which the party adopted from 1947.

We recall that the 'Left line' was based on two premises. One was that a new depression was in the offing. A new economic crisis was expected to lead to a radicalisation and move workers towards the CPA. The second premise was that the Labor Party was more and more openly becoming a tool of the bosses because of the coming economic crisis – which would eliminate any basis for reformism – and the growing political polarisations of the Cold War. The CPA believed that it could, and must, present itself as a political alternative to Labor on every front.

The first premise was, of course, badly mistaken. Australia was about to participate in a worldwide economic expansion. No one could have foreseen this development; even bourgeois economists reckoned with the prospect of economic downturn.

As for the Labor Party, it was doing its best to fulfill Communist predictions.

Militants remembered that, in the last depression, the federal Scullin Labor government had presided over a wage cut, and the NSW Lang Labor government had evicted the unemployed and sent the police to break up their demonstrations. In the performance of postwar ALP governments, state and federal, they saw little promise of anything better if a second depression occurred.

Chifley maintained wage-pegging after the war until forced to abandon it. He fought long and hard to delay a victorious end to the Victorian metal trades strike. In Queensland, during the rail strike, the Hanlon government invaded strikers' homes and beat up picketers and demonstrators. Under these circumstances, a certain hostility to the ALP leaders did not seem unreasonable. Now, what exactly do CPA leaders feel was wrong with the 'Left line' of those days?

Ralph Gibson attacks it as embodying the view that 'the united front of the working class could be built only from below and only against the Labor leaders'.[34] Given the record of the Labor leaders, does this seem unreasonable? Was it even remotely possible to build a united front with Chifley or Hanlon, except at the expense of workers' interests?

Gibson cites a particular example of the evils of leftism: the Victorian draft resolution of 1946 which the Central Committee rejected. Gibson probably picks this resolution, written before the actual left turn was taken, because he prefers to attack its author Jack Blake rather than the Central Committee of the late 1940s. This is consistent with the decision of the party leaders, taken in the early 1950s, to make Blake and Jack Henry the scapegoats for a policy that was, in fact, the policy of the whole leadership. But that need not concern us now. Blake's views of 1946 are the same as the Central Committee's views of 1949 and may be examined in their place.

Blake himself has identified the particular passage which the Central Committee and Gibson disliked:

> The sentence in question ... read: 'The workers will gain from Labor governments, only that for which they are prepared to unite, organise and fight.' My line of thinking was directed against the wartime wage pegging regulations which the Chifley government continued to maintain in force.[35]

There is nothing very radical in the sentence Blake quotes. In the face of Labor's consistent and vehement opposition to strikes and union demands, how could any militant worker expect to make gains without a fight? Miners reflecting on the 1949 coal strike could only have considered Blake's prediction accurate. As for Blake's enthusiasm for fighting the wage-pegging regulations, for which he was condemned as ultraleft ... on this question, the workers had the last word.

The wage-pegging regulations finally ended as a result of the Victorian metal trades dispute, precisely because the Metal Workers were 'prepared to unite, organise and fight', not only against the employers but against Chifley.

I dwell on this question to make it clear that the long-standing condemnation of the CPA 'ultraleftism' of 1947–49 is also an attack on militancy itself. In building up the conventional wisdom about the 'ultraleft policies' of that period, the CPA leaders simultaneously established the ideological basis for the right-wing trade union practice which they followed in the 1950s and 1960s.

That is not to say, of course, that the party policies of the late 1940s were free of ultraleftism – or of sectarianism towards the Labor Party. Many of their formulations, and no doubt some of their practices, were overly aggressive and overly confident. But what is certainly needed is a more balanced view than has been presented in most histories.

The coal strike: anatomy of a defeat

Early in 1949, Communists and other militants in the leadership of the mining unions began planning for a major dispute.

They believed that a new depression was imminent, and this shaped their thinking considerably. At the start of the last depression, precisely 20 years earlier, the coal owners had used a lockout to gravely weaken the unions and drive down wages and conditions. Now, the employers were again becoming aggressive. The militants believed that the unions must take the offensive themselves while conditions were still reasonably favourable.

The Miners' Federation adopted three main proposals. A log of claims was to be drawn up. An intensive campaign was planned to explain the log to the rank and file, build support and prepare them for struggle. Finally, an attempt was to be made to win support among other workers.

The log boiled down to four demands: long service leave, 30 shillings per week rise, 35-hour week and provision of amenities. These claims were endorsed by the Coal Mining Unions' Council (CMUC) and served on 22 April, and a campaign to build support on and off the coalfields was launched immediately.

The coal owners proved very hard-nosed, but F. Gallagher, chairman of the Coal Industry Tribunal, announced that he would grant some form of long service leave and would publish a draft award setting out the terms. This move might have postponed the dispute, had not the employers gained a no-strike order from the same Gallagher. The no-strike order polarised the situation and made a strike inevitable. On 16 June, aggregate meetings of miners voted for the strike by 7,995 to 882.

At first, miners believed that the government might intervene in their favour, but they were soon disillusioned. Ben Chifley declared that he would come in 'boots and all' against the strikers, and the government froze union funds and jailed union leaders. Finally, on 27 July, troops were sent into the open-cut mines. The amount of coal the troops could mine was trivial, but their presence convinced miners that they were up against the full power of the state.

The miners were also facing a united front of the government, the media and the bulk of the trade union officialdom. With coal shortages leading to massive layoffs in mid-winter, public opinion also swung against them. By mid-July, the strike front began first to fray, and then to crack.

Firstly, small mining communities on the fringe of the struggle began to weaken: Collie (WA), Blair Athol (SA), Ipswich (Qld) and Tasmania. By the end of the month, trouble was also brewing in the Northern District of NSW. Beginning in the town of Muswellbrook, Northern District miners began to demand new aggregate meetings to reconsider the strike. This demand was taken up by the Northern District Executive, a body on the right wing of the national union. The call for new aggregate meetings began to gain support throughout the union.

The central leadership held out against this demand for a time, but the pressure mounted. The Northern District Executive called a conference of lodge delegates, which displayed such strong sentiment for aggregate meetings that the militants dared not openly oppose them. A motion calling for an end to the strike was narrowly carried.

The militant Central Area Committee attempted to counter this development by calling meetings in Bulli and Wollongong – expecting pro-strike motions to be carried. They were disappointed. Militant motions were only narrowly carried at Wollongong and were overwhelmingly lost at Bulli.

The central leadership was now forced to call aggregate meetings. They put forward a recommendation to remain on strike for another week, hoping to find a face-saving formula to resolve the strike in the meantime. They hoped to gain approval for this recommendation, though the vote was expected to be close. They were disappointed. The recommendation was rejected by 6,974 to 2,378, and every district except Wonthaggi voted for a return to work.

What are the lessons?

CPA leaders have devoted much attention to the lessons of the coal strike. Predictably, they place the blame on 'ultraleft and sectarian' policies. Let us look at some of their arguments. Laurie Aarons writes:

THE COMMUNISTS ON THE OFFENSIVE 75

1949 coal strike. *Clockwise from top:* Miners at Wonthaggi, Victoria, receive strike pay; Prime Minister Chifley confronted by miners; Striking miners at a meeting organised by the ALP; Pamphlet by J. D. Blake.

> The Communist Party over-estimated the level of political awareness of Australian workers and the support for revolutionary socialism. We under-estimated the influence of reformism and the effect of a Labor government's strike-breaking, whose severity surprised communists and militant ALP workers.[36]

For Ralph Gibson, the main problem was lack of unity with the ALP and the entire trade union bureaucracy:

> Looking at the strike in retrospect, one compares it with the waterside workers' national strike of 1956, which, following years of united front work led by Jim Healey, was supported for three weeks by the ACTU, by all Trades and Labor Councils, by the whole Federal and State Labor Party machine, and by a large section of the general public.[37]

Gibson admits that 'such a high degree of unity would not have been possible in 1949' but insists that 'much more could and should have been done to find a broad basis for the waging of the struggle'. He blames the CPA's failure to do so on its 'Left line'.[38]

It might be well to point out at the start that one cannot, as Aarons seems to do, reduce the failure of the strike to wrong policies by the CPA. Gibson points out that the party was in a minority in the union leadership; nor was that leadership always in control of events. It came under considerable pressure from the rank and file from the start. Idris Williams reported on 9 June:

> Since we adjourned last Thursday's stopwork meeting, we have had hundreds of protests from lodges against adjournment. It may be that the rank and file will take charge itself, and as a consequence we will have a worse situation to face than otherwise.[39]

One lodge called on miners everywhere to hold weekly stoppages, to force the leadership to hold these meetings.[40]

However, to the extent that the CPA or Miners' Federation leaders were responsible for the defeat, it is not quite for the reasons advanced by Aarons and Gibson.

Gibson insists that more could have been done to broaden support. In a sense, this is undeniable: more can *always* be done. But just *where* could that broader unity have been built? The federal Labor government was quite consciously out to smash the miners and the Communists. ALP parliamentarians were touring the coalfields, spruiking against the strike. The ACTU leadership devoted its energies to securing a return to work. Some ALP union leaderships were dominated by Groupers. Under the circumstances, a 'broader basis for the struggle' would clearly have to be built among the trade union and ALP *rank and file*. Any strategy for breaking a section of the Labor Party or Labor trade union leadership away from Chifley would depend on pressure from that rank and file.

This would be precisely that 'united front from below' which Gibson does not approve of. However, the strike leaders did make a considerable effort to build unity on that basis. A full two months before the strike, a major campaign was underway to build support throughout the working class:

> It was not long before tens of thousands of Sydney's industrial workers were acquainted with the miners' campaign and ready to support it with enthusiasm ... At one rally in the Sydney Domain on 15 May, over 4000 people attended and carried a resolution calling on the Federal Government to grant the claims of the mineworkers.[41]

In the course of the strike, considerable opposition developed within the ALP to Chifley's actions. When a special regional ALP conference was called in Maitland to organise the anti-strike campaign, it only narrowly endorsed the government's stand. On 21 August, about 200 ALP members met in Sydney to form a Committee for the Defence of Labor Principles and Platform. It won support from several branches, especially in East Sydney and Lithgow.

The CPA and the miners could probably have done much more to exploit this situation, to 'drive a wedge between the right and left wings of the ALP', as one writer puts it.[42] This, however, raises further questions.

To what extent was the unrest in the Labor Party the *product* of agitation by the CPA and the miners? To what extent do they deserve credit for it? The conventional accounts do not even raise these questions, let alone answer them.

Aarons' suggestion that the CPA underestimated the severity of ALP strike-breaking is transparently wrong. For the previous two years, party leaders and publications had repeatedly stressed the reactionary nature of the Labor leaders. Blake, as we have seen, stated that nothing could be won except in struggle against them. The party declared that a depression was imminent, and severe repression inevitable, if the workers did not act quickly to forestall it.

Moreover, they believed their rhetoric. Edgar Ross, CPA member and editor of the miners' paper *Common Cause,* was so convinced that fascism was coming that he buried his books.[43] It is unlikely that Ross or any other CPA leader had illusions about the ALP's capacity for strikebreaking.

The price of bureaucracy

Aarons' argument is transparent, but it is significant all the same. It reflects the actual line of argument which CPA officials took when speaking to miners before the strike began. There was a widespread belief in the ranks of the miners that the government did not want a prolonged dispute and would step in and force the coal owners to meet the unions' demands. CPA officials encouraged this illusion, although their entire political perspective suggests that they could not have believed it themselves. Idris Williams told one meeting:

> We are not asking you for a general strike. If members demonstrate they are united and strong, I think the authorities will settle this within a week.[44]

It is hard to avoid the impression that the CPA wanted this strike at all costs, to achieve a confrontation with the ALP. And the party was prepared to lull miners into a mood of overconfidence in order to get it. This impression is quite consistent with a general pattern of manipulative and bureaucratic behaviour, both before and during the strike. Seeds of doubt about the democratic principles of Communists had already been sown before the dispute began. L. J. McPhillips, a Communist official in the FIA, had been jailed in early April. Phillip Deery recounts the response from CPA officials in the Miners' Federation:

> In an unprecedented move Williams and Parkinson recommended a general twenty-four hour stoppage in the coal industry

without consultation or ratification from the general secretary, the Central Council, or the membership ... [T]he political nature of the attempted stoppage demonstrated that union officials who were also communists were prepared to allow their ideological affiliations to impinge on union policy and even determine industrial action. This was remembered by union moderates in the months to come.[45]

The union leaders effectively kept information from their members about the actions of Gallagher, Chair of the Coal Industry Tribunal. Gallagher had proposed to publish a draft award on long service leave, but the fact was obscured by the no-strike injunction that was granted immediately after. The union leaders made no serious effort to inform their members about Gallagher's proposal.

Of course, it is unlikely that Gallagher's proposals would have been accepted. Knowledge of them would not, in itself, have postponed the strike – because the no-strike injunction made it inevitable (although, at one meeting where they were discussed, some 30 percent voted against striking, an unusually high figure). But the failure of the officials to make these facts clear was later used by the right wing as a handy stick to beat the left with. At Muswellbrook, the centre of early back-to-work agitation, one miner told a meeting:

Wharfies defend the CPA Sydney headquarters, aka 'Marx House', from police raid, 8 July, 1949.

> We struck before we knew what Mr. Gallagher was going to give us. Now, no-one knows what we are fighting against.[46]

This statement was unreasonable, but it could be damaging in a situation where the officials' credibility was in doubt.

One of the major issues in the last weeks of the strike was the reluctance of the leadership to hold aggregate meetings. They resisted the demand for such meetings, in the hope of holding the strike front for another week or two. They were apparently animated by the belief that the coal owners or the government were themselves about to crack. But by refusing to call meetings, they only played into the hands of the right wing.

As early as 30 July, representatives of mechanics and shotfirers (blasters) had seized on the refusal of the more militant unions to call aggregate meetings as a pretext for walking out of the CMUC. Two days later, a meeting of AEU shop stewards from all Northern District Collieries declared no confidence in their representatives on the CMUC over the same issue. On the same day, 300 miners signed a petition calling for meetings, and a miner was quoted in the *Maitland Mercury* as declaring: 'Why should we sit down while these men in Sydney won't give us aggregate meetings?'[47]

This denial of democracy became a very sore point. Deery records:

> In a recent interview Frank Manning said numerous rank and file miners – 'and I was at the grass roots level, I was one of them' – kept asking him for aggregate meetings. After the strike Manning realised, along with many other communists in the industry, that the meetings should have been called earlier.[48]

When the Northern District conference of lodge representatives called for a return to work, the Communists resorted to a very dubious bureaucratic manoeuvre. The Northern District Board of Management, which they controlled, met within 30 minutes and rejected the decision of the conference – an entirely unprecedented move.

Their justification was that the large minority of the lodge representatives who had voted against the resolution represented a larger total number of miners. This was a shaky argument. It was true that most large lodges had voted to stay out. On the other hand, some of the representatives who had voted against a return to work did not reflect the views of their members.

All in all, the CPA and their allies in the Miners' Federation established a pattern of manipulative and bureaucratic behaviour that must have contributed greatly to the collapse of the strike.

Alas, if only it were an isolated case. But this very style of work, in the unions and in the party, was an important reason for the massive defeats the Communists were about to suffer from one end of Australia to the other.

4
A Party Besieged

> Some soldiers in a train were eating bananas, and one of them threw the skins out of the window. His mate said: 'You shouldn't throw the skins out there. Someone might slip and get hurt'. The thrower of banana skins replied: 'Don't worry, the Communists will get the blame for it'.
>
> *Fred Paterson, Communist MLA[1]*

From about 1947, when the CPA took the offensive, a ruling-class counter-offensive was also gaining momentum. It had its roots as far back as the meeting of 14 right-wing groups called by Robert Menzies in 1944 to found a new conservative party, but it began in earnest with the onset of the Cold War. By 1950, the new Liberal Party had a membership of 150,000 and provided the main focus for a right-wing revival. Others included the ALP Industrial Groups and employers' bodies, including especially the bankers and insurance executives. The scope of the mobilisation is most obvious if we examine the struggle over bank nationalisation. This was a coordinated offensive by the political and industrial wings of the ruling class:

> The mobilisation extended far beyond the Liberal Party, with business publicity and financial resources being coordinated by the banks – the chief manager of the National Bank, L.J. McConnan, working practically full time on the campaign. The Liberal president R.G. Casey, a scion of Mt. Morgan money, raised large campaign funds from English capitalists; Menzies built the

issue into a general campaign against rationing and government controls as a foretaste of socialist dictatorship – and the Labor cabinet went down to defeat in 1949, hardly knowing what had hit it.[2]

The ALP leadership did its best to facilitate the right-wing offensive, even though it meant paving the way for its own downfall. Victorian Labor Premier Cain had fought the Metal Workers tooth and nail in 1947, and Queensland Labor Premier Hanlon had used violence against the railway workers. Chifley backed them both and spearheaded the great counterattack that broke the coal strike. He also amended the *Conciliation and Arbitration Act* to allow appeals over union elections, a provision that was soon used by the right wing to take over the FIA.

Labor governments, however, dependent as they are on trade union organisation and working-class votes, are poorly placed to carry out *open* assaults on the working class. By 1949, Australian employers had turned decisively to the Liberals and the extreme right to carry out the task.

While Menzies was winning power in the arena of federal politics, the ALP Industrial Groups were carrying on a growing campaign in the unions. Behind the Groups stood the shadowy 'Movement', whose social base lay among rightward-moving Irish Catholics. Its leader, B. A. Santamaria, was a professional anti-communist whose magazine, known first as *Freedom* and then as *Newsweekly*, warned the nation that the Communists were 'now in supreme control of the Australian trade union movement ... Australia stands one step from revolution'.[3]

With the appeals provisions – introduced by Chifley – and further

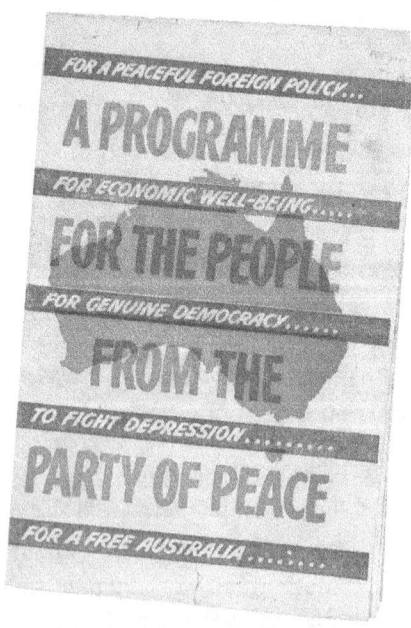

CPA program for 1949 federal election.

legislation from Menzies making it easier to get court-controlled ballots in union elections, the Groupers were able to displace the Communists in a number of unions. Some of them, notably the Federated Clerks and the Ironworkers, remain under extreme right-wing control to this day. The Groupers even won temporary control of the Melbourne Waterside Workers and, for one year, forced the CPA out of the leadership of the Miners' Federation.

The anti-Communist campaign soon expanded into an anti-militant campaign, with anyone who tried to be a good trade unionist seen as fair game. Ultimately, as the Groups gained in strength, they began to campaign against anyone who would not support them, an orientation which Santamaria made quite explicit:

> Firstly they [the Groups] opposed Communists. Secondly they opposed men who helped Communists, even though they might call themselves 'good Labor men'. Thirdly, they opposed men who considered themselves anti-Communist but who, for their own various reasons, wished to destroy the ALP Group organisation by withdrawing ALP endorsement from the Groups.[4]

By 1951, with the unions greatly weakened by this onslaught, Menzies was ready to hit them with legislation imposing severe penalties for militant action. These were the notorious Penal Powers which hamstrung the more militant unions to a considerable degree, until they were effectively defeated by the Clarrie O'Shea strike of 1969.

Finally, the Federal government used economic policy to weaken the union movement by increasing unemployment:

> The 1951 'Horror' budget was the first post-war attempt to repress economic activity through fiscal measures. The 1952 budget, though less drastic, continued policies of restraint ... The significance of Menzies' fiscal policy lies not in its effects on demand, but rather in its impact on the level of unemployment, which increased dramatically during the recession.[5]

The ruling-class offensive was successful in its main objectives. Union militancy declined markedly after 1950. Strike days lost, which had been about two million in 1950, fell to under 900,000 the following year and remained around one million for the following period. Labour's share of the national product fell dramatically during 1952 and stabilised at a level about four percent lower than before the recession of that year.

The success of the ruling-class offensive was fairly central to laying the basis for the postwar economic expansion and political conservatisation of Australian capitalism. The rate of exploitation was raised, and a climate of reaction was created in which trade unionists felt powerless. Politically, the rule of the Liberal Party was established for over two decades.

Simultaneously, there was a quite specific campaign against the CPA, waged on many fronts.

Lance Sharkey spent 18 months in jail for the crime of answering a journalist's question about a hypothetical invasion of Australia by Soviet troops. Sharkey did reply that 'Australian workers would welcome Soviet forces pursuing aggressors as the workers welcomed them throughout Europe', but added that such a prospect was 'very remote and theoretical' and insisted that 'the job of Communists is to struggle to prevent war'.[6] The disclaimers did not save him from imprisonment.

Cecil Sharpley, a member of the CPA's Victorian State Committee, broke with the party and wrote a series of sensational 'revelations' in The *Herald* (Melbourne), charging it with ballot-rigging and other crimes. The Victorian government seized the opportunity to summon a Royal Commission, only to find that the Commission became a minor victory for the Communists, because the government had made the mistake of appointing a Commissioner with a certain amount of intelligence and integrity. Mr. Justice Lowe found that the CPA did not advocate a minority seizure of power, and that strikes led by Communists were waged genuinely 'for the advantages sought in the men's demands'. He found no evidence that the Communists were 'foreign agents', paid or unpaid, and he found all but one charge of ballot-rigging unproved. Indeed, on several counts – ballot-rigging, the level of internal democracy and subservience to the USSR – Lowe was rather more generous to the party than some of its members have been in their memoirs.[7]

Another pathetic attempt was made to frame prominent Communist Ken Miller on a charge of molesting a little girl, but the case collapsed ignominiously when the girl admitted under oath that she had been put up to making the charge.

But temporary victories could not stem the anti-Communist tide. There was a wave of petty legal harassment. Ralph Gibson was arrested in Geelong for speaking in the street. Councils cancelled CPA bookings for use of their halls. In Sydney, the Lord Mayor even banned the Central Council of Railway Shop Committees from holding a meeting in the Town Hall, on the grounds that they were 'not a registered union'.[8] The real reason, of course, was Communist influence in the shop committee.

Left activists resorted to ingenious devices to circumvent the bans. When the Melbourne Town Hall was denied to Mr. John Rodgers for a speech about the Soviet Union:

> Mr. Rodgers announced that he *would* speak and a crowd gathered on the Town Hall steps. And he DID speak. The crowd heard a five-minute recorded address blaring from a microphone in an upper storey of a building nearby. The crowd was then advised to adjourn to the Unitarian Church where Mr. Rodgers spoke at leisure.[9]

While legal harassment could be dodged, it was less amusing dodging the missiles of hecklers. The Returned and Services League of Australia (RSL) systematically mobilised hecklers in country towns, plied them with beer and sent them to break up Communist meetings. Police stood idly by. Gibson observed wryly of one such episode:

> it was the tomato season, and before the meeting the local fruiterers were doing a roaring trade in tomatoes. This was a good sign, as tomatoes are actually the softest form of missile.[10]

The campaign against the party reached its climax with Menzies' attempts to ban the CPA altogether. He firstly introduced a bill to that effect, only to find it held up in parliament for a time by the Labor-dominated Senate, then later ruled unconstitutional by the High Court. He called a double dissolution to remove the first obstacle, then called a referendum with the hope of overcoming the second. Australians would vote on 22 September 1951 on whether the CPA had a right to exist.

The CPA had taken the threat of illegality very seriously from the start. They had gained some experience in underground work during the war and now

CPA poster attacking Bob Menzies, 1951

Page 2   TRIBUNE—Wednesday, September 26, 1951.

Communist Party Secretariat statement . . . . . continued from Page 1

LESSON OF THE REFERENDUM IS UNITY, AND STILL MORE UNITY

The great mass movement of opposition to fascism and war revealed in the Referendum campaign confirms the correctness of the perspective given in the Party Program adopted at the recent 16th Congress of the Communist Party.

Here was revealed the power of a united working class arousing and leading all other sections menaced by the dictatorial ambitions and war plans of Menzies.

Rex Chiplin Says..

FOR SALE: One brand new dictator's uniform, complete with whip, one cross of hand cuffs, 20 rolls of barbed wire, 8 dozen bottles castor oil and one complete home kit for making smoke screens. Apply Liberal Party headquarters, Ash Street, Sydney.

ABOVE organisation also willing to trade one rather worn red herring and flock of publicity men to state headers for rabbits.

STATEMENTS are going round that when the Sydney sailed for Korea recently she was one officer and was left behind when the Bataan arrived back from Korea the crew — over 200 — were lined up and when volunteers to return were called for only six stepped forward. It is in the public interest that Mr. Menzies should either confirm or deny these rumors.

MR. L. NAPIER THOMPSON, President of the Rural Democracy League, was franker than most of the YES men.
On August 21 he wrote to selected 'teachers' that "I am truly alarmed that our friends seem to think the Referendum is lost.
"Please find enclosed with "please act at once" and in ink he indicated the amount of the "push." One bloke down for £70 gave £2.

IT is not true that Menzies dropped his English butler when he gravely woke him on Sunday with "Nice morning, sir?"

"PROPERLY considered, the referendum should be carried by 10 votes to one." Menzies said in Tasmania last Wednesday.
One of his heelers, a Sydney newspaper columnist, took him seriously and laid two colleagues £10 to £1 his nonsense has been reflected in his column since.

A READER phoned on Monday to say that the Americanists Government has been referendum-founded.

TAKE your pick. "There could be no stronger way of showing the falsehood of Communist charges that the US nation is warmongering than to consider this magnificent ship. The United States is not a mighty battle-wagon. It is a passenger ship built for operation by a privately-owned American company." — Senator Tom Connally at recent launching of "United States".
"We care the solemn fact that we are in a period of world confusion and crisis. Against the possibility of such a crisis this mighty ship was conceived, planned and constructed basically and primarily as a naval transport for immediate use as a troopship." — John H. Franklin, president United States shipping line, same ceremony.

A WIDE unity in action was established between the Communists and the ALP members in the factories and unions.
The trade unions entered the fight in a way unparalleled in the history of unionism in this country. Trade unionists organised and fought on the NO committees as well as sponsoring their own radio and written material. Teams of union speakers visited many country centres.
This powerful unity and activity of the working class was the main basis of victory. It aroused the small farmers and middle class. It convinced the wavering sections.
It is this powerful unity and leadership of the workers on which is based the perspective outlined in our Program for People's Power and Socialism. We have seen in the beginnings of this great people's movement in the fight against the Referendum.
The lesson is: unity and still more unity, and the routing of sectarianism, narrowness and Leftism.
The importance of allies was shown in the considerable influence on the outcome exercised by the support for "NO" on the part of groups of university professors, clergymen and middle class people.
The powerful popular movement must be strengthened and further united in the fight to realise the Five-Power Peace Pact, against the rearming of Japan and conscription, for the defence of the economic interests of all the people, and for the removal from office of the Menzies Government.

Big blow to splitters

ALTHOUGH the Labor Party was divided because of the sabotage of extreme Rightwing groups, the campaign for "NO" conducted by the Labor Party leadership, headed by Dr. Evatt, helped to correct this.
The cause of unity scored a success in the campaign when it revealed the isolation from mass sentiments of the Keon-Mullens groups in Victoria and similar groupings elsewhere.
These reactionary elements who were enemies of unity and the chief splitters working within the Labor movement. They are the chief vehicle for spreading Menzies propaganda and anti-democratic policies within the Labor Movement.
They have received a severe blow in the NO vote, and the task of all honest members of the Labor movement is to destroy whatever influence they still have and drive them into their true home, the ranks of the Liberal Party.
To establish unity calls for the defeat of the enemies of unity and the splitting of their ranks.

the mass movement shows the way to victory against a still more powerful unity of the people. This can be achieved by pressing forward in the struggle for peace and for the Five-Power Pact.
It opens up the perspective of really going forward to the achievement of the objective of our Program — People's Power and Socialism!

Wouldn't be a bargain at any old price

(By a correspondent)

WHAT is the lady selling Daddy?" asked the three-year-old boy of his father as they walked past a Yes table on Saturday.
"She's trying to sell Menzies, but the people won't buy him," the father replied.

Win new members

The Communist Party membership responded to the call of the Central Committee and worked harder than ever before; not only that, but in a broader way than for a long time.
The conditions have been created for new thousands of workers to join the Communist Party. It becomes a main task for each Party committee and every Party member to bring new members into the Party, and in the first place, the industrial workers. It is particularly important to strengthen factory organisation.
Every Party member must draw the lessons from this wonderful experience and resolve still further to extend the united front with the ALP workers in particular and to reach out to ever new sections of the Australian people.
The Referendum experience of the mass movement shows the way

Domain crowd cheers victory; "proud of Australian people"

"I feel proud of our Australian people for their decision. Today Australia's name will be to the forefront throughout the entire world wherever people are fighting for liberty."

CPA General Secretary L. L. Sharkey said this amidst the cheers of hundreds of people at the Communist Party's Victory Rally in the Domain on Sunday.
The people had shown the warmongers that they were for peace, Mr. Sharkey added.
"A huge army of workers poured from one end of the continent to the other has dealt a crushing blow to the Menzies Government.
He called for a vigorous campaign to defeat the Crimes Act which had been condemned by the ALP Federal Conference—highest ALP body

—and the ACTU Congress.
Points made by other speakers: Mr. A. Watt: "This is one of the most important democratic victories ever won in Australia."
Mr. Dr. Evatt has played a valuable part but it is not his victory."
"It is the victory of those who trudged the streets night after night distributing leaflets, of the waterfront teams who took the NO message far and wide to distant parts of the country, of the pensioners who gave their pennies and the mothers who paid their endowment money in to swell the NO funds."

"Build unity"

Mr. C. Jones, Secretary of the Sydney District Committee:
"In Australia's first big battle with fascism, the democratic traditions live on.
"This doesn't mean that from now on we fold our arms. We have

only just started. Now is the time to build even higher the unity so achieved."
Mr. J. B. Miles, who was greeted with rousing cheers: "The Liberals made their slogan 'For or against Communism' but, whatever yesterday's vote showed, it was not an anti-Communist majority.
"A barrier has been raised to fascism, but this not the end. It can only be stopped by the united efforts of the people."
Mr. R. Morant: "This is a victory over big business, over the US warmongers, over the daily newspapers and over the extreme rightwing of the ALP.
"It is the first time the Australian people have been successfully rated if they favor a ban on the Communist Party and they have answered NO."

Referendum victory greetings to Party

The Communist Party received many messages of congratulations on the Referendum result.

"CONGRATULATIONS on Newcastle Trades Hall executive and trade unions on victory for democracy and peace," Mr. A. Dowling, Newcastle Trades Hall Secretary, wired CPA General Secretary L. Sharkey.
"Shipboard meeting congratulates Party on victory in Referendum," wired Mr. N. Troy for the Dunnoon NO Committee.
"The Victorian State Committee of the CPA wired Mr. Sharkey "warmest greetings on great victory."
Mr. Tom Dowling said that the ALP victory showed that the Australian people do not want Menzies' Fascism and war; they want peace, freedom and progress.
He said that in the Balmain area

the YES supporters were completely routed. "They deserted their tables very early on Saturday."
Mr. Dowling said that ALP and Communists unity was a feature of the Referendum. ALP workers in Balmain worked hard for a NO victory.
"In all, 17 people in the Balmain area joined the Party during the Referendum campaign.
Mr. Dowling said that Birchgrove did the most consistent work in the area during the campaign. Party members collected over £50, held 14 successful parties, collected over 200 signatures to the Peace Pact Appeal, gained 10 of the 12 new recruits and won many new Party supporters.

Wharfies' books are still open

THE books of the Waterside Workers' Federation at 60 Sussex Street are still open for new members.
Applications for membership, said Mr. Stan Moran, should state their name, address, age, union, place of work, and make personal application to 60 Sussex Street not later than 4 p.m. Thursday, September 27.

Air pollution serious at Newcastle

(By a correspondent)
NEWCASTLE — Between 1936 and 1948 there have been 1132 deaths in Newcastle due to diseases of the respiratory system. This statement was made by Chief Health Officer Meddows.
He pointed out that for every one of the tons of coal burnt in Newcastle it had been calculated that 40 pounds of "pollution" were discharged. This means that Newcastle sends a receptacle for up to 10,000 tons of pollution each year.
"It appears that Newcastle's respiratory disease death rate is 41 per cent higher than for the rest of the State."

proceeded to make use of it. Several party leaders went 'into smoke' to avoid likely arrest, a Comintern document on illegal work appeared in the *Communist Review*, and the *Review* itself ceased legal publication for a time. Four illegal issues, on a trial basis, were published by the 'Henry Lawson Press' supposedly operating out of Eurunderee, NSW.

Attempts were made to consolidate and 'purify' the membership. Members whose political affiliations were not publicly known were sought out to provide accommodation for Communists who had to stay clear of the authorities.

Nick Origlass at a trade union rally, c.1969.

Above all, the party made a determined campaign to establish unity with anyone who would oppose banning the CPA. Repeated attacks on sectarianism appeared in the party press, with an olive branch even being extended to the Balmain Trotskyists. A few months earlier, they had been 'fascist rats'; *Tribune* now announced with delight that Trotskyist leader Nick Origlass was the chairman of the Mort's Dock 'Vote No' Committee.[11] Summing up the struggle in late September, the paper headlined: 'Lesson of the Referendum is Unity, and Still More Unity'.[12]

The most important allies were to be found in the Labor Party. H. V. Evatt, who followed Chifley as leader, had decided by 1951 that if the CPA could be banned, the same measures could be used against the ALP. The Federal Executive of the Labor Party voted by eight to four to oppose the referendum, and Evatt threw himself into a vigorous campaign, warning:

> It is the Hitler technique all over again. First the Reds, then the Jews, then the trade unions, then the Social Democratic parties, then the Roman Catholic Centre Party, then the Roman Catholic and Lutheran Churches.[13]

The ACTU voted to oppose the most objectionable of Menzies' proposals and indicated its unease about all of them. A broad spectrum of intellectuals and public figures stated their opposition, and a Democratic Rights Committee held a rally of 2,000 in the Melbourne Town Hall. Above all, the Communist rank and file threw itself into the struggle. Letterboxing, painting slogans, stuffing envelopes, became a day and night activity. Even the football grounds were leafletted. And no wonder; John Sendy has recalled the grim future that party members felt might be in store for them:

> Central Committee Secretariat member Jack Henry visited Adelaide several times that year ... Henry attended our state conference, held in a small hall in Coromandel Valley ... I remember him enthralling the delegates with his account of probable illegality and the dangers which existed for active Party members. 'There may be sacrifices,' his voice rang out, 'there *will* be sacrifices, there *need to be* sacrifices to inspire the masses to struggle'. So as we marched into the red dawn it seemed that some of us might be left to languish in prison or fall before blood-stained walls.[14]

The defeat of the referendum by about 50,000 votes marked the end of Menzies' all-out offensive. While severe repression continued, the party was never again in such immediate danger. But the results of the onslaught were bad enough. Membership had fallen by half, from 12,000 to 6,000. Vic Williams, long-time Footscray Section Secretary, remembers once standing outside the party bookshop in 1952 and watching seven people walk by one after another, all ex-Communists![15] And as serious in the long run as the numerical losses were the effects on morale, consciousness and the style of party work.

Internal factors in the party's decline

How had the party fallen so far so fast? Repression is, of course, part of the explanation, but it does not seem enough to explain the severity of the setbacks, because a communist organisation is supposed to be able to face repression. The period of setbacks after mid-1949 revealed a number of serious weaknesses within the CPA that had lain hidden beneath the surface.

Retreat is a more complicated and difficult exercise than taking the offensive. All sorts of new and, for those accustomed to militant action, distastefully slow and unrewarding areas of work have to be entered. Above all, reality has to be looked squarely in the face, and the *need* for retreat fully accepted. But the party found it hard to accept reality and was ill equipped for the complexities of retreat.

For 18 months after the defeat in the coal fields, the CPA leadership pressed on with a perspective of immediate gains just around the corner. The coal strike itself was claimed as a victory, on the grounds that the miners had exposed the 'ALP traitors inside and outside their organisations',[16] and *Tribune* went so far as to declare:

> The way is open for taking *further offensives* in future to see that the capitalist class never again escape with their callous policy of unloading their depression losses at the expense of hunger and want for the working class. [Emphasis added.][17]

The party held out similarly unrealistic hopes for what could be accomplished in the 1949 federal elections, arguing:

> there is little doubt that we can achieve a big swing to Communists as the only real alternative to treacherous Labor politicians ... we are out to win.[18]

The CPA did pick up some extra votes from militants outraged by Chifley's role during the coal strike. But, of course, the winner was Menzies. The CPA reacted to his victory by calling for a united front and immediately claimed the most outlandish successes for it, announcing in *Tribune*: 'Bosses Wilting Under United Front Pressure'[19] and reporting that Communists in the factories had been besieged by Labor Party workers clamouring for a united front. As late as April 1951, Jack Henry told an unbelieving world that 'the time is approaching when the factories can be made fortresses of Communism'.[20]

It is no wonder that members were quickly exhausted or demoralised, when they had to face workmates or political contacts armed with such an unrealistic political perspective.

A second basic weakness was that the style of leadership, both in the party and in the unions, was bureaucratic, manipulative and elitist. There was a cult

Tribune, 7 January, 1950.

surrounding Sharkey and Miles. When Sharkey was jailed, a pamphlet was produced about his life concluded by comparing him to Lenin.[21] Speeches at Central Committee meetings and Congresses often began with the words, 'I fully agree with the remarks made by Comrade Sharkey' or something to that effect. The same adulation was extended in more moderate form to other leaders. For example, in Frank Hardy's book *The Hard Way*, we read: 'Ralph Gibson will not die, rather he will wear himself out in the service of the people then lie down to rest'[22] and, of Ted Hill:

> There is an air of tremendous strength about him that inspires others to greater fortitude. He can hold a situation together and prevent panic. He can be ruthless when the struggle calls for ruthlessness, yet he can be warm and sympathetic, making allowances when the luxury of tolerance can be afforded.[23]

If a man of Hardy's ego could write that way about the leadership, it is a comment on what the average party member was expected to think. Sharkey later grudgingly admitted: 'The idea was created, flowing from Stalin and his cult, that the workers had to have leaders in whom they could have confidence'.[24]

This idea was applied in similar measure to trade union officials. Every effort was made to turn Jim Healy and Ernie Thornton into folk heroes. The thoroughly *elitist* nature of the cult emerges best from the passage in John Morrison's novella *Black Cargo*, in which the Communist union official Manion is pictured looking at wharfies in the pub:

> He was seeking courage in the soiled and lively faces. Ill-informed no doubt, but staunch as cradled brothers and forthright as children. Easily led as long as the path had all the outward appearance of loyalty. Easily baffled by the plausible and hypocritical scheming of the [right-wing] Nesses and Heffners. Indomitable under the [Communist] Healys and Elliots.[25]

The personality cults were backed up by the use of pseudo-Marxist 'science' to dazzle the naïve. By 'science', they meant a kind of absolute truth that was the property of the experts. Zelda D'Aprano no doubt expressed the feelings of many when she wrote:

> Our leaders made lengthy reports and speeches and I never questioned what they said. I was always overawed by their intelligence, ability to express themselves and their composure. I never questioned a doctor when giving a diagnosis, and it was the same in the party. One never questioned the experts.[26]

Elitist attitudes went hand in hand with undemocratic practices in the party and in the unions. That is not to say that party conferences were not *formally democratic*. It is sometimes imagined that the CPA was an armed camp with whip-wielding commissars; in reality, the mechanisms of control were normally relatively subtle. Rather than a reign of terror, there was often a reign of speechifying, with all the top leaders making lengthy reports which pre-empted any serious discussion. Anyone bold enough to disagree was as likely to be attacked by the membership as by the leaders, as one activist remembers:

> [T]o oppose views from people in leadership positions ... was seen incorrectly as the voice expressing views of the class enemy. This

was seen as planned disruption ... and was not to be tolerated by the 'party'.

The general approach was to rally to the leadership and deal blow after blow at the malcontents.[27]

Just as often, potential critics were dissuaded in advance – again, by their fellow rank-and-file members. W. J. Brown noted: 'Too often when somebody raises a criticism we hear the phrase, "You'll get done". Then fear of "getting done" becomes a fetter on criticism'.[28]

A similar pattern emerged in the unions, with drastic consequences in some cases. When CPA officials were defeated in union elections after 1949, Ted Hill found himself forced to record the reaction of the rank and file in these terms:

> I have heard it said that it will do some of these trade union officials good, that they be defeated in these ballots and be returned to the workshops ... I have heard it said that they have been guilty of bureaucracy, that they have failed to develop Party organisation down below, that they are economistic and various other phrases about trade union officials.[29]

In an attempt to save themselves from the challenge of the Industrial Groups, Communist officials sometimes resorted to ballot-rigging. Daphne Gollan, who worked in the office of the FIA, has confirmed this and explained the elitist justification:

> Those who argued for adjustment of union ballots, recognising it as an evil necessity of course, said that beleaguered as we were in the unions ... we could not allow the enemy into policy-making bodies ... After all, the long term objectives of the socialist movement could not be jeopardised by the errors or failures of our short term policies, or halted because the rank and file were temporarily misled by the overwhelming barrage of lies from the reactionaries ... The use of dishonest expedients to gain time brought its own punishment ... the time gained never was used to reassess policies ...

Adjustment of ballots continued, with the hope that sooner or later, the rank and file would catch up, come to realise the correctness of party policy. Needless to say, the perspectives of party and masses, far from converging, drew further apart.[30]

Political initiatives were forced on union memberships bureaucratically, while bread and butter issues were neglected; so, in 1951, Dixon could attribute electoral setbacks on the wharves to 'neglect of the economic issues, the day-to-day questions' while concentrating on political strikes.[31]

The party was also paying the price for dampening militancy during the war. In their all-out push for war production, CPA officials had weakened the shop committee movement; now, with the right wing on the offensive, shop committees were one important way Communists could retain influence on the shop floor even if official positions were lost. In some areas, such as the power industry in NSW, the CPA was able to do just this. In other areas, it proved very difficult to revive shop committees that had lost their dynamic quality during the war. Even worse, as Ted Rowe discovered, many left officials had become afraid to do so:

> [A] certain temerity had emerged within some of us in union jobs who were inclined not to relish the enfilading from the flank, which was very often very healthy working class criticism.[32]

The elitism and bureaucratism in the unions led to setbacks for two basic reasons. Firstly, they discredited Communists in the eyes of the rank and file and gave ammunition to the right-wing opposition. Secondly, and probably most importantly, they demobilised the militants who were the party's own base or, at least, discouraged critical thinking and imagination among them – qualities that are especially important in a period of retreat.

Within the party, the same weaknesses led to decline for similar reasons. Members trained in parroting dogma, unaccustomed to open debate, were ill equipped to defend the party in the face of intense ideological attack. Abuses were hard to correct: Vic Williams remembers raising problems of minor corruption among the union officials in his section, only to find that 'people at the top were just closing their eyes'. He discovered that, if you relayed criticism from your branch members, 'it was immediately imputed that you held that criticism yourself'.³³ Perhaps the most scandalous example was the 'Party Consolidation' episode of 1954. In that year, when the worst defeats were over, and the situation had stabilised, the party leadership attempted to produce some assessment of the period 1949–51 and explain the setbacks, with an eye to consolidating the party on a new course. The result was very sad indeed.

The blame was, predictably, placed on 'ultraleftism' and sectarianism. This was, as we have seen, a very one-sided approach; but what was worse was that the whole responsibility was dumped on the doorstep of two individuals, Jack Blake and Jack Henry. The Central Committee disinterred the Victorian draft resolution of 1946, written by Blake, to show the historic roots of his errors. It blamed him and Henry for leftism in general, for leading the party astray when Sharkey was in jail and even for attempting to seize control of the party while Sharkey was out of the way. Now, several years later, these alleged sins were suddenly brought to light. Blake and Henry were removed from the Secretariat, even though they had 'given no sign of resuming their earlier activities'. The two scapegoats were then obliged to publish grovelling statements approving the verdict. Blake admitted that 'my activities in the period referred to were a grave menace to the Party, and the Party owes a great debt to Comrades Sharkey and Dixon who led the Party out of this danger'. He promised to correct his errors and to 'eliminate all forms of subjectivism from my make up'.³⁴

Jack Blake

Nothing about the appalling manipulation by Communist union officials; no assessment of the internal life of the party. In fact, the scapegoating of Blake and Henry could only make the real problems worse. It could only reinforce the authoritarianism of the remaining leaders and make middle cadres wary of taking initiatives. As for the substance of the criticism – the attacks on ultraleftism and sectarianism – it only paved the way for an increasing conservatism and timidity in party work, including, in some cases, a positive fear of industrial militancy.

The focus on unity that arose with the struggle against the attempt to ban the party found its reflection in the practice of running 'unity tickets' for union

The Canberra Times, 25 August, 1961.

office. These were joint tickets of Communist and Labor Party supporters with policies based on the lowest common denominator. Care was taken to avoid initiatives that might alienate ALP officials and to avoid excluding them from leadership in unions where the CPA was strong. By this means, the party rapidly regained its strength in the union bureaucracy. By 1958, it had won back most of the ground lost since the 1940s. But at what price?

It is instructive to note that, while party membership grew for a time in the mid-1950s, it by no means grew as quickly as the party's bureaucratic union strength. And it fell again after 1956 without substantially affecting that hold on official positions. There were two factors at work here. On the one hand, a combination of increasing prosperity, the defeat of the left offensive of the late 1940s and the sustained ideological and legal onslaught from the right had reduced both the urgency and the appeal of radical *politics* in the eyes of many workers, while militant trade unionism around economic issues still offered tangible rewards. Workers without radical politics might, therefore, elect Communist officials who were seen as effective union leaders. (To be sure, many workers had always adopted this attitude, but postwar conditions were designed to intensify the problem.)

At the same time, it seems clear that the CPA was now winning union positions, not by distinguishing itself from the ALP officials, as it had generally done in decades past, but by merging into the mainstream. This might win union jobs but would not provide workers with any reason to join the CPA. But, if the numbers of officials grew, without a corresponding growth among the working-class rank and file, that could only mean that the party's industrial work would be increasingly dominated by the bureaucrats, with a consequent tendency to conservatise the work.

The consequences have been well summarised by Jack Mundey, who described the postwar union work of the CPA in these trenchant words in 1970:

> when a group of workers was involved in a struggle ... after a few days or a week an array of union officials ranging from extreme right to extreme left would turn up and urge them ... to return to work to avoid the penal powers being slapped on ... the 'left' officials usually justified this as being 'in the interests of the class as a whole' ... There was too much readiness to *settle* rather than set out to *win* disputes.[35]

It is worth discussing one specific example of what this style of work meant in practice. Vic Williams, then a power worker, got together with a few other Communists to set up a shop committee at Melbourne's Newport power station. They were 'practically begged' by the workers to set it up and were soon able to contact other stations and establish shop committees in them as well. After prolonged agitation about the fact that wages were lower among these workers than their counterparts in NSW, the stage was set in 1961 for a 24-hour strike. The strike would be illegal, but it was obvious that the militants had mass support. 'Prior to that,' says Williams, 'there was a sort of Communist leadership in the SEC [State Electricity Commission] but all it did was make pronouncements ... They were so afraid of the SEC'. Now, this section of the working class – previously neglected by the mainstream union officials – was about to enter a major struggle, with the CPA on the ground floor, after two years of work by its members. How did the party leadership respond?

> Right on time came the 24-hour stoppage ... and the State Executive decided otherwise! I did my block and went off in high

dudgeon. I remember a great delegation of trade union officials coming out to Newport power station, they came over the bridge. I saw them coming, and went out to meet them. And as they came down the steps I called out to them, 'It's no bloody use, the stoppage is going on'. Laurie Carmichael was in front, and he just laughed and said, 'Oh yes, I guess it is'. He was a bit of a realist.[36]

And the strike did go ahead against the desires of the CPA leadership, setting the stage for a historic period of militancy among Victorian power workers that culminated in the 1977 Latrobe Valley strike. But the party leaders would have stifled it at birth.

Turning inward

In a period of defeat, the greatest danger is that the activists will turn inward. It is hard to talk to non-Communists and tempting to spend all your time talking to comrades. From here, it is only a short step to bitterness and contempt for other people. This is the road to sectarian isolation, and not a few Communists travelled it, as Jack Blake made clear as early as 1951:

> The conditions of the early post-war years ... led to a defensive spirit among some party members, linked with a turning inwards for the comfort of being among like-minded people.
>
> Of course this tendency was not consciously thought out in this way – it expressed itself mainly in evading the political struggle, shifting ground under pressure ...
>
> Basically our sectarianism is related to an inability or unwillingness to undertake political work among the working people who are not Communists or who are not even close to the Communist Party.[37]

Blake was writing about the late 1940s – when things were polarised, but the left was at least winning some victories. How much worse these tendencies must have become in the early 1950s! The passage suffers from the usual CPA leaders' habit of placing all the blame on the rank and file, but it is insightful, nonetheless.

If members were evading the political struggle, they had some good reasons. The wages struggle on the job was something Communists could agree about with fellow workers fairly easily, and they could even win support and popularity among other militants on this account. Getting a hearing for Communist politics was far more difficult. Winning an argument about the merits of Soviet Russia was well-nigh impossible, except in isolated left-wing bastions like the Seamen's Union. But even the peace movement propaganda, which had a moderate language and popular appeal, did not excite much real enthusiasm in a working class battered by a series of defeats.

After a period of frustration, many Communists began to turn bitterly inward. An internal party document of the time offers a graphic account of their sentiments:

> [There is] a lack of faith in the strength and potentialities of the Australian working class and the Communist Party. 'They [the working class] will not accept Socialism – they may in the distant future after the capitalists have kicked their guts in.'

Having turned away from the masses, the next step was to leave politics altogether. The internal document indicates quite bluntly how many comrades were tempted to do just that, quoting members' statements:

> 'I've done my bit in the past (or I'll do my little bit now), let others have a go … I've been a fool so long – depriving myself of things while the rest of the so and so's looked after themselves – now it's my turn'.

> Some comrades spoke of fearing to come out openly as a Communist for fear of being 'branded' and suffering the social stigma associated with being a Communist in the eyes of many today, thus ruining their chances of 'becoming something' socially … Others leave jobs where they have won considerable mass influence for jobs with higher pay, or where the struggle appears to be easier.[38]

The party was also pervaded by paranoia, understandably. Communists faced one witch-hunt after another, were often victimised at work and found their children being harassed. Frank Hardy's account in *The Hard Way* of the repression and harassment he faced while writing *Power Without Glory* is only a somewhat more spectacular version of what others faced. But, while the Communists' fears were understandable, a fascination with security could only hamper recruitment. Potential members were not likely to feel comfortable in a party that was constantly looking over its shoulder, and branches often approached potential recruits with more suspicion than enthusiasm.

In 1956, W. J. Brown went so far as to say that the fear of spies was hurting democracy in the organisation because, whenever someone raised a critical viewpoint: 'Very quickly some party member suggests there might be more behind such criticism than meets the eye'. Brown pointed out that the best guarantee of security is free political discussion:

> Quick stifling of criticism provides the atmosphere in which police agents can flourish.
>
> Genuine criticism that could lead to uncovering a police agent remains unspoken. Chance incidents that might lead to uncovering a provocateur go unmentioned because we have failed to create a free atmosphere for exercise of criticism.[39]

Given the setbacks and problems, however, it is remarkable how many Communists survived the Cold War with their confidence in socialism (of some kind) and the working class intact. Unfortunately, they often did so at the cost of a retreat into blind and dogged faith, a process which the Italian Communist Antonio Gramsci summed up very well:

> When you don't have the initiative in the struggle and the struggle itself comes eventually to be identified with a series of defeats, mechanical determinism becomes a tremendous force of moral resistance, of cohesion and of patient and obstinate perseverance. 'I have been defeated for the moment, but the tide of history is working for me in the long run.' Real will takes on the garments of an act of faith in a certain rationality of history.[40]

This 'mechanical determinism' is an expression of perseverance and dedication and so contains a healthy element. But, for cadres forced to live with it for two decades, it inevitably leads to permanent distortions: they get in the habit of thinking in terms of slow, gradual change. In the late 1960s, when both students and young workers produced explosive struggles and were bursting with anger and impatience, far too many Communists, shaped more than they realised by the years of downturn, responded with annoyance at these ignorant youngsters who didn't understand that 'things take time'.

Even in the 1950s, while 'mechanical determinism' could be forgiven in the rank-and-file activist, it could hardly be forgiven in those who formulated party programs. In the passage quoted above, Gramsci went on to explain that, if it

'Marx House', Sydney, 1950.

were taken up by the leadership and made into a political principle, 'it becomes a cause of passivity, of idiotic self-sufficiency'.[41] Yet, the leaders – more, perhaps, than the rank and file – were fascinated with a number of articles of political faith that bore little relation to the reality around them. One was the perspective for building a 'mass' party in the immediate future, a perspective which Jack Blake later recalled with some acerbity:

> In 1958 the 'mass party' conception was embodied in the Party membership target of several tens of thousands; the idea being some forty or fifty thousand members, or twice our best wartime figure. By 1961, still pursuing the same conception, the slogan calling for doubling the Party membership was put forward ... [42]

The fantasy of massive growth prospects was based in turn on the belief, held to grimly throughout most of the postwar boom, that a cataclysmic economic crisis was imminent. Sharkey's prediction of 'growing political as well as economic crisis',[43] made in 1958, is a sample of the splendid disregard which the party leadership entertained for economic reality.

Such pronouncements produced a remarkable sort of behaviour among the membership. Some members, no doubt, simply laughed them off. Others tried to act on the basis of them. Most, however, inevitably were of two minds: in one compartment, they accepted them, believed them, and would even sometimes defend them heatedly; at the same time, they did little – if anything – about them. They were articles of faith, not perspectives for action.

The unfortunate consequence was that even perspectives that *deserved to* be acted upon got the same treatment; for example, the peace movement of the 1950s, whatever political criticisms one might make of it, certainly

did arouse popular sympathy, as the huge meetings and massive signature campaigns proved. Yet, it was hard to get the party membership enthusiastic about building it, leading Jack Blake to complain that it took some time even for the Central Committee to 'grasp the central position which the struggle for peace must occupy', let alone the rank and file.[44] Similarly, on the question of sexism, then called 'male supremacy', there were continual exhortations from the leaders for male members to take work among women seriously, or to do housework and so free their wives to do political work. One reason these appeals were disregarded was undoubtedly that the personal record of the individual leaders did not match their own rhetoric, but another was that these pronouncements appeared as simply another abstract ideal to which lip service must be paid – and little else.

Party work tended to get into deep ruts. Vic Williams recalls that he was always dismayed by the fact that 'too often you'd find people who should have been doing the work couldn't see beyond making a general pronouncement' and were incapable of 'the sort of spark that generated leaflets here and committees there'.[45] Branches clung to tried and true methods of work, and every meeting was like every other. In her novel *Bobbin Up*, Dorothy Hewitt has portrayed the atmosphere of a CPA branch in the 1950s. Nell, the heroine, is a shop steward in a textile mill. She wants to put out a job bulletin with a lively style.

> 'Well, I don't know, Nell,' said the section secretary. 'I don't like the tone of it much. Doesn't sound ... dignified to me ...'
>
> 'There ought to be more of the Party's policy in the thing.' Mick Shannan was laying down the law. 'There's not a straight-out political article in the whole bulletin. Now when I was gettin' out a political bulletin in the AWU ...'
>
> 'It doesn't sound nice,' Rae said firmly. 'I don't think the girls would like it. Nell often exaggerates, and she hasn't got anythin' about peace in the bulletin.'
>
> 'Have you taken it down to the Centre yet, Nell? The Centre ought to see it before it's roneoed.'

'It's got to be out by tomorrer,' Nell said stubbornly. 'Anyway we can't always be wet-nursed by the Centre.'

'It'll probably all fizzle out anyway.' Rita shrugged her plump shoulders. 'When I was in the clothin' trade ...'

'I move we pass onter the political discussion. We haven't had a decent political discussion since I came inter this branch.'

'Oh! Snow, for Christ's sake shut up,' Nell thought, but she only said quietly, 'This *is* the political discussion, Snow.'[46]

Just as Nell found her branch more hindrance than help, so did many activists find party campaigns an obstacle to real work. Dulcie Mortimer remembered:

> For a long time we had Party-building drives – in themselves narrow, inward-looking – absorbing a great deal of time of most members of local organisations in a fruitless search for a magic formula; while on the other hand a thinning band of mass workers, who were gaining valuable experience among real people, were becoming more and more frustrated. Nobody was interested in what they were doing; it didn't seem to have any bearing in the arid atmospheres of local discussions.[47]

Still a major force

Of course, we must not overstate the case. For all the setbacks, both in numbers and in consciousness, the CPA remained the most important organisation outside the ALP promoting progressive and radical causes and able to do so on a large scale. In fact, considering the conservatisation of most of society, its role became perhaps proportionately more important. And its members were involved – indeed, the moving force – in a great many activities.

Vic Williams says:

> It didn't matter what happened ... if some school committee hit the headlines, you could bet your life, there'd be some Communist Party member at the school, and he'd be organising. I used to pick

up the paper when I was a Communist Party organiser and I'd be amazed; I'd see all these issues and I knew someone who'd be running them.

He even recalls a story, probably apocryphal, that the CPA had a fraction in the Masons. When called upon to report, they replied that they couldn't do so because, as Masons, they were sworn to secrecy.[48]

To get a sense of the scope of the party's mass work in this period – but simultaneously of its limitations – let's look at some concrete examples.

Peace was an obvious and urgent issue in the 1950s, because both superpowers were developing gigantic nuclear arsenals. Lest one imagine that this country could remain on the sidelines, there was Menzies to declare that 'Australia must be ready for war in three years'[49] and the participation of Australian forces in the Korean conflict. The prospect of nuclear warfare was immediate and moderately terrifying, and we must remember that people in those days had not yet had decades to become used to the idea of nuclear weapons. The left, and especially the Communists, could thus build a sizeable campaign against the war danger.

A World Peace Council had been formed in Paris in 1949 after a meeting that attracted 2,000 delegates. By October of that year, there were committees in 70 countries. In Australia, a peace organisation was relatively easy to establish; a section of its natural constituency among intellectuals and clergy was already more or less organised. These were the groups that had campaigned for free speech and the right to use public halls for various leftists. Many of their members moved directly into the peace movement.

The movement held its first Peace Congress in April 1950, featuring Dr. Hewlett Johnson, the 'Red Dean of Canterbury' and author of *The Socialist Sixth of the World* as guest speaker. Hewlett attracted crowds of 10,000 to the Melbourne Exhibition Building twice in one week, and the organisers raised £10,000 – a lot of money in those days. Two years later, the Eureka Youth League, youth section of the CPA, and other organisations sponsored a Youth Carnival for Peace and Friendship, which became a centre of controversy when Menzies refused to allow the Chinese delegates to enter Australia. But despite – or perhaps because of – such official opposition, the Carnival was a massive success, attracting 2,364 participants and crowds as large as 30,000.

These successes were achieved, moreover, despite proscription of the movement by the Labor Party. After the split with the Groupers in 1955, Labor moved back towards the left, and it became possible for peace organisations to make new overtures to ALP members. To this end, the movement was reorganised, both to get around the proscription and to present something of a new face to the world. A Congress for International Cooperation and Disarmament was held in Melbourne in 1959, and leading Labor and union personalities were induced to attend. This ought to have been the beginning of a new period of growth.

The potential was not realised, and part of the reason appears to be that the CPA was increasingly tied up with divisions over the Sino-Soviet split.[50] By the time it had put that problem and the split with the Australian Maoists behind it, the Vietnam War had appeared on the scene, and the old peace issues and organisations began to merge into a new anti-war movement. The power of the movement against the Vietnam War seems to have totally overshadowed previous peace work in public awareness.

Yet, the older movement had its importance. At a time when the world seemed to be moving rapidly towards nuclear war, and the Cold War atmosphere was being used to erode civil liberties, the peace campaigns undoubtedly represented an important check on the Menzies government. When considering later mass movements against nuclear weapons internationally and in Australia, it becomes especially important to look at the political lessons of these earlier experiences. Unfortunately, the peace movement of the 1950s reflected all too clearly the CPA's drift to the right.

The central political thrust was multilateral disarmament, with Andrei Vyshinskii, the Soviet representative at the UN, calling for a peace pact with the five great powers.[51] The world's ruling classes would somehow, under pressure from their populations, agree to eliminate war. *Unilateral* disarmament, the slogan that lent such a radical cutting edge to the disarmament movement in Britain, was never seriously considered in Australia. Had it been, the CPA would undoubtedly have seen it, as did its sister party in Britain until very late, as upsetting the orderly progress of big power negotiation. Nor did the Australian peace movement have any class politics: there was a clear assumption that only lunatics could favour nuclear bombs, and so all the people of the world, bar a few evil conspirators, could be united against them. 'All the women in the world want peace, and ... a thousand million women can't be wrong.'[52] In consequence, the peace propaganda was often remarkably insipid. One could not, of course, expect the CPA of the 1950s to have more than a dim recollection of Lenin's viewpoint:

> An end of wars, peace among the nations, the cessation of pillaging and violence – such is our ideal, but only bourgeois sophists can seduce the masses with this idea, if the latter is divorced from a direct and immediate call for revolutionary action.[53]

But one would have hoped for something a bit feistier than this proposal for anti-war struggle, which appeared in the Victorian newsletter of the CPA-influenced Union of Australian Women (UAW):

> Let us teach our children that there are other ways of settling differences than by war ... Let us teach them above all, to be human, and to do as they would be done by ... If we cannot reach the children of tender years through their mothers, then let us try to reach them through other ways.
>
> *Example One.* School teachers who belong to the UAW or perhaps their husbands who are school teachers could work the Peace Plan into their history, explaining to them after a lesson on Battles how wrong it is to kill, especially people who are undefended.
>
> *Example Two.* By approaching the teachers of Sunday School classes. I approached my son's Sunday School teacher ...
>
> *Example Four.* By getting up a Petition to be signed by members of the Community to say that they lie in dread of their little children passing school age, in case they are claimed for war.[54]

This rather passive quality in the propaganda went together with a certain fascination for petition campaigns – the most passive form of political expression. Of the eight million signatures collected for the Vienna Peace Appeal internationally in 1954, Australia contributed 300,000. One man, W. J. Ross, made his run for the Guiness Book of Records by collecting 6,000 all by himself. Unfortunately, unless there is some form of struggle, such expressions of public opinion do not overly impress the power brokers of the world, although they do manage to consume the energies of countless activists.

A second political problem was the implicit pro-Sovietism of the movement. The peace organisations contained large majorities of non-Communists; but, between the superior organising ability of the CPA and the naïve illusions cherished by their liberal allies about the 'socialist camp', the peace organisations nevertheless clung to the belief that the Western powers were the only threat to peace. While it was undoubtedly correct for the peace movement to direct its concrete agitation against Western nuclear weapons – because it was operating in the West – the uncritical attitude to the Russian bomb and to Russian policy in general was a drawback. It meant that right wing charges that the peace movement was only a Trojan horse for a foreign power appeared plausible to many people. After the events of 1956, it also cost the peace organisations the support of some activists.

In the work among women many of the same political features emerged. Here, too, we must emphasise at the start that the UAW, formed after the decline of the NHA and noticeably less militant, was nevertheless far in advance of any other group of women in Australian society at the time. They carried on the battle for equal pay and other aspects of women's rights in a society that was increasingly hostile. They demonstrated in the face of police repression and published magazines that took up such issues as women's rights at work. Yet, little could be achieved in these areas for some time. For most of the membership, there was a retreat into charitable work, making sandwiches for the school canteen or raising money for nurseries.

'Nearly every UAW woman was a member of a mother's club, if they had children,' says one of the longest-standing UAW activists. We would not want to suggest that such work is wrong in principle: communists must be prepared to work just about anywhere in a difficult period. But the effects of a decade or more of luncheons and charity work on the spirit and consciousness of Communist women must have been deadening; worse, it came to be seen as the normal way for Communists to operate. And when, in the late 1960s and early 1970s, women really *did* begin to be radicalised, the new Women's Liberation movement simply bypassed the UAW, which could not cope with the new style of work and new attitudes towards politics and personal life. The same activist remembers:

Miners' Women's Auxiliary members hold a thank you sign from a coal miners sit-in (known as stay-puts). Photo probably from Great Greta or Glen Davis strike, New South Wales, 1952.

UAW equal pay demonstration in Melbourne, early 1960s.

When Women's Lib started, some of the older women were a bit shocked by some of the things that went on in Women's Lib, and they wouldn't have a bar of that. The younger women felt this, and they sort of felt that the UAW was old hat. They didn't want to have a bar of it or anything to do with it.[55]

The New South Wales Waterside Workers Federation Women's Strike Committee, 1956. It distributed donated food to striking families and other activities.

The CPA also put a lot of effort into establishing trade union women's committees, more or less on the model of the Miners' Women's Auxiliaries. These committees helped to inform wives of the principles of trade unionism and about their husbands' work experiences, for example, by organising workplace tours. Sometimes they were mobilised for strike support. All too often, however, they remained largely in the role of 'hewers of cake and drawers of tea' or engaged in charitable activity designed to ease the loneliness of seamen's wives or help the children of strikers.

Such activities have their place, of course. Moreover, some committees that began life this way went on to more political activities; for example, the Waterside Workers' women's committee was first agreed to by the union 'mainly to assist in the union canteen'. By 1956, it was playing a militant support role in the wharfies' national strike, and its members were being invited to stopworks.[56]

However, to the extent that Communists found themselves trapped in relatively passive and apolitical roles, the work among women became part of the trend towards stagnation, conservatism and, ultimately, accommodation of the party to mainstream Australian life.

5
The Monolith Cracks

Faced with a hostile political climate in Australia, the Communists often consoled themselves with the thought of their comrades' triumphs abroad. The Communists had come to power throughout Eastern Europe, replacing fascist rule and beginning reconstruction; they had won a great civil war in China and achieved control of parts of Korea and Vietnam. John Sendy has related just how important these victories were for one member of the CPA:

> George Robertson found great solace in the Chinese victories. He literally cheered them on. 'You bloody beauty,' he would yell as the fall of Soochow or Hangchow was announced on the radio. Yet George did not know where any of these places were. After cheering he would look confused – 'John, where in the bloody hell is Soochow?'[1]

Immense faith in the world movement was tied to an immense faith in Joseph Stalin. That famous grandfatherly face, peering out reassuringly from countless walls, and the simple, Grimm-Brothers writing style lulled you naturally into a sort of complacency. The CPA rank and file undoubtedly accepted at face value, therefore, the first articles in the party newspaper that insisted: 'Don't fall for press stories of attacks on the late J.V. Stalin at the 20th Congress of the Communist Party of the Soviet Union'.[2]

But the complacency was soon to be shattered. Khrushchev, the rising new Soviet leader, *had* attacked Stalin only three years after his death, in guarded terms at public sessions but much more bluntly in a secret speech – which was soon leaked to the *New York Times*. While the public speech only criticised the 'cult of personality' that had surrounded the leader, the secret speech told a tale of horror: murder of political opponents, political terror, criminal irresponsibility during World War II, distortion of history. Everything that the Western press, as well as the Trotskyists, had been saying for decades was revealed to be true.

And Communists who read the secret speech could not really doubt its authenticity, as Sendy makes clear:

> Jim Moss and I took it in turns to go to the public library on North Terrace to read the speech in the *New York Times*. Each of us returned ashen-faced, believing that what we read was authentic. It seemed to explain so many things which had been difficult to comprehend – the fact that so many old Soviet Communist leaders had been found guilty of spying, the unanimity which marked the proceedings of the CPSU, aspects of Soviet literature, the doctors' plot, the excommunication of Yugoslavia, and so on.[3]

It was a shock to the system. Later in the year, another was to follow, when Soviet armed forces intervened to crush a workers' uprising in Hungary. An entire dream world that had been so crucial to the morale of Australian Communists was under threat, and the party leadership waged a determined battle to save it.

Unlike some Western parties, the CPA refused to admit publicly that the secret speech was genuine. The British party had a major debate forced on it by dissidents – and their own newspaper correspondent supported the workers of Budapest, but the CPA was able to suppress any real discussion of the Hungarian events. Critics soon found themselves expelled, if they did not resign, and this general closing of ranks around support for the Kremlin was largely accepted by the party's cadre.

Even so, there had to be some discussion at leadership level and some assessment of the issues that had been raised. In the course of this process, the seeds of future change were sown.

There were several closely linked issues: firstly, the attack on the 'cult of personality' that had surrounded Stalin; secondly, a criticism of the previous attitude of Communists to parliament and the social democratic parties; and thirdly, the Hungarian events. The last two points were closely tied to the first; they were both blamed in large part on 'errors' of the Stalin regime.

The CPA's account of these issues and of its own response was summarised in a booklet called *Basic Questions of Communist Theory* published in early 1957. This contained speeches and resolutions from the party leadership which were so closely interlinked that they can be taken as a single document.

The experiences of 1956 were portrayed as essentially positive: 'One might even say we are reaching a turning point, a leap to a new higher stage in the historical development of international Communism.' This was because the errors of the past had been exposed and overcome. Scorn was poured on those who 'cannot perceive the great leap forward of our movement'.[4]

Tribune, 31 October, 1956.

Having performed this necessary ritual, the documents then took up the past 'errors', beginning with the cult of personality. The CPA was 'surprised to learn that Stalin, whom we had always regarded as a model of revolutionary virtue, had fostered and encouraged the cult of the individual and placed himself above the party'. Under the impact of this discovery, the CPA had seriously examined its own practice and found that there had indeed been 'tendencies toward exaggerated praise and adulation of individual party leaders'.[5] 'But it never grew to any proportions amongst us ... it was rather alien to the Australian outlook for one thing'.[6]

If the CPA had escaped the worst aspects of the personality cult, it had been no less fortunate in escaping the worst of the other 'errors'; for example, Stalin had been attacked for his theory of the 'main blow', a sort of bowdlerised Leninist concept that, at any given time, some particular political current should be singled out for intense attack. Typically, this concept had been used whenever it was felt necessary to aim the 'main blow' at the social democrats. Now, Khrushchev had announced that the social democrats were to be allies, and the Communists could collaborate with them in finding a parliamentary road to socialism.

The CPA leaders happily pointed out that they had been pursuing a united front policy with the ALP since 1951. So much for that error!

Regarding Hungary, the CPA leadership could even turn the events there to its advantage. On the one hand, the Hungarian events were blamed, to some extent, on blind copying of Soviet methods, an error of which the CPA had already decided it was comparatively innocent. On the other, the very fact that 'socialism' in that country had been so seriously threatened showed the importance of strong Communist leadership, said the CPA leaders:

> If the Hungarian events proved anything, it was the need for the dictatorship of the proletariat, in fact, a major criticism of the Rakosi-Gero regime was that it failed to deal a timely blow and destroy the counter-revolutionaries financed by U.S. imperialism.[7]

It was not hard to translate this into Australian terms: here, in this country, we need a strong central leadership in the party and strong discipline to ensure that 'counter-revolutionaries' (read: dissident CPA members who were unhappy about the Stalin revelations and Hungary) did not subvert the party:

> If democratic centralism did not exist, then these comrades perhaps feel they would have a better chance to impose their revisionist, petit-bourgeois-idealist and Browderite views on the Communist Party.[8]

Certainly, the party made short shrift of most of the oppositionists who did raise their heads. When the intellectual Jim Staples circulated a document demanding discussion of the secret speech, he was forced to withdraw it; after the Hungarian events, he was expelled. Helen Palmer was kicked out when she moved to set up an independent journal called *Outlook*. Ian Turner was expelled some time later in Melbourne, and figures like Stephen Murray-Smith left in solidarity with him. These were only the most prominent individuals among hundreds of intellectuals who left the party or were driven out.

Nor was the exodus limited to middle-class elements, as the CPA leadership claimed. These were in the majority of at least the explicitly political cases; but, given that the party membership slumped from about 8,000 to less than 6,000 in the aftermath of the events of 1956, it seems clear that a significant number of workers must have left too. The experience of one branch in West Como, NSW has been documented. One intellectual was expelled, and the whole branch of 16 members promptly collapsed. Two ex-members of the branch wrote:

> In fact, W. Como branch was made up mostly of industrial workers ... in a primarily working class area ... West Como branch is now almost non-existent, with a total of two members ... A branch destroyed ... and the C.C. can boast of another complete victory.[9]

Of course, losses of this magnitude could not be explained away as the defection of 'a few individuals in the Party who have lost their balance',[10] but the CPA leadership had another explanation: throughout the 1950s, it consistently pointed to the intensity of Cold War repression as the main reason why the party's mass membership was falling away. Sharkey quoted Khrushchev in 1956 as saying that the parties in the West 'had been passing through a most difficult and trying time',[11] and such explanations could be put forward again for the losses suffered after 1956. Alistair Davidson has rightly challenged this explanation, pointing out that many of the people who left at this time had already weathered the worst of the Cold War successfully. He argues that the 'large number of defectors of the years 1956–58 ... left not because of persecution, but because of disagreement with the policy and organization of the party'.[12]

Both explanations seem one-dimensional and suggest a third: that many of the people who had survived the worst of the Cold War had done so precisely because of their faith in the triumphs of 'socialism' on a world scale; in surviving, they had nevertheless suffered a great deal of damage to their morale; and the impact of the Stalin revelations, followed by Hungary, was the final blow. Nor was the blow merely psychological: the events of 1956 brought a new and intense isolation to Communists. 'We were like a besieged fortress,' writes Sendy. 'Our shop windows were smashed and Party members were abused by neighbours and work-mates as had happened during the coal strike.'[13]

There *were* dissidents who managed to remain within the party. Of these, the most vocal was W. J. Brown, who published a remarkable series of articles in the

Communist Review. Brown sought to build on the positive features of the Stalin revelations, as he saw them, and to use them to strengthen the party within the context of official policy. This was a delicate high-wire performance, and Brown suffered a bruising at the end of it.

He was careful to surround his criticisms with disclaimers. He mentioned Stalin's positive features, noted that the CPA had already taken 'appropriate steps' to rectify all possible problems and declared J. B. Miles to have provided 'sterling service as general secretary'. Nevertheless, Brown was prepared to be truly critical.

There had been an 'excessive adulation of leaders,' he said,[14] and some comrades had adopted 'an almost instinctively hostile attitude to even the most moderate criticism of the leadership'.[15] Praise of the USSR in the party press was 'overdone'[16] and Communists had to 'learn how better to talk in the language of the people'.[17]

This was heavy stuff, coming from a prominent party member, and it received boots-and-all treatment from Ted Hill. Brown was accused of being divisive, undermining democratic centralism and advancing a portrayal of the party that was 'not in accord with reality'. The tenor of the whole article can be conveyed by one masterly passage:

> Dissent in the sense of complete disagreement with the line of the party is not so common because Marxism–Leninism is directed to the correct working class solution of the problems that face the working class and the people. Unanimity of voting is quite a common occurrence and naturally so because the Communist Party is a Marxist–Leninist Party based on the Leninist principle of democratic centralism. All the efforts of all Party members are devoted to serving that purpose.[18]

In the face of such subtle reasoning, what could Brown do but publish a grovelling retraction, not only admitting his own metaphysical, undialectical, compromising, anarcho-syndicalist, bourgeois liberalism, but thanking Hill for pointing it out.[19]

Between Moscow and Beijing

Yet, if the liberal dissidents received a hammering, there lay concealed beneath the surface another kind of dissent among large sections of the leading cadre of the party: a *Stalinist* dissent. The leadership of the party had been conscious Stalinists, having risen to power with Stalin's direct support and having been associated with him and his regime for decades. Exposure of his failings automatically reflected on them. Further, the political changes inaugurated by Khrushchev were by no means to their liking. Some of the rank and file shared these feelings.

Khrushchev had proposed that the CPs attempt to improve relations with the social democratic and Labour parties, with an eye to transforming society by parliamentary means. This new strategy for the Communist movement was closely tied to the needs of Soviet diplomacy, which was now firmly set on a course of 'peaceful coexistence' with the West. The CPA leadership had not, of course, pursued a really *revolutionary* orientation for a very long time. However, a certain 'leftism' had remained in the make up of the Australian party's leaders since the days of the 'Third Period'; they preferred to distinguish themselves from the social democrats and to retain a formal commitment to revolution (some examples will be considered in Chapter 6). Nevertheless, the Australians would undoubtedly have followed loyally after their Soviet masters, had not another important ruling party dared to challenge Moscow. This was the Communist Party of China.

The Chinese had found Soviet tutelage oppressive and considered that the Russians wanted to turn them into a satellite on the East European model. At the same time, they feared that peaceful coexistence would bring an accommodation between Moscow and the West at their expense. By the late 1950s, the Chinese were moving towards a position of aggressive independence and attempted to rally support for their position in the world movement. They appealed to Communists in the West for support, not only on international questions, but on a platform of greater militancy, hostility to reformism and a more 'balanced' appraisal of Stalin.

The Australian party had always felt a great respect for the Chinese.[20] Now, they found that Beijing was voicing doubts that they had already felt. At first, the Chinese expressed themselves with a certain circumspection, and the differences seemed to be no more than a comradely disagreement in which the CPA could take sides without any lasting consequences, and both the national leadership under Sharkey and also the group around Hill in Victoria lined up with the Chinese. It appears that they all remained in the Chinese camp until very near the time of the final, public split. The leaders of the New Zealand party later described the attitudes of Sharkey and Dixon in 1960:

> We would remind them that, early in 1960 ... they cabled asking our General Secretary to come to Sydney urgently for what was obviously regarded by them as an important discussion. Cde. L. Sharkey had just returned from China ... L. Sharkey (in his own garden – Cdes. R. Dixon and L. Aarons also being present) reported on discussions he had had in China, in particular with Mao [Zedong]. The core of Cde. L. Sharkey's report was to warn us not to fall for the new view being advanced that imperialism would die easily, not to fall for the illusion of world-wide peaceful transition to Socialism. Basically, it was a call to reject the many incorrect assumptions arising from uncritical acceptance of the decisions of the 20th Congress of the Communist Party of the Soviet Union ...
>
> Later ... did you not many times compliment, through a number of New Zealand comrades ... Cde. J. Manson for his firm stand in refusing to be associated with the attack of Khrushchev and others on the Chinese Party leadership?
>
> When the New Zealand Party delegation to the 81 Parties' Meeting in Moscow passed through Sydney, did you not discuss your views with both Cde. V.G. Wilcox and Cde. G.E. Jackson? ... We talked well into the night. *And was not the key note of your approach the need to have a common stand against the revisionist danger at Moscow?* And Cde. L. Sharkey, do you not remember that when we arrived in Moscow you said, 'I'm in the dogbox' and that a Russian comrade well known to both of us 'no longer loved you'? [Emphasis in original.][21]

The 81 Parties' Meeting was a last, temporary attempt to paper over the differences between Moscow and Beijing. Soon, each side was interpreting the meeting's declarations differently and attacking the other. As the battle hotted up, Sharkey began to swing around to the Soviet position. Davidson notes:

> an observable difference in the tenor of Sharkey's and Hill's writings before April 1961. Sharkey stressed unity, attacking leftism; and Hill emphasised the need for Marxist–Leninist purity, attacking moderate communism and revisionism.[22]

This was the beginning of a growing division between Hill and his supporters and the bulk of the party.

The background to the shifting attitudes of the CPA leadership is complex and obscure,[23] but the pressures moving Sharkey back towards Moscow seem clear enough. There was, firstly, the ingrained loyalty to the USSR built up over decades – combined, perhaps, with the fact that the vast majority of the parties internationally were sticking with the Kremlin. As it became clear that a real split was inevitable, Sharkey drew back from the prospect of international isolation. Secondly, there was strong sentiment among sections of the secondary leadership in both Melbourne and Sydney against supporting China; this grouping included Laurie Aarons and Eddie Robertson in Sydney and a group around Bernie Taft and Rex Mortimer in Melbourne.

Thirdly, and probably most importantly, the extreme leftism of the Chinese rhetoric had no appeal to most of the party rank and file, who had spent the past decade learning to be restrained, moderate and, above all, devoted to a pacifist struggle against war. The Chinese, after all, opposed disarmament. Their real reason was that they wanted the bomb; for international consumption, they posed the issue in terms of class struggle and the fact that war was built into the imperialist system. To justify an indifference to the dangers of nuclear war, in turn, it was necessary to portray the world as being perpetually on

The Australian Women's Weekly, 12 May, 1945.

John Sendy (right) in Moscow, 1972.

the brink of revolution. The average CPA member was unlikely to be sympathetic to a point of view expressed in terms like these:

> The workers, peasants, petty bourgeoisie, patriotic and revolutionary national intellectuals, and patriotic and revolutionary national bourgeoisie of various countries who constitute more than 90 per cent of the world's population, are always for revolution.[24]

In domestic terms, the issues became those of a strategy for Australia, styles of work and attitudes to the ALP. Sendy recalls that, at a Political Committee meeting in 1961, Ted Hill:

> advanced ideas, influenced by the Chinese experience, which would have involved turning our party into an underground, clandestine, revolutionary detachment, working in an illegal fashion, rather than as an open political party.[25]

This was no more attractive to the CPA rank and file than the Chinese equanimity about World War III. But, above all, debates about how to build a CP in Australia centred around the strategic attitude towards the Labor Party.

Stalinism has traditionally had difficulty coming to terms with its attitude to mainstream reformist parties. The underlying thrust of Soviet policy since the mid-1920s had always been towards either opposing, or attempting to ally itself with, particular Western ruling classes, and this fact was the most important factor in shaping the strategies towards reformist parties. The parties' central concern has normally been what attitude to take towards the *official structures* of the reformist organisations and towards their *leaderships*. It is, after all, the officials and the politicians who have an influence with the ruling class; and, conversely, it is they who attempt to carry the ruling-class point of view in the labour movement. The CPs thus moved between two basic attitudes: either immense hostility towards reformist leaderships (in periods, like the late 1940s, when the world movement was in open conflict with the Western bourgeoisie) or an attempt to conciliate them (for example, during the Popular Front).

However, there is also the reformist *rank and file* to be considered. In theory, and to a limited degree in practice, the CPs differentiated between the leaders and members of reformist parties. During periods when they were on a 'left' course, they called for a 'united front from below', in which Communists were to attempt to maintain common activity and dialogue with the supporters of social democratic parties while lambasting their leaders. During more moderate phases, they still made some carefully couched criticism of the reformist leadership in order to differentiate themselves in the eyes of rank-and-file workers who might be moving leftward.

As long as the CPs remained tied to the Kremlin, the main concern for them was to advance the foreign policy of the USSR. Attempting to win rank-and-file workers to Communist politics was a secondary consideration, subordinated to the needs of Soviet diplomacy in theory and practice. This had its consequences for the bulk of the CP members, who have always had trouble remembering to differentiate between party attitudes to reformist leaders and to their rank and file.

Consequently, Stalinism has tended to oscillate between two poles: hostility to social democracy as a whole, and accommodation to it. In the split in the CPA, each faction seized on one of these two poles.

According to the Maoists, most of the party were guilty of accommodation to Laborism. This was not a hard charge to substantiate, although the most explicit formulation by the majority on the ALP question – the one which I will quote in order to make the exposition as clear as possible – appeared just after the split itself. This was Laurie Aarons' pamphlet, *Labor Movement at the Crossroads*. The pamphlet took the form of some friendly advice to the ALP leadership, particularly Arthur Calwell, who was described rather favourably:

> Mr. Calwell is neither of the extreme right, nor the left, of the Labor Party. He is openly and proudly a reformist. He outlines lucidly and persuasively the philosophy and policy of Australian reformism.[26]

The failures of the Labor Party to win government were assessed as a consequence of the errors of the ALP leadership: 'Most Labor Party leaders will not come out boldly and campaign for their own Party platform. Thus, they get the worst of both worlds.'[27] The ALP and ACTU socialist objectives were quoted without comment, as if Calwell were privately committed to them but had simply neglected to campaign for them out of a mistaken tactical approach. The next section was headed: 'How to Make a Start On the Road to Socialism' – as if the ALP leadership would give such a project their earnest consideration.

There was no suggestion that the Labor leaders supported capitalism – that, in government, even the best of them would operate the system at the expense of the working class (indeed, Calwell had been a minister in the Chifley government which crushed the coal strike of 1949) and that, consequently, there might be some need for workers to organise independently of them. And there was most certainly nothing in the pamphlet to suggest seriously to a worker that he or she should consider changing allegiance and joining the CPA.

Hill seized on this pamphlet as summing up everything he had alleged about the party's capitulation to reformism. Yet, the Maoist approach to the Labor Party was at an equally unrealistic opposite extreme. For Hill, the Labor Party was a capitalist party, and there were no grounds for preferring it to the Liberal Party. One simply built the CP as the alternative.

Each side could quote Lenin against the extreme views of the other. But, as prisoners of the foreign policy of Russia and China respectively, neither could seriously consider Lenin's own positive approach, expressed in his famous pamphlet *Left Wing Communism*. According to this approach, one supported Labor against the open parties of the bourgeoisie, but critically, with the aim of winning away their rank and file:

> [W]e must, first, help [Labour leaders] Henderson and Snowden to beat Lloyd George and Churchill ... second, we must help the majority of the working class to be convinced by their own experience that we are right, i.e., that the Hendersons and Snowdens are absolutely good for nothing ... third, we must bring nearer the moment when, *on the basis* of the disappointment of most of the workers in the Hendersons, it will be possible, with serious chances of success, to overthrow the government of the Hendersons at once ... I want to support Henderson in the same way as the rope supports a hanged man[28]

The vast majority of the CPA rank and file, anxious to find a way out of isolation after years of the Cold War, was unlikely to be attracted by the Maoist approach. The central leadership could count on winning the debate on this crucial question.

At first, the faction fight had been conducted, at all levels, as merely a struggle within the inner circles of the parties. The Soviets had attacked the 'Albanians' when they meant the Chinese; the Chinese vilified the 'Yugoslavs' when they meant Moscow. Only a chosen few could follow such Aesopian language. It was only when a split became inevitable, and the broad membership had to be prepared for it, that the issues were discussed openly. This was certainly true in the Australian party. At first, only an inner circle was aware of the extent of the differences, and these were debated in public forums only in an indirect manner. Vic Williams recalls:

> People would go to branches and give reports, and people would give other reports, and fair dinkum, quite often the branches wouldn't appreciate the difference ... And it finally got to the hilarious stage that a conference was called, and Sharkey was at this conference, and there were two different lines given to the conference – and the conference didn't even appreciate it. So I stood up and said I wanted to ask a question of Comrade Sharkey ... I asked him would he comment on the fact that there were two different lines being put forward ... [one] was the line of the Chinese Communist Party. And on the other hand there was the line of the Central Committee ... He sidestepped the issue. But

there was an absolute furore. I remember Vic Little confronted me on the floor and there was a bit of a yelling match, and all sorts of people said I shouldn't have done it – I'd split the party![29]

Williams had not split the party, but it was split. When it became clear there was no healing the breach, the central leadership did appeal to the membership. It knew that it could count on their support. Large cadres' meetings were held which recorded overwhelming majorities for the Central Committee. Finally, things were brought to a climax at the 1963 Victorian state conference. The Hill forces, aware they could not win, aimed less at gaining votes than at making the maximum organisational impact.

Hill had already resigned as State Secretary some time before, leaving behind Frank Johnson, who attempted to hide his Maoist sympathies. Now, a week before the conference, prominent Tramways Union leader Clarrie O'Shea resigned from the party. Hill and his supporters addressed the conference itself for two hours, only to receive a derisory 16 votes out of 159. Johnson was thrown out and replaced with Ralph Gibson, while John Sendy was brought over from Adelaide to be State President. A new layer of people came onto the State Committee, many of them known enemies of Hill.

Nothing was left but for the Maoists to depart – comparatively quietly at the end – and establish a new organisation, the Communist Party (Marxist–Leninist; CP(ML)). This group had a considerable strength at the official level in Victorian trade unions, which has eroded as the officials retired, leaving only the BLF as a Maoist bastion. The CP(ML) also assumed a certain importance in other spheres in the late 1960s and early 1970s, when it won the allegiance of numbers of students inspired by the Chinese Cultural Revolution and used them to build a nationalist Australian Independence Movement. This movement subsequently declined because the CP(ML), following Chinese foreign policy, became obsessed with campaigning against the USSR, even where it meant aligning themselves with the Fraser government. Although in the mid 1980s, Hill and his followers indicated a desire to break with the most dogmatic of their past policies, they did not have much idea what to replace them with.

The 'Coalition of the Left'

Years after the Hill split, Dave Davies told a joke about the time he had trouble finding the question mark on an unfamiliar typewriter. 'Ah, comrade,' said a young smart alec. 'It's an old typewriter – about your age. It dates back to when you didn't ask questions in the party'.[30]

One might tell stories like that about any section of the party; but, in the old days, none had been so rigidly authoritarian as the Victorian organisation. Sendy has even revealed that Hill had his own private spies and was prone to extreme paranoia about police agents within the party. Many individuals have since commented that they were glad to see the back of him. It was fitting, therefore, that his fall became the signal for a new era of open debate and critical thinking within the CPA.

In Victoria, Hill's departure – along with a big chunk of the leading cadre – brought to power leaders of a new stamp. People like Bernie Taft and Rex Mortimer, who had opposed the pro-China policies of Hill (and also Sharkey) early on, were not simply uncritical supporters of the USSR. The influence of the Italian CP had begun to make itself felt in Victoria from as early as 1953, and the grouping around Taft had discussed them with considerable interest in 1959–60. The Italians were developing a policy of 'polycentrism' in the world movement and were no longer prepared to accept the tutelage of any other Communist Party. In their own strategic thinking, they were developing the ideas that have since come to be called 'Eurocommunism'.

The Taft group had been temporarily broken up by the Sharkey leadership, at the time when Sharkey was still in alliance with Hill. In the aftermath of the Victorian split, the central leadership was forced to look to these very people to lead the state organisation. Rex Mortimer, a strong supporter of the 'Italian line', became editor of the *Guardian*. And, in the course of the 1960s, Taft himself emerged as a moving force in the organisation.

Mortimer soon set the new tone by participating in producing the independent Marxist journal *Arena*, together with ex-Communists of the 1956 vintage. He then proceeded to enter into a dialogue with Melbourne Jews about Soviet antisemitism. While he still apologised for Soviet policy, he openly admitted the existence of antisemitism in the USSR and called for a vigorous campaign to eradicate it. In 1966, Sendy wrote an article for the first issue of the new CPA journal *Australian Left Review* attacking monolithism in the party. And the new journal was significant in itself: unlike the old *Communist Review*, it was to be open to critical input from outside and even included non-Communists among its editors.

The Victorians were the trailblazers, because they had developed a relatively coherent point of view in their study of the Italians. In the national leadership, new ideas grew up more slowly at first – and more impressionistically. Yet, in the final analysis, it was among the national leaders that the central ideas which informed the new strategic approach adopted by the CPA in the latter part of the decade were developed.

The national leadership had also seen a change of personnel. In the course of the Sino-Soviet split, Sharkey had become politically disoriented and had also fallen into ill health. The prosecution of the fight against Hill had been left largely to Laurie Aarons; by the end of it, Sharkey was in effective retirement. In May 1965, Aarons replaced him as General Secretary.

Aarons had been a hardline Stalinist for many years. In the aftermath of the Stalin revelations, he had been one of the leaders in cracking down on dissidents and had published a pamphlet called *Party of the Working Class*, which made ferocious attacks on liberal ideas. Aarons had characterised such ideas as follows:

> 'There is no need for a social revolution to achieve socialism, which will come gradually. The working class does not need to set up its own political power, its own state organisation to consolidate its rule and build socialism.
>
> 'Not the class struggle but propaganda of general truths and moral maxims will bring about socialism. From this it follows that not the working class but intellectuals are the leaders of the socialist cause.' These and similar ideas are called 'revisionism', because they would 'revise' Marxism–Leninism in such a way as to get rid of its class-conscious spirit and revolutionary meaning.[31]

It was ironic that the same Laurie Aarons was now to lead his party rapidly in the direction of adopting just such ideas. He and his supporters took the first major step in this direction by formulating a new strategic concept, the 'Coalition of the Left', which became party policy at the 1967 Congress.

For a concept whose implications proved so far reaching, the 'Coalition of the Left' first appeared in a surprisingly modest set of documents. The 1967 Congress documents devoted six pages to outlining the contemporary situation as the party saw it and another three and a half pages to setting out a 'Program for Peace and Social Advance'; only in the last couple of pages was there any attention devoted to the 'unity of the left', which was supposedly the thrust of the new orientation. Moreover, very little in the documents departed sharply from established phraseology.

To be sure, the documents faced up to the reality of the postwar boom and the social changes that had accompanied it, noting particularly the growth of the white-collar sector. This was a major development in itself for a party that had denied these changes for many years. Still, these were facts that could no longer be evaded, rather than a theoretical revolution. In any case, the industrial workers were still referred to as 'the decisive class'.

The documents stressed the importance of a democratic concept of socialism that could appeal to the Australian 'national tradition'. Yet, this could be considered an extension of the traditional national-democratic approach of the Popular Front; certainly, the talk of democracy did not extend to open criticism of the Eastern Bloc regimes.

As for the section discussing unity of the left, it called for unity in struggle against reaction, expressed the hope that a 'far-ranging discussion' would emerge and suggested that this could lead in turn to the possibility of a 'commonly agreed program and course of action'. These notions appeared at first glance to be nothing more than a re-run of the traditional ideas of the united front or popular front.[32]

No wonder that Lloyd Churchward, a sophisticated Communist academic, concluded that 'the present documents are clearly in the Dimitrov tradition',[33] and another member described the new concept as embodying the classical definition of the popular front.[34] In fact, there *were* new ideas hidden in the documents, and some members sensed as much. D. Beechy of NSW wrote in the pre-Congress discussion:

the impression given to many comrades, especially in our branch is that the Communist Party will become submerged, and this creates a fear of a loss of identity.³⁵

What was Beechy driving at? Laurie Aarons answered this question for the membership at the Congress itself, in a speech that was quite explicit and so possibly more significant than the official documents:

> New features of this concept can be seen if we consider the ideas expressed in the present party program: 'Such experience, together with frank and free discussion of policy and aims by all sections of the labour movement will ultimately lead to the formation of a single mass working class Party based on the principles of scientific socialism.'

and

> '[Transformation] ... will be possible through the strength of the organised working class firmly united and in alliance with the small farmers, under the leadership of the marxist party and with the organised co-operation and support of the majority of the people.'

Compare this with the concept in 'Towards a Coalition of the Left':

> 'This co-operation in action for social change [by working class parties] would continue as the centre of different social and political groupings which would share the leadership of the new society.

> 'These may well include besides trade unions and other people's organisations, other political parties which formed to represent interests of classes and social groups other than the working class.'³⁶

Quite clearly, the intent was: firstly, to water down the working-class content of party strategy; secondly, to modify the class content of the socialist state power that would follow a social transformation; and thirdly, to remove any concept of the leading role of the party. A coalition of proletarian and non-proletarian forces was to arrive at a common approach, transform society and rule in concert. The Communists were to be only one force among many.

These were policies designed to allow the CPA to blend into the political mainstream by blurring both its distinctive politics – indeed, its claim to have any special vision at all – and also its stance as an independent organisational force competing for influence. A second major step in this direction was taken the next year, when the party published a Draft Charter of Democratic Rights.

In 1968, John Sendy related comments a wharfie had made to him:

> Democracy might be a class question. But when we talk of democracy, that's what we've got to mean. If an author writes a book we don't like, or people refuse to toe our political line, that's too bad. When we talk about bloody democracy, that's what we've got to mean – it's as simple as that.[37]

This rather straightforward, commonsense approach was in striking contrast to the traditional Communist view. For decades, Communists had been told that democracy was a class question. And so, for Marxists, it must be. The working class, in the Marxist view, has the right to exercise a political dictatorship over its opponents, and it will not shrink from censorship or other forms of repression in emergencies – any more than capitalist governments have done. But this is meant to be the dictatorship of the proletariat *as a class*, 'democracy for the working class', and a transitional phase to a free society in which all forms of repression would wither away. Under Stalinism, the 'class question' became something else: the dictatorship of the party and state bureaucracy over the working class itself. The atrocities that this involved were stupendous, the implications horrifying. When CPA members became aware of them, they were rightly repelled. But what *analysis* were they to make of the problem?

I have suggested in Chapter 1 and will attempt to develop further in Chapter 6

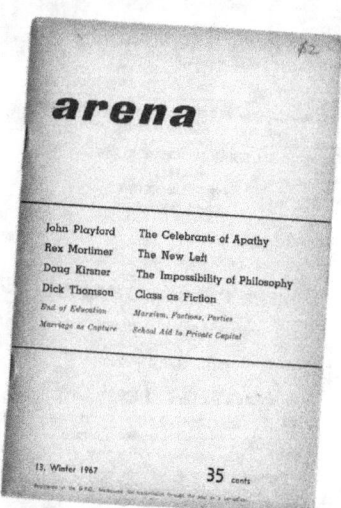

Arena, No. 13, 1967.

an analysis of the USSR as essentially capitalist. The bureaucracy dominating Soviet society is seen, in such an analysis, as an exploitative ruling class – and its repressive behaviour as flowing from that fact. It follows that, to end the repression, what is required is the overthrow of the bureaucracy and its replacement with the social rule of the working class. On the basis of such analysis, it becomes possible to oppose Stalinist repression, defend democracy and yet see democracy in class terms.

This analytical framework had no appeal for the membership of the CPA, for the simple reason that it suggested that they had spent their lives defending a capitalist state. Rather, they preferred to continue regarding Russia as some sort of socialist society, to which democracy needed to be somehow added as an extra ingredient. As we will see in the next chapter, this is precisely the position of liberal critics of Stalinism. The CPA wanted a more democratic socialism, in the East and in the West, and quite rightly; unfortunately, the idea of democracy that they developed inevitably had a liberal cast.

The Charter of Democratic Rights approached these questions from the point of view of Australian society, but there was no mistaking its relevance for Eastern Europe as well.

The Charter complained that, in Australia, 'our democracy has never been fully realised'. It assured the reader that 'Australian Communists work in a democratic way' and expressed regret over the 'declining role of parliament'. It referred to 'our independent judiciary'. The security organisation ASIO was to be replaced by 'men whose responsibilities will be strictly confined to defence and security matters under the control of a parliamentary committee'. Finally, it insisted that, under socialist rule, anti-socialist parties would be guaranteed their freedom.[38]

Quite obviously, the authors of the Charter conceived of socialist democracy as simply an extension and completion of the existing, bourgeois democracy of

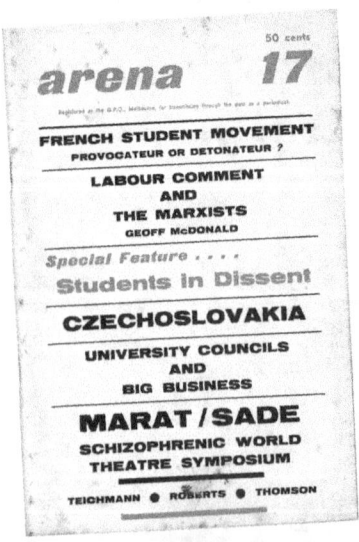

Arena, No. 17, 1968-9.

modern Australia. Regarding restoring the power of parliament, they appeared to want a return to older practices. A statement that the CPA worked 'in a democratic way' could only mean repudiation of revolution, and this was quite logical, because revolution in the West means precisely a dramatic rupture between bourgeois democracy and workers' democracy – a distinction which the Charter was designed to blur.

The draft aroused considerable hostility, especially among those who were soon to form a pro-Soviet opposition. Its critics made arguments against it which were formally Marxist and worth examining:

> Is it fair to say 'the Communist party should be legal under capitalism, but the capitalist parties should not be legal under socialism'? One could give a quick mechanical 'no'. But it is a dialectical answer we want, and that answer is: 'the working class is the rising new force, the capitalist class is the dying old force which nevertheless will fight desperately to turn back history's clock. Therefore the fight for a legal Communist Party under capitalism serves human progress. The fight to prevent the capitalists forming parties under socialism to rally their forces and bring capitalism also serves human progress'. Are we then for human progress, or 'nice', 'democratic' but nonsensical formulas of a fair go for all – worker and boss alike?[39]

Despite an element of overstatement (such as seeming to say that bourgeois parties would necessarily always be banned), this was, as CPA cadres well knew, more or less the traditional Marxist view. Yet, they were also becoming aware that, in practice, this view had been used in Eastern Europe as a pretext for repressing all dissent, from the workers themselves as well as from the bourgeoisie. They did not wish to project such an unpleasant future for a socialist Australia. Unable to develop a Marxist critique of the Eastern Bloc states, they were forced to effectively abandon the Marxist concepts to the Stalinists and collapse into liberal democracy. This became quite clear in their response to the Czechoslovakian events of 1968.

Tribune, 28 August, 1968.

The consequences of the 'Prague Spring'

In 1966, two Soviet writers, Sinyavski and Daniel, were imprisoned for dissident writings, and the CPA broke new ground by expressing its disapproval. To be sure, the disapproval was carefully qualified: the writers were declared to be guilty as charged, but:

> we consider it would have been far better to rely upon publishing the truth of their double standards and dealing, and allow public opinion and that of their fellow writers to decide.[40]

Yet, even this mild statement drew critical letters from among the membership, one of whom even insisted on remaining anonymous for 'fear of reprisals'.[41]

The following March, Lloyd Churchward published a lengthy critique of Soviet democracy, which drew fire from Alf Watt and sparked a short debate in the letters page of *Tribune*.

Until 1968, the criticism was limited and vague, and the debate could be kept within bounds. This all changed with the Czech events. Quite early in the year, it became clear that a very far-reaching process of reform and even upheaval was in train in Czechoslovakia. The CPA, which had been groping towards some kind of democratic socialist concept with no obvious example to point to, was absolutely enraptured by the 'Prague Spring'. An anonymous correspondent from Prague summed up the feeling:

> This country has taken an enormous step forward – and I am so glad ... Here we stand on firm ground to beat the whole concept of 'Western way of life' in its entire ramifications. This is the 'cultural revolution' which is utterly and completely invincible! There will be no H. G. Wells society; there will be, however, a free cultured, dignified mankind – much more wonderful than William Morris dared to dream.[42]

Here, it seemed, was the socialism with a human face that the party had been searching for ... and it was crushed by Soviet tanks in August of the same year. The CPA's response was correspondingly angry and agonised; within its own ranks, it also led to a severe polarisation.

The party's National Committee voted to condemn the Russian invasion by a vote of 37 to 2, and a special *Tribune* supplement was published to get the message out. A mass protest meeting was held in the Sydney Town Hall at which speakers included Laurie Aarons, Malcolm Salmon (who had previously been in Prague) and – ironically, given his later pro-Soviet stance – the leading trade union figure Pat Clancy. Aarons told the meeting:

> The Communist Party of Australia has protested against the invasion of Czechoslovakia by the Soviet Union and four other socialist countries because we support socialist democracy and national independence for all countries in the world.[43]

This stand sparked immediate controversy within the party and helped to cohere an open, pro-Soviet opposition. Jack Henry sounded the most blindly religious note, declaring that, as a result of the Russian invasion:

> once again good has triumphed over evil; brotherly love over the foul witches' brew; enlightenment over the knights of darkness whose fortresses are in the quagmire of imperialism.[44]

Many others, although they might not write of fortresses located in quagmires, also expressed their point of view in terms of irrational faith in Moscow. However, there were those among the Stalinist critics who made points worth looking at, because they exposed underlying weaknesses in the majority approach.

Lulla Davis wrote to *Tribune* to point out that the alacrity with which the party had rallied around the Czechoslovakian issue was a bit suspicious:

> it seems strange to me that the National Committee was able to get cracking really fast on this question and throw all its resources and organisation into condemning the Soviet Union, when questions vital to the Australian people never seem to get off the ground.[45]

In other words: was the party perhaps anxious to attack the Russians in order to prove its respectability in the eyes of bourgeois public opinion? We will have occasion in the next chapter to suggest that there is a grain of truth in Davis' suggestion.

THE MONOLITH CRACKS

Bernie Taft (right) and Richard Dixon (left) with Czech leader Alexander Dubček (centre), March 1969.

Then there was the question of national self-determination. Quite obviously, the Russian invasion was a violation of Czech national sovereignty, but the question then arose: was self-determination an absolute principle, or was it expendable in pursuit of higher ends? Neither for Marx nor for Lenin had national independence been an end in itself. Marx had supported the national movements of the Irish and the Poles but opposed that of the southern Slavs because he saw it as a stalking horse for Russian tsarist reaction. Lenin had been equally emphatic in insisting that national self-determination was not an abstract, absolute principle. Rather, he saw the 'nationalism of the oppressed' precisely as a strategic device for attacking imperialism. The revolts of colonial countries, he argued, could undermine the power of the imperialist bourgeoisie. That Lenin saw national sovereignty as a consideration secondary to the defence of workers' power in Russia was made quite clear by his preparedness to invade Poland during the Russian civil war.[46]

In 1968, however, the problem seemed posed in a new manner. Here was one supposedly socialist state invading another. For Kremlin supporters, this was justified on the grounds that the socialist regime in Prague was allegedly threatened by counter-revolutionary forces. Opponents of the invasion might simply have denied this claim, but they went further, contending that, between socialist states, the right of self-determination was something like an absolute principle. Lenin's own views were distorted to make them dovetail with this view, which is that characteristic of liberal democracy:

> Self-determination is one of the main principles, not something of relative importance. Lenin regarded it as the principle of democracy in relation to the national question, an essential part of the democracy he considered the key question in the struggle for socialism.[47]

In reply, the opposition could, and did, simply quote Lenin himself:

> But no Marxist, without flying in the face of Marxism and socialism generally, can deny that the interests of socialism are higher than the interests of the right of nations to self-determination.[48]

Here, again, was that vexed question: democracy and socialism. Again, a Marxist solution was possible on the basis of an analysis of the East European countries as a form of capitalist society. One could defend Czech self-determination on Lenin's grounds, by regarding the USSR as a capitalist *imperialist* power and perceiving the fight for Czech independence as a blow against that power. But, for the reasons already indicated, the CPA could not consider this solution. As in other situations, two dismal alternatives arose: having accepted that the Eastern Bloc regimes were in some sense socialist, one had either to accept the brutal actions of the USSR as legitimate

Laurie Aarons (left) and Bernie Taft (right) representing the CPA in Moscow, June 1969, following the invasion of Czechoslovakia.

(and defend them in formally Marxist terms) or collapse into liberal-democratic ideas to avoid such a fate.

The party splits

The Czech crisis proved the catalyst for the worst split in the history of the party, with a sizeable section of the membership in several states departing to form the new Socialist Party of Australia. After Czechoslovakia, the pro-Soviet elements who had been vaguely uneasy about the party's development began to perceive a pattern to the changes in policy, a pattern which they did not like at all. Their understanding of it can be roughly summarised: The Aarons brothers and their supporters had been a bad element for at least 15 years, ever since they came back from China. The Aarons brothers had hidden their 'sympathies with Mao's opportunist theories' during the split with Hill, in order to climb into power when Sharkey retired. But:

> privately, their pro-Mao sympathies remained. As the Aarons brothers increased their influence in the leadership, their real position emerged. This was not expressed in open pro-Mao terms. It was seen in increasingly hostile attitudes towards the international communist movement in general and the Soviet Union in particular together with an increasingly opportunist line in Australia.[49]

The leadership had gone through a 'right opportunist' phase in the late 1960s, said the opposition, pointing above all to the Charter of Democratic Rights. However, as the party entered the 1970s, they claimed, it was moving into an ultraleft phase. This latter phase was associated with irresponsible politics in industry, most notably on the part of the NSW BLF. It was made worse, they said, by an excessive openness to the more radical elements of the new student and anti-war movements, whose actions 'smacked more of political lairising than of serious activity'[50] and only made it harder to achieve the main task, electing a Labor government:

[I]t is certain the decisions to withdraw the troops [from Vietnam] and end conscription must be made, in the final wash-up, by a government and not by some queer form of workers' control.[51]

Perhaps most horrific of all, the CPA was falling under the influence of Trotskyism. It emerged that one Denis Freney, a supporter of the French Trotskyist Michel Pablo, had been visiting Laurie Aarons for years and discussing the evolution of the CPA. Freney hoped that the party would evolve in a revolutionary direction and, by the early 1970s, he was sufficiently satisfied with its progress to join it. Aarons, meanwhile, had clearly been influenced by Trotskyism, largely via the ideas of Pablo and the historian Isaac Deutscher.

For some sections of the CPA's old guard, these trends were simply anathema. They had been trained over many years to regard Trotskyism as counter-revolutionary and even as associated with fascism. To see its influence growing in the CPA helped add a frenzied quality to much of the minority's criticism. But, by this time, the majority had worked up a fair bit of steam too.

It seems clear that, by 1970, the Aarons group had made a conscious decision to drive the minority out of the party. Formally speaking, they had organisational grounds to do so, because the minority had established their own publication, *The Australian Socialist*, and were refusing to abide by party rules. These grounds were cited to justify expulsions of key leaders of the opposition. But the leadership also had its political reasons. Sendy put it convincingly: 'The leadership was mesmerised with the false belief that the opposition was the main impediment to a growth in size and influence'.[52]

The CPA leadership believed, rightly, that society was changing rapidly around them. New layers of people were being radicalised. The old, tired Stalinist politics could only be a hindrance to recruiting these new people and building new influence. But what exactly did the CPA have to

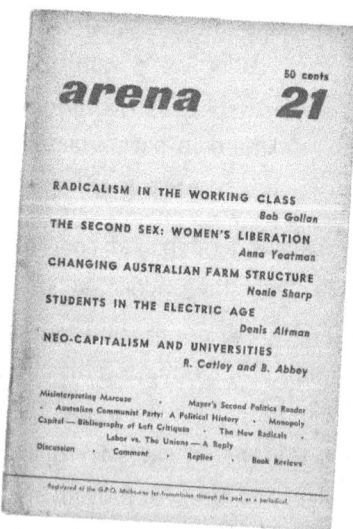

Arena, No. 21, 1970.

offer, and just how was it going to relate to the new radicalisations? In the following two chapters, we will consider, firstly, the theoretical basis of the party's new ideas; then just how the CPA faced up to the challenges of the new decade in practice.

6
A Revolution in Theory?

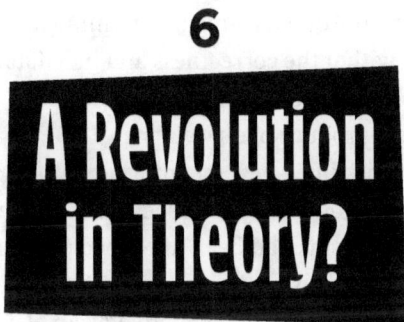

In discussing the traditional views of the Communists, I have sometimes used the term 'Stalinism', not as a term of abuse but with a specific meaning. The methods and ideology of the Communist movement under Stalin arose from the needs of the Soviet bureaucracy and the peculiar circumstances of its program for building an industrial society on the ruins of a workers' revolution.

Stalin set out to industrialise Russia on the basis of a planned economy under totalitarian control and to harness the international Communist movement to defend the Soviet Union while the industrialisation took place. In the beginning, at least, the Soviet leaders may have still been animated by the belief that they were in some sense 'building socialism'; certainly, the popularity the regime retained outside Russia derived partly from its revolutionary past. What arose was an ideology of totalitarian collectivism clothed in concepts derived from that past, concepts that were formally Marxist.

The substance of Marxism was, of course, transformed. Democratic centralism, which for Lenin had meant freedom in debate and unity in action, was now taken to mean authoritarian control. Internationalism meant defence of Russia at all costs, even the cost of blinding oneself to harsh realities or carrying out dizzying changes of line. The Leninist concept of leadership degenerated into a personality cult of the leaders.

The dialectical quality of Marxism was flattened out. From a living critical method designed to *overthrow* oppressive social relations, it was transformed into a series of mechanical formulas suited to *justifying* existing Soviet society. Marx's theory of history was broken into two opposing extremes: on the one hand, an extreme voluntarism, according to which plans could be and were forever over-fulfilled; on the other, a vulgar determinism proving the 'inevitability' of socialism – and with it the correctness and inevitability of existing policy. In the latter case, ideas were sometimes reduced to mere reflections of reality: 'put crudely, gasometers produce poetry via men'.[1]

The concept of class assumed new meaning as well. For Marx, class analysis was a tool to identify antagonisms within society. In Stalin's Russia, the regime insisted that such antagonisms had been abolished (although 'remnants' of the old ruling classes remained to justify the activities of the secret police). The USSR *as a whole* was now said to embody proletarian class interests. The 'class line' could therefore be drawn between Russia and its allies on the one hand, and the Western bourgeoisie on the other.

This had several consequences. It justified subordinating the world Communist movement to the cause of defending the Soviet Union and its program of industrialisation. It also led to a blurring of class divisions in the West. Those among the Western bourgeoisie who could be won to an alliance with the Kremlin were included in the 'people's front' and became allies of the working class. Those among the working class who made a Marxist critique of the Soviet bureaucracy – the Trotskyists in particular – were labelled fascist agents and treated as such.

This entire ideological structure began to crumble when the Communist movement started to fragment in the 1960s. With the Sino-Soviet split, there was no longer any single source of wisdom, nor a monolithic 'socialist camp' to defend. With the drift of the large European and Japanese parties away from Moscow and nationalist stirrings in the East European parties, Communists were presented with myriad conflicting political lines. As Russia developed a sophisticated modern industry, and therefore needed a workforce capable of flexible behaviour, the police terror began to be modified even in Russia itself, and Western liberal ideas began to penetrate there.

With the growth of the class struggle and the student radicalisation in the late 1960s, new ideas and new people entered left movements in the West. Often, the CPs were outflanked by radical new forces. Communists were forced to rethink.

The most obvious and powerful alternative sets of ideas which presented themselves were liberalism and social democracy. By liberalism, we mean an ideology that places *individual* rights and *individual* freedoms at the centre of politics. For Marxism, though these had been important questions, they were traditionally placed firmly within a broader context of *collective* self-emancipation and *class* struggle. Stalinism, however, had given the latter concepts a totalitarian content and hence, ironically, given a new appeal for Communists to its formal opposite, liberalism.

In politics, liberalism is closely tied to *pluralism,* a view of the state that sees its proper role as reconciling the competing claims of the individuals and groups. Marxism is also meant to accept that, in a free society, a plurality of views would contend without compulsion. However, for Marx, this was to be achieved with the withering away of the state. As long as the state machine continued to exist, it embodied the domination of one part of society – and hence its point of view – over others; this was axiomatic for him from his early critiques of Hegel onwards, and it applied to a proletarian state as much as a bourgeois one.

By social democracy (or 'reformism'), we mean the view that socialism, or profound social change, can come about through extending the control of the existing state over the economy; that this can be done through parliament, helped along perhaps by protest action; and that the best vehicle for doing so is a political party that embraces the masses of the working class in a loose organisational framework. In Australia, Laborism is the obvious example. Although there are differences between Laborism and classical social democracy, they need not concern us here.

Liberalism and social democracy appeared as the main alternative to Stalinism for two basic reasons. One was that the logic of their situation impelled the CPs towards their own domestic bourgeoisie and the dominant ideas in the labour movement that were associated with class collaboration. We have outlined this dynamic in Chapter 1. The second reason was that the other alternative that should have attracted CP militants – a revolutionary approach that sought to revive the tradition of Marx and Lenin – did not present itself to them in a very attractive form in the 1960s, anywhere in the world.

The organisations that had kept revolutionary Marxism alive throughout the Stalin period, largely the Trotskyist groups, were tiny before the late 1960s and still comparatively small in the 1970s.

Militants accustomed to a mass party were not likely to be attracted to them. Moreover, years of isolation had made most Trotskyist groups ingrown and sectarian; they sometimes reminded CPers of the worst periods in their own history, only rendered more comic than tragic by the small size of the groups.

We must also remember that many Communists simply could not tell the difference between genuine Marxism and Leninism and the Stalinist forgeries which they had only just begun to reject. The revolutionary groups spoke of building vanguard parties, democratic centralism, smashing the state – and CP members were irresistibly reminded of how the same phrases had slid off the tongues of their own Stalinist leaders. They also remembered the content with which these phrases had been invested and which they had not liked. Why should the revolutionary groups be different?

By contrast, social democracy and liberalism offered apparent benefits: individual freedom and access to mainstream politics. No wonder most Communists moved in that direction.

In Australia, the ideological shift was carried out, in broad outlines, between 1963 and 1971 and, despite apparent moves back to the left in the early 1970s, has proved to be permanent. In this chapter, I will trace some of the roots of the new ideas in the experiences of Australian Communists, then devote some attention to the work of an individual, Eric Aarons. I do not mean to suggest that the role of Aarons, or any other individual, was decisive; had he been absent, the same general trend would undoubtedly have emerged. But, because Aarons made it his task to attempt to think through at a theoretical level the issues we are about to consider, his work provides a convenient framework in which to discuss them.

The belated impact of the postwar economic boom

One important factor impelling Australian Communists to rethink their ideas was undoubtedly the postwar economic boom. The boom flew in the face of everything they had been taught to expect. The Communist International had been founded in the belief that 'the epoch of final, decisive struggle ... has arrived'.[2] The grim Depression of the 1930s appeared to be a decisive confirmation of that thesis. After World War II, Communists firmly expected a second depression, and their leaders continued doggedly to predict it for a decade or more after they had been proved mistaken.

Had the boom only meant a refutation of the CPA's theories, however, it would not have been such a blow. Much more seriously, it brought a historic decline in the class struggle. Strike levels had been up to two million days lost in 1950; in 1951–56, they averaged around one million; from 1957 to 1967, they averaged well below that. The decline was even more serious than these figures suggest, given the rapid growth in the size of the workforce. The decline in industrial militancy was only the most obvious feature of a general conservatisation of Australian life, which included anti-Communism and conservative government as well as a dominant ideology – a woman's place was in the home.

The boom and the decline in the class struggle naturally produced theories that Australia was a 'classless society', capitalism had overcome its contradictions, and Marxism had become outdated. The CPA opposed these theories, but only on the basis of dogma. In 1958, attacking those who had left or been expelled from the CPA for just such 'revisionist' ideas, Sharkey said: 'In the light of the growing crisis of capitalism we can only hope they will realise the erroneous character of their views'.[3] What was needed was a theory that faced up to the reality of the boom and also sought to identify the contradictions within it which would eventually bring it to an end. Attempts of this sort were made overseas, by Marxists outside the official Communist movement.[4] Unfortunately, the CPA possessed neither the sophistication nor the theoretical framework to attempt it.

This is also true of the notion that the class struggle had ceased to be the central motor of change. In a period of downturn in industrial struggle, a left party needs to face up to the fact and find other places to work, other layers of society from which to recruit. In doing so, however, it needs to retain its long-term working-class orientation. The CPA, in the face of a changing world, simply dug in its heels. Indeed, it often exhibited an increased suspicion of non-workers, especially intellectuals, that was later to be referred to as 'proletarian sectarianism'. This suspicion arose partly out of the rapid departure of middle-class elements from the party at the onset of the Cold War. Many workers in the party felt that middle-class elements had proved unreliable – and, to some degree, they had a point. There is no substitute for a working-class base. But any recruitment is better than none; and it *is* essential to win as many intellectuals as possible to a serious revolutionary stance.

The suspicion was also consciously bred into the party by the leadership to explain away the loss of large numbers of intellectuals after 1956. Here, the danger was that it could give rise to anti-intellectual prejudices as a substitute for critical thinking and allow important issues to be swept under the rug. Either way, the result was inflexibility.

In the short term, dogmatism of this sort, either on economics or on the question of a working-class orientation, could only lead to isolation. In the longer term, ironically, once the hold of such ideas was broken, they were quickly replaced with their diametrical and equally unfortunate opposites.

In the 1960s, the CPA finally accepted that there had been a postwar boom. So far, so good, but the CPA now proceeded to invest it with a permanence it did not possess. In 1966, in the first issue of the new journal *Australian Left Review*, Bernie Taft wrote:

> The question is: Are there new features which have changed the pattern of cyclical development and brought an accelerated rate of growth of a transient character, or do they reflect fundamental changes in the world? Can we expect a return to the old types of crises and to a drastically reduced rate of growth, or are these new features likely to be with us for a long time, *possibly for the transition period between capitalism and socialism?* ...
>
> If the former view is adopted, there will be tendencies to wait for change; if the latter, marxists have to find the way to win wide popular support in present conditions. [Emphasis added.]

Taft clearly believed the latter and was prepared to draw the political conclusions:

> the problems created by capitalism, economic, social, moral and cultural are greater and more varied than ever. Insoluble within the framework of the capitalist system, objectively they make the need for socialism ever more urgent ... New needs created by modern life remain unsatisfied[5]

A theory which accepted that capitalist economic stability would persist right up until socialism arrived necessarily meant a political strategy based as much on 'moral or cultural' as on 'economic and social' issues. Such a shift in political program has traditionally been associated with a downgrading of the central role of the working class in the struggle for socialism. Sure enough, early the following year, Ron Hearn, apparently writing under the influence of Taft's article, expressed quite clearly the link between the prospect of capitalist stability and that reorientation to the middle class that was embodied in the 'Coalition of the Left':

> Because of several factors operating on Australian conditions the possibility of a change to a socialist form of society without passing through a deep economic crisis exists ... the effects of automation and the influence of socialist trade, etc., which are dominating social changes today, are two very important factors which could stave off deep economic crisis for a long period. If this does occur, then a decline in socialist influence on a mass scale is likely ...
>
> On the other hand there is established a very fine and mature growing of left forces particularly noticeable among academics, students, the clergy and within the ALP itself ... this left trend is a forward moving development which will grow in depth and later in size to mass proportions.[6]

It was a wide swing of the pendulum: from denying the boom to granting it virtual immortality; from dogged 'workerism' to placing one's hopes in academics, students, the clergy and the ALP. What is striking is the speed with which the CPA leaders were able to make the shift. The basic reasons why this was possible have been suggested in previous chapters. However, there is one interesting additional factor that contributed to shaping the political make up of the party leaders and their supporters, which may perhaps justify a brief digression: the peculiar experience of training in China.

The experience of China training

In the early 1950s, a small group of Australian Communists travelled secretly to the People's Republic for a political education, and they were followed by other groups throughout the decade. Among the first group was Eric Aarons, who found among his teachers a flexibility in political thinking which neither the Russians nor the CPA leadership of the time had often displayed.

The Chinese party had met a bloody defeat in 1927 because of mistaken instructions from Moscow, and Stalin had never shown much enthusiasm for the Chinese revolution. Moreover, Beijing was wary of Soviet domination. The Chinese Communists were thus critical of Moscow from the start. The differences did not become public before the late 1950s but were reflected in an insistence by Beijing on the importance for Communists in each country of making a concrete study of local conditions.

At the same time, the particular nature of the Chinese revolution led to theoretical innovations. The working class had played no role whatsoever in Mao's rise to power. For Mao, therefore, class politics had not needed to display any connection with the working class at all.

Already, the Soviet rulers had drawn the class line more between Russia and the West than between the proletariat and the bourgeoisie. Moscow had to lead a world movement of workers' parties. China did not, and was thus free to transform the content of class politics much more thoroughly. In Mao's thought, it was reduced to extreme subjectivism. Nigel Harris writes:

> Mao uses the terms 'proletariat', 'peasant', 'capitalist' in a ... loose fashion. The terms do not refer to objective categories, but to political attitudes, degrees of support for the Communist Party (which is itself the 'proletariat') ... Thus the 'dictatorship of the proletariat' can arrive in 1956, ending the 'New Democracy', somehow disappear along the way, and then become the prize in the Cultural Revolution.[7]

Chinese society was also different from Russia: it was far more backward. Stalin had been able to carry out an industrial revolution in Russia, mobilising the resources of the nation through ruthless compulsion. Mao had neither the material nor the cadre resources to construct a comparable repressive apparatus or to mobilise comparable masses of capital. The peasantry could not be driven, so it had to be coaxed; the same, to a lesser degree, applied to the urban population. The situation demanded a considerable flexibility on the part of the party cadres – a flexibility that tended to find an ideological reflection. Hence, the comparative open-mindedness that Eric Aarons found in his teachers. If it was not really Marxist, neither was it 'Stalinist' in the sense Australian Stalinists were used to:

A REVOLUTION IN THEORY?

Ted Hill meeting with Mao Zedong, China, 1968.

The Chinese lecturers we had, and the cadres we met, evidenced considerable flexibility of thought and non-dogmatism (or anti-dogmatism) especially when compared with the Soviet lecturers ... Particularly noticeable, though hard to specify precisely, was the emphasis on things of the mind and emotions. This is hard to define also, but it stood out in marked contrast to our Australian brashness, lack of consideration for dignity and feelings, and over-riding emphasis on 'objective causes' with much playing down of 'subjective' ones, which we had thought to be one of the main hallmarks of 'Marxism–Leninism'.[8]

This general climate found a rather remarkable expression in the Chinese teaching methods. These sometimes resembled Western encounter-group therapy. One writer explained that the emphasis was heavily on individual and subjective factors:

> Ideological remoulding through introspection (to give it its full title) began ... with the study of a particular topic, say, the role of

a Communist Party. Then, the class committee ... would pick out one theme for intensive study ... The choice ... may have been the notion of the Party as a vanguard ... Group members would then reflect on this 'centre of gravity'. They would ask themselves how well they had observed this principle in practice. And eventually they might come up with examples, however trivial, where they, as members of the party, had gone beyond the level of the consciousness of the masses. From this they would conclude ... that they had been guilty of 'commandism'. At this point, someone would probably point out that 'commandism' ... constituted a serious breach of the Party's mass line ...

[T]his fault would be traced back to one or another of the variations of bourgeois ideology ... most likely, 'individualism' or 'contempt for the masses' or maybe both. The group member would then be obliged to dig up other examples of his 'bourgeois individualism' or 'contempt for the masses' from both his present and past behaviour. Finally ... he would try to overcome these particular shortcomings in practice.[9]

This process approaches the strengths and weaknesses of cadres as a moral and individual problem; the 'masses' appear only as a backdrop, or as passive herds towards whom 'contempt' or a correct 'mass line' is expressed by the individuals. There is a strong flavour of guilty liberalism, and it is almost a relief to discover that later tour groups displayed a 'healthy scepticism' towards this ideological remoulding, with Claude Jones declaring, 'if you have a guilty complex, a uselessness complex, how can you be a good Communist?'[10]

I have dwelt on these experiences because they were an important formative influence on the generation that transformed the CPA, including Eric Aarons. They came away from China with a number of new ideas: the fallibility of the Russians; the value of flexibility and studying the local conditions in one's own country; an approach to the education of cadres that was a bit fixated on the individual as against the social aspect; and perhaps, finally, the Maoist tendency to free Marxist categories from any fixed content. Commenting later on his own China experiences, Rex Mortimer described them as a 'liberal education'.[11] If that is what it was, then no doubt it made some modest contribution to the liberal *theory* that Eric Aarons, also the recipient of such an education, began to develop in the course of the 1960s.

A revolution in philosophy?

Aarons began his rethinking of Communist ideas with a study of philosophy. He was most impressed with the Western thinkers whose books were recommended to him by academic friends. Compared with the tedium dished out by Soviet sources, they were lively and refreshing and appeared to have made new insights. He concluded:

> [T]here was no likelihood that the burgeoning knowledge in this and other fields could be squeezed without damaging surgery into any glass slipper, however elegant, and that the easy divisions into 'bourgeois' and 'proletarian' ideology we were in the habit of making were a major aspect of confining thought within old pre-determined bounds and could no longer be accepted in that form.[12]

The old notions of bourgeois and proletarian ideology, of course, had virtually amounted to Western and Soviet ideology. Not surprisingly, when Aarons published the fruits of his studies in a book called *Philosophy for an Exploding World*, he announced almost at the start that he was taking up problems that were common to both East and West: The people of all countries – socialist and capitalist, 'East and West', industrially advanced and undeveloped – are for the first time simultaneously involved, all driven by problems that are at least substantially similar, however different the starting points.[13]

This could have been the signal for an important breakthrough: if the USSR is 'driven' by the same fundamental problems as the Western capitalist societies, one might begin to question the socialist nature of the USSR. Further, a Marxist who saw in the prosecution of the class struggle the answer to social problems might be led to discover the presence of a class struggle in the Eastern Bloc societies. From here, it would be a short step to a class analysis of these societies, perhaps in terms of state capitalism. Unfortunately, Aarons' concerns are far removed from the class struggle. Instead, he writes of a 'values revolution':

> There is mounting evidence that a revolution in thinking and, perhaps more important, a revolution in feeling, is taking place in industrially developed societies. It is a tide which cannot be stemmed ... It is potentially socialist since the new values emerging involve man taking conscious control of his relations with his kind and with nature [14]

This passage represents a decisive departure from Marxism. The suggestion that a revolution in feeling can be more important than a revolution in thinking already suggests a retreat from scientific thinking; the notion that either can be a 'tide which cannot be stemmed' is wishful thinking rather than analysis. The idea that societies that are already socialist need to develop a 'potentially socialist trend' removes any content from the term 'socialist' itself, as does the suggestion that there can be socialist societies in which 'man' has not yet 'taken conscious control of his relations with his kind and with nature'. Nevertheless, the passage might be simply dismissed as vague and muddled, were it not coupled with a conscious shift of emphasis away from the working class and the class struggle. Aarons identifies three major areas of his values revolution: the ecological crisis, women's liberation and industrial democracy. It would be difficult to find three more vital issues for revolutionaries today, but what leaps out at you from the pages of the book is that it does not relate any of these questions to the class struggle.

The struggles of third world and Indigenous peoples are given their due, but the working class does not appear to have anything to do with them. Women's liberation is treated simply as an issue between women and men, as if the women of the bourgeoisie did not have class interests which might get in the way of women's liberation, and as if working class women's position in the process of production did not impinge on a strategy for their liberation as women. The emphasis in Aarons' treatment is on sexuality and lifestyle – important issues, but dealt with largely in psychological terms that are not really anchored in a social, let alone class, analysis.

In the discussion of industrial democracy, there is no mention of unions! Nor is there a critique of 'workers' participation', as opposed to workers' control. Indeed, there is no discussion of workers' *struggle* at all (how else will industrial democracy be achieved?). *Rydges*, the management magazine, is quoted, and so is an academic. Jack Mundey, the prominent Communist who was leading workers' control struggles in the building industry at that very time, is noticeably absent.

Can all these be simple oversights? No indeed. Aarons has consciously and explicitly rejected class politics:

> [I]t is not 'the workers' or 'the intellectuals' or any other stratum as such, but the revolutionary-minded elements from among them all that must make themselves into a social force, grow to a majority or near enough to it, and impress upon society new revolutionary values which permeate all spheres of society.[15]

For Marx, the workers were to seize power and transform society. For Aarons, the most revolutionary-minded from *all* sections of society are to impress new values on it. Quite logically, therefore, he embraces political and philosophical *pluralism:*

> Pluralism has come to stay in political commitment, in life style, and in philosophy and theoretical approach in general. A common core of thought and feeling which can only spring from shared values must be achieved ... This process would be hampered rather than furthered by attempts to constrict it within a highly ordered edifice of thought and organisation.[16]

Lenin had stood for a disciplined party of the working class, which allowed the workers as a class to exercise political hegemony over their allies among the rural and urban petty bourgeoisie. Aarons wants an alliance of diverse elements, all of which he considers equally important, based on shared values rather than political agreement. Quite logically, he must oppose both a 'highly ordered edifice of thought' (that is, a coherent political program) and anything but a very loose form of organisation.

Within the first few pages of his book, Aarons laid the philosophical basis for a shift from Stalinism to liberalism in thought and to social democracy in organisation. He was no less forthright in translating the philosophical shift into political terms.

The nature of the Soviet Union

One of the first questions he had to consider was the nature of Soviet 'socialism'. In the 1960s, Communists had begun to reconsider their previous blind loyalty to the Kremlin. They felt a growing need for a new analysis of Soviet society.

There are several options open to leftists trying to develop a critique of Russia. The followers of Chairman Mao contend that Soviet socialism was betrayed by Khrushchev and that capitalism was restored in the USSR after 1956. But this explanation had little appeal for Communists. If the Russian workers, after decades of socialism, could allow the restoration of capitalism without a struggle – and there was no visible struggle against Khrushchev – then only very pessimistic conclusions follow about the ability of the working class to govern society at all.

My own contention, indicated in previous chapters, is that the rise of the Stalinist bureaucracy represented the liquidation of the Bolshevik revolution. The Stalin regime carried out the tasks of capitalist accumulation on the basis of a state-run economy; Russia is therefore best defined as a state capitalist society. But this analysis, too, is a hard one for veteran CP members to accept. Who wants to feel that they have spent decades defending a capitalist regime, without even knowing it?

There remained the theory elaborated by Leon Trotsky. Trotsky broke with Stalin in the 1920s and denounced the bureaucracy which Stalin represented as repressive and counter-revolutionary. He nonetheless defended the Soviet state against the West on the grounds that it still retained socialist property forms. The state industry represented a fundamentally socialist aspect of the regime, said Trotsky, but the society was held back from achieving genuine socialism by the bureaucracy. The USSR was a 'degenerated workers' state'. In the Stalin period, Trotsky had been labelled a fascist for putting forward this analysis; but, by the 1960s, it began to have an appeal for CP intellectuals, particularly in the modified version advanced by Isaac Deutscher.[17]

Deutscher followed Trotsky in declaring Russia a degenerated workers' state and agreed that the Stalin regime was repressive. But he argued that Stalinism had been a historically necessary phenomenon. Great revolutions, said Deutscher, have a heroic phase represented by personalities such as Lenin and Trotsky. After that, they must be *consolidated,* and this task falls to less appealing but more practical realists, such as Stalin. Essentially, he saw the Russian revolution as analogous to the French Revolution: firstly, the heroic upsurge led by the Marats, Dantons and Robespierres; then a consolidation under Napoleon. This consolidation, he said, leads to a loss of some of the original progressive content of the revolution and to a loss of democracy. This is regrettable but unavoidable. It is up to later generations to rectify the situation.

For Communists, this version had a greater appeal than Trotsky's implacable anti-Stalinism. It suggested a perspective of reforming, rather than overthrowing, the Eastern Bloc regimes. It also allowed CP members to feel that they had still been part of a historically progressive movement throughout the Stalin period, while criticising specific features of the contemporary USSR. It is probably no accident, therefore, that Eric Aarons' major document on this question cites Deutscher more than once, while mention of Trotsky is avoided.[18]

By 1970, under the influence of such ideas, the CPA was prepared to define the Soviet Union and similar societies as 'socialist based' rather than 'socialist' and to declare:

> Conditions for man's liberation were created and these countries have challenged imperialist domination in the fields of production, science and technology; but the actual liberation of man in the main has yet to be accomplished.[19]

Among the negative features of Soviet society, the party cited 'over-centralised control of the economy', the 'existence of bureaucracy', 'curtailment of political democracy and individual freedom', a shortsighted nationalism and 'dogmatic ideologies'. And it warned:

> In some countries these problems and their various manifestations are leading to the build-up of social pressures and tensions which will eventually lead to crisis and upheavals while present policies remain.[20]

This prediction was borne out the same year by a massive revolt of Polish shipyard workers. The CPA was obviously on the right track. But, as the 1970 statement itself conceded, the analysis was far from being coherent; for example, Laurie Aarons suggested in 1971 that the genuine socialist alternative to bureaucratic Stalinism was 'public ownership plus democracy, plus liberty, plus workers' control plus self-management'.[21] As a list of desirable features, this might suffice; as an alternative social program, it was rather fragmentary and eclectic.

It was left to Eric Aarons to attempt to raise the discussion to a theoretical level. His document, circulated in 1974, was more sophisticated than anything else the party has produced before or since. For just this reason, it is perhaps more revealing. Aarons elaborated a reformist perspective towards the Eastern Bloc states which, given his previously declared emphasis on the similarity of problems facing East and West, had implications for CPA strategic thinking in Australia. He began his discussion by examining the term 'socialist based', which he said was intended, on the one hand, to acknowledge the fact that private (capitalist and feudal) ownership of the means of production no longer existed, having been replaced by social ownership; and on the other, that the political forms were not of the kind to which Australian socialists aspired.[22]

This formulation is clearly derived from Trotskyism, but Aarons took it a step further, because he pointed out a contradiction in the Trotskyist approach. He noted that it drew a sharp dividing line between the (supposedly progressive) economic base of the society and the (undemocratic) political superstructure. Such a sharp division is unusual in Marx and foreign to his basic method, although it was common enough in the vulgar Marxism of the Stalin period. Moreover, it is particularly unsuitable to a society in which the means of production are in the hands of the state, as Aarons makes clear:

> Private ownership of the means of production and the relations of production which go with it may have been abolished, but 'public ownership' does not, and cannot, by itself fully establish new relations of production. For without actual decisions (by the state) no production, distribution or reproduction will take place.
>
> The decision making process, then, in the very nature of things, becomes an essential part of the relations of production, or if you like, of the economic base.[23]

A REVOLUTION IN THEORY? 159

Josep Broz Tito (centre) with Laurie Aarons (left) and Bernie Taft (right), 1969.

This is a most important insight, but it can lead in two opposite directions. We recall that Trotsky's analysis, as modified by Deutscher, tended to blur the distinction between a revolutionary opposition to the Soviet regime, aimed at overthrowing it, and a reformist one, aimed at gradual change. Nevertheless, the reformist tendency is partially restrained by the sharp distinction between a progressive economic base, which one supports, and a repressive political superstructure, which one is still committed to transforming. Once that distinction is dissolved, you either have to accept the whole of society as essentially progressive or consider the whole as reactionary.

The revolutionary response would necessarily be to conclude that Russia has no socialist base at all. If the decision-making process is part of the relations of production – and a rather vital part – and this process is controlled by the bureaucracy without any hint of workers' democracy, then clearly, these relations of production are not themselves socialist. By this line of reasoning, one arrives in fairly short order at the conclusion that the Soviet Union is an exploitative class society.

We have seen, however, why this conclusion was unacceptable to most Communists. Aarons therefore moves to the exact opposite conclusion. From denying a sharp division between base and superstructure, he moves to blur the distinction between the idea of a 'socialist based' society and socialism itself. His portrayal of Soviet society is noticeably more favourable than those which had appeared in party documents in the period immediately before. He identifies two mainsprings to the Soviet system:

> For the Soviet Union it appears that the two things mentioned above – the material living standards of the people and the influence and power of the nation ... are these springs.[24]

This is a key test. For the Communist movement under Stalin, the concept of 'socialism in a single country' promised to combine just these features: growing power for the Soviet state to enable it to survive in a hostile capitalist world; at the same time, a society where the needs of people were to take precedence over accumulation – unlike capitalism, which is characterised precisely by the subordination of human needs to profit and the subordination of consumption to accumulation.

There is no doubt that the second of the two 'mainsprings' nominated by Aarons has indeed been a constant feature of Soviet society. Stalin himself had made the central logic of Soviet economic development quite clear in a famous speech in 1931:

> No, comrades ... the pace must not be slackened! ... To slacken the pace would mean to lag behind; and those who lag behind are beaten ... We are fifty or a hundred years behind the advanced countries. We must make good this lag in ten years. Either we do it, or they crush us.[25]

The historic problem, of course, was to combine this with a social order in which human needs ('living standards') were nevertheless the main priority. This, the Soviet Union has manifestly not done; on the contrary, the Stalin regime turned the society directly away from such a priority. Consumer goods constituted 64.9 percent of industrial production in 1928, dropping to 38.8

percent in 1940, and plummeting to 27.5 percent well after the end of the war in 1960.[26]

In fact, the only evidence Aarons advances to show that improving living standards is a mainspring of the Soviet system is the statement that 'material well-being is fairly consistently advancing'.[27] But this is hardly a decisive argument. Material wellbeing may rise as a by-product of economic development in a society whose central dynamic is entirely different. In fact, many Marxists today would agree that the historic tendency in capitalist society is for living standards to rise. Certainly, at the time Aarons' document appeared, material wellbeing in Australia had been 'fairly consistently advancing' for two decades. To conclude from such evidence that improving living standards was a 'mainspring' of Australian capitalism would lead one straight to reformism. And that is where it led Aarons in the case of the USSR.

The idea that Russian society can be reformed was not stated explicitly in this document, but it did not need to be. For CPA members trained for many years to be sympathetic to the Kremlin, one needed only to refrain from an explicit call for revolution and to hint that, basically, Russia wasn't too bad. And Aarons certainly goes out of his way to find positive things to say about the Soviet regime.

The ruling group in the USSR, we are told, 'cannot *(and probably do not want to)* amass wealth in its general form' [emphasis added].[28] They display this remarkable lack of interest in worldly goods because they are 'to one degree or another bound and/or motivated by at least some of the ideals of the revolution'.[29] The most concise means of refuting this fantasy is perhaps to quote the experience of journalist Alexander Werth, who observed conditions in different layers of Soviet society in 1942.

It was the height of the war, when sacrifice was especially called for. Werth spoke to a maid whose children had to live on bread and tea, but he also recorded his experience at luncheon with the elite:

> That lunch at the National today was a very sumptuous affair, for, in spite of the food shortage in Moscow, there always seems to be enough of the best possible food whenever there is reason for any kind of big feed, with official persons as guests. For *zakuski* there was the best fresh caviare [*sic*], and plenty of butter, and smoked

> salmon; then sturgeon and, after the sturgeon, chicken cutlets *à la Marechal*, then ice and coffee with brandy and liqueurs; and all down the table there was the usual array of bottles.[30]

For Aarons, not only are the Soviet bureaucrats a spartan lot, but even their nuclear weapons have virtues. The Soviet nuclear capacity has 'created possibilities of averting world nuclear war'.[31] By this logic, even Stalin's terror would have its positive features; it was, after all, essential to building the industrial capacity for nuclear weapons.

Given this general background, it is hard to see any but a reformist meaning to the one passage Aaron devotes to the possibilities for change in the USSR. The structures of this society must be 'negated', we are told, but this is 'not to call for the "overthrow" of socialism'; rather it is to 'speak up *for* socialism, it is to urge the completion of what has been called "The Unfinished Revolution"'.[32] That, however, will not happen quickly:

> Change will not be easy, and all the indications at present are that it will not be quick. No sober assessment could hold that the present system *must* give way in a shorter time than it has taken to develop to a considerable degree of maturity (that is, 25 or 30 years).[33]

Aarons had raised the discussion of the USSR to a higher level – only to turn it back in the direction of accommodation to the Soviet ruling circles. When he turned his attentions to socialist strategy in the West, the thrust of his argument was similar, except that the reformism was much more explicit.

The transition to socialism

Before 1870, Marx and Engels had believed that the existing state machinery of capitalism could be taken over by the workers and used to introduce socialism. The Paris Commune changed their minds. Marx wrote, soon after the Commune:

> the next attempt of the French Revolution will be no longer, as before, to transfer the bureaucratic–military machine from one hand to another, but to *smash* it.

After quoting these words, Lenin added that they 'briefly express the principal lesson of Marxism on the tasks of the proletariat in relation to the state during a revolution'.[34] For the Communists of Lenin's day, this was a central part of their concept of revolutionary politics.

In practice, revolution ceased to be Communist policy by 1935, at the very latest, with the adoption of the policy of the Popular Front. The Popular Front involved collaboration with a section of the bourgeoisie and even brought Communists into governments in some places. However, this strategy was limited to specific aims: immediate reforms, the defence of democracy, defeating fascism. The transition to socialism was put off into the dim future, but, in theory, it still involved revolution. Ralph Gibson has made this quite clear:

> In past years, when we spoke of the workers' 'united front' and the broader 'people's front', we thought of them as directed to winning peace, progress, democratic liberties, not to winning socialism. This was, I remember, my own treatment of the matter in Party discussions over many years.[35]

A new stage was reached after World War II. Throughout Eastern Europe, the Soviet forces had imposed governments to their liking. These were coalitions involving not only the CPs but also social democratic and bourgeois parties. The CPs held key ministries and had the backing of the Red Army, but the public position was that the governments were 'people's democracies' rather than the dictatorship of the proletariat. So far, this was consistent with the conception of the Popular Front as outlined above.

After 1947, Moscow tightened its grip. The commanding heights of the economy were placed in the hands of the state, and the CPs became openly dominant. It was announced that the East European states were on the road to socialism. To Communists who did not perceive the iron hand of the Red Army and the Kremlin as the moving force behind the changes, accepting the democratic pretensions of the East European regimes as genuine, it seemed that the transition to socialism had been achieved through peaceful reform with the cooperation of sections of the bourgeoisie. The smashing of the capitalist state and the dictatorship of the proletariat appeared to have been superseded by the Popular Front as a method of achieving socialism itself. Khrushchev made this new view

Popular front politics are clearly encapsulated in these posters for May Day 1962 and 1963.

official in 1956 when he announced that the 'parliamentary means of achieving socialism are now possible'.[36]

Even now, however, Communists still clung to tattered remnants of Leninism as they understood it. Gibson, in his memoirs, writes at some length about the virtues of Lenin's work *State and Revolution* and about how it showed the need for revolution. He then proceeds to fill Lenin's terms with reformist content:

> If in our day it has become more possible, in certain conditions, on the basis of a powerful mass struggle, for the people to win power peacefully, take over the basic means of production and turn parliament into an instrument of their own will, the change involved is still a revolutionary one.[37]

Gibson was only concerned with retaining the *term* revolution. According to John Sendy, many CPA leaders retained secret hankerings after a real revolution well into the postwar period:

Certainly to my knowledge leading Communists took a tongue-in-cheek attitude to our stated 'preference', in various party programmes, for a peaceful road, while others have long regarded with disdain such strategies as those of the Italian Communist Party. Following the 1956 20th Congress of the CPSU, Party leaders laughed about Spanish Communists considering a peaceful road as possible in Spain. The same leaders, and those who followed, ridiculed the possibility of structural reform in Italy.[38]

Even Eric Aarons' brother, Laurie, could declare in a short-lived left period as late as 1972 that the election of a Labor government 'cannot change anything, because the real power does not lie in the government and parliament'.[39] If the CPA was to become a left reformist party, someone would have to wage a struggle against this residual revolutionary sentiment. Eric Aarons took up the task.

The problem became acute after the fall of the Allende government in Chile. Allende had stood at the head of a 'coalition of the left' and had argued that the existing capitalist state could be manipulated in favour of the workers. He promised that the army would remain neutral and even invited some generals into his cabinet. The generals responded with a military coup and the annihilation of the left. This experience might have given some pause to the advocates of a parliamentary road to socialism, but Eric Aarons stoutly defended Allende's strategy:

> So far as one can judge, the strategy of the Popular Unity was correct enough in the respect that they planned to use (and did use) various laws ... to erode the economic power of capital, and to assist mass mobilisations ...
>
> They also spoke of not ultimately counting on the neutrality of the army or adherence to 'the law' by the opposing classes.[40]

While not 'ultimately' counting on the neutrality of the army, Allende had trusted them enough in the short term to include them in his government! At the same time, he systematically dampened workers' struggles. But Aarons would only make the most minor criticisms, referring to a 'hesitation in relying sufficiently on the workers and an apparent [!] failure of work in the armed forces'.[41] The only major criticisms he made were made from the *right*. There was sectarianism towards the church, he said. And, while the fragmentation of the left was regrettable:

> Nor should the later consequences of such a political evolution to a single party as revealed in the Soviet Union in particular be forgotten.[42]

If the strategy of the 'coalition of the left' proves incapable of meeting the threat of capitalist violence, never mind: the main thing is that the hypothetical threat of Stalinism is staved off! The CPA's inability to criticise the Soviet regime except in terms of liberal democracy now bore fruit in the form of a failure to face up to the lessons of the Chilean defeat. And Aarons was absolutely determined to learn no strategic lessons from it:

Eric Aarons, 1965.

> The most one can say is that a combination of all available means, with flexible shifting from one to the other as occasion demands, will probably emerge.[43]

Some time later, Eric Aarons turned his attentions to the question of socialist strategy in Australia, in an article that showed definite signs of Eurocommunist influence. Entitled 'The State and Australian Socialism', the article contends that the capitalist state has changed qualitatively since Lenin's day. Its institutions now contain large numbers of employees who can be mobilised against the system, writes Aarons – and this is undoubtedly true. Yet, the very example he chooses to hammer home the point reveals the fundamental error behind his train of thought:

> There are even examples in history of armies – the ultimate core of the state – being influenced by the prevailing social sentiment and political situation to refuse to fire on strikers.[44]

Again, the statement is undoubtedly true, but what does it prove? One might quibble about whether the army is the 'ultimate core of the state'; certainly, it is vitally important. The point, however, is that splits in the ranks of the armed forces have been a feature of every great revolution in modern history. Whole sections of the army came over to the Bolsheviks in 1917. Would Eric Aarons, had he been present in Petrograd in 1917, have concluded that the Russian state was being democratised; that Leninist-style revolution was outdated?

Aarons seems to imagine that the traditional Leninist concept of smashing the state somehow means the physical liquidation of its employees and a general bloodbath all round. On the contrary, it means breaking up the authoritarian structures of the state machine. To this end, the mobilisation of state employees is vitally important, of course, but the fact that these employees are numerous and can be organised does not mean that the state has been democratised. Ask any public servant!

Aarons goes on to identify another supposed change in the capitalist state:

> The claimed 'impartiality' of the state, which is a vital ideological prop ... has to be given some lip service. This creates avenues for ideas and actions which don't prop up the existing order.[45]

Once again, the statement is quite true, and yet it proves nothing whatsoever. The capitalist state claims to be impartial, and this claimed impartiality opens up contradictions that socialists can exploit. But there is hardly anything new about this situation. Engels wrote in 1884, not just about the capitalist state but about all past states, that, because of the existence of class struggle, 'it became necessary to have a power, *seemingly standing above* society ... and this power ... is the state' [emphasis added]. Lenin quotes these words and comments that, after the February revolution in Russia, all the Mensheviks and Social Revolutionaries 'descended at once to the petty-bourgeois theory that the state reconciles classes'.[46] In any case, we are only dealing with a *claimed* impartiality that needs to be exposed, not with a *real* democratisation of the state. Surely it is Aarons, with his theory of democratisation, who builds illusions about the impartiality of the state.

The most audacious part of his article concerns the transition to socialism. For some reason, he attempts to cite Lenin to justify his own theories, offering the following paraphrase of *State and Revolution:*

> The state consists, [Lenin] pointed out, of a separate body of people whose function is to rule. The aim of marxists in respect to the state is not to make it all powerful, but to 'do away' with it.
>
> How can this be done? By having everyone partake of the function. We call this self-management, and see it as a great extension of democracy. A 'democratic road to socialism' might therefore be briefly characterised as the process in which more and more people in more spheres of life act over things that affect them.[47]

The first paragraph correctly reproduces Lenin's view of the 'state in general', of *all* states. The second is made to follow on so as to suggest that all states can be 'done away with' by 'having everyone partake of the function', then generalises this into a 'democratic road to socialism' which is made to appear consistent with Lenin's own views. It is a rather squalid exercise in sophistry.

Lenin's pamphlet, after making general points about the state, proceeds very pointedly to distinguish two very different kinds of state with which communists have to deal. On the one hand, there is the capitalist state, which must be smashed; on the other, there is the workers' state, which is to be progressively democratised, with 'everyone partaking of the function' until it 'withers away'. These propositions, the core of Lenin's argument, are belaboured tirelessly through the work and are so well known on the left that one can hardly believe Aarons is unaware of them.

Beginning with a healthy desire to criticise Stalinism, where have Aarons and his co-thinkers ended up? With liberalism in philosophy, with reformism in strategic thinking, with sophistry in the presentation of ideas. This theoretical progression is the reflection of and, to some degree, a contributing factor in, the evolution of CPA practice from Stalinism to a kind of left reformism. In the following pages, we will see how this basic trend, despite a left lurch in the early 1970s, reached full fruition as the party entered the 1980s.

7
Left Turn, Right Turn: The Party in the 1970s

The Communist Party entered the seventies smaller and more divided than it had been for decades, yet there was one saving grace: it was also able to respond, though somewhat sluggishly at first, to a powerful radicalisation that began to sweep Australia from about 1967. The party was engulfed in a great upsurge of industrial militancy and by a student radicalisation which was at the heart of a powerful movement against the Vietnam War. Following closely on the heels of these developments came the explosive growth of women's liberation.

How did each of these aspects of the radicalisation contribute to a turn to the left in the CPA's orientation?

The *trade union struggle* took off like a skyrocket from 1967. Days lost in strikes, which had been below one million per year for a considerable period, grew by leaps and bounds:

Strike Days Lost (thousands)[1]

Year	Days Lost	Year	Days Lost
1967	705	1971	3,068
1968	1,079	1972	2,010
1969	1,958	1973	2,634
1970	2,393	1974	6,292

One aspect of the general militancy which was to have particularly important political consequences was the widespread participation by women, whose

Laurie Carmichael addressing mass demonstration in support of Clarrie O'Shea, Hyde Park Sydney, May 1969

willingness to fight led to a narrowing of pay differentials with men and, ultimately, to a historic equal pay decision by the Arbitration Commission in 1972.

By the beginning of 1969, the CPA's central leadership had grasped some of the implications of the industrial trends and concluded that it was possible to wage a major struggle against the Penal Powers which had hamstrung the entire trade union movement for most of the postwar decades. In January of that year, the CPA National Committee was induced to call for a perspective of confronting the Powers, despite resistance from those of its trade union leaders who were soon to depart with the SPA. The party prepared itself for what it

believed would be a major fight. It was proved correct within months, when Victorian Tramways union leader Clarrie O'Shea was jailed in May for refusing to pay fines imposed under the Penal Powers. One million trade unionists stopped work; a mysterious anonymous donor paid the fine; and the Powers had become a dead letter.

The O'Shea victory opened the way for a generalised working-class offensive, in which CPA-led unions and workers played an important role. Among the most important areas of work were the building industry, the NSW power industry and the workers' control movement.

The NSW BLF became something of a legend, beginning with a hard-fought strike in Sydney in 1970 which was, in many ways, a model of organisation.

Mass demonstration in support of Clarrie O'Shea, Collins Street, Melbourne, May 1969.

Jack Mundey and other officials, who had already agreed to receive salaries no higher than those earned by workers in the industry, did not get their salaries at all during the strike, subsisting on strike pay. The dispute was run by an elected committee, and measures were taken to involve the many migrant workers in the organisation. However, the most famous action was the forming of vigilante 'de-scabbing' groups, which occupied building sites until non-unionists were withdrawn. No amount of state government or press hysteria were enough to defeat such an enthusiastic group of workers, especially in the runaway boom conditions that then existed in the Sydney building industry, and 'Mundey's marauders' became a household word.

Next came the 'Green Bans', beginning with the defence of Kelly's Bush in Hunters' Hill. This was a piece of land in an upper middle-class area; but battles to save the Rocks and the struggle for Woolloomooloo, both inner city areas of historic importance, followed. The bans eventually extended to the area of sexual politics, when union action defended the rights of a homosexual student at Macquarie University and then helped to ensure the establishment of a women's studies course at the University of Sydney. These were inspiring and historic

LEFT TURN, RIGHT TURN: THE PARTY IN THE 1970S   **173**

Jack Mundey, 1970.

actions. If I do not dwell on them here, it is because they have been well chronicled in other places.²

Less publicised but also quite important were the workers' control tactics pursued by the BLF: the BLF were given to 'sacking' their foremen and reorganising the work process to attain some desired end, such as greater safety.

Workers' control was also the new watchword in the NSW power industry. The power stations have a long history of shop committee organisation, derived originally from their links with the railways, and the CPA had enjoyed a considerable presence in the shop committees since the 1930s. The committees were linked together in the Electricity Commission Combined Union Delegates' Organisation (ECCUDO), a strong body that was well to the left of the official union structure and enjoyed considerable freedom of action.

In the early 1970s, ECCUDO led a series of struggles for the 35-hour week, employing innovative tactics. They remained in the stations rather than walking out, attempting to control the flow of power; when the state government told certain industries to shut down, aiming to divide the working class by putting sections of it out of work, ECCUDO took out newspaper advertisements advising trade unionists to simply replace fuses and continue work. Power, they said, was available, whatever the government might claim.

Workers' control ideas were spreading widely, encouraged by the CPA. A left journalist captured the prevailing mood:

> An ABC TV 'Monday Conference' interview in 1972, in which
> Jack Mundey elaborated on some of the ideas of the Builders

Labourers' Federation, brought a flurry of congratulatory phone calls and letters. A lot of these were particularly enthused about the concepts of new forms of strikes; for instance, keeping trains and buses running but not collecting fares, or workers keeping factories producing food and other necessities but distributing the goods to pensioners and others in need. The idea of workers using that sort of radical initiative appealed to people's imagination.

Later in that year, workers and others were jubilant about what workers at South Clifton coalmine (on the NSW Southern field) did: with the US-controlled mine owner pronouncing the mine closed and the workers sacked, some 90 of them worked the mine for three days, producing coal without a boss.

Earlier, at the Harco Steel plant in outer Sydney, boilermakers who had been sacked by the boss continued working there in a defiant weeks-long work-in.[3]

In the same year, the CPA put a great deal of effort into a series of conferences. Beginning in Newcastle, they aimed to establish a workers' control movement modelled somewhat on the Institute of Workers' Control in Britain, led by Tony Topham and Ken Coates. The Newcastle conference was a considerable success and attracted many workers, some of them delegates from jobs. Conferences elsewhere had uneven results: in Melbourne, it became apparent that the CPA could not control the direction of the discussions because there were too many people from the revolutionary left present; the party therefore simply did not turn up for the second day and allowed the Melbourne end of the project to collapse.

The *student and anti-war movements* were, in some ways, even more spectacular than the industrial upsurge. In 1966, the ALP had declared against the war in Vietnam and campaigned against it in the federal elections. While the electoral results were poor, the campaign did mobilise an important activist minority. After the electoral defeat, these activists swung sharply to the left and towards direct action, especially on the campuses.

By 1969, the issue had become a rallying point for masses of youth, interwoven with other aspects of a general youth rebellion. The campuses became tinderboxes: students revolted against authoritarian structures, the ideological bias of course content, sexual repression and the values of the society around them. At Monash, students collected aid for the Vietnamese National Liberation Front. On all the bigger campuses, an important minority moved towards an explicitly socialist – and even revolutionary – stance.

In doing so, they moved well to the left of the CPA. The CPA was still associated with Russia and still contained a substantial pro-Soviet minority, at a time when the young activists perceived that the Kremlin was nothing resembling a force for revolution. Further, the party was seen, correctly, as associated with those traditional Old Left and pacifist forces who sought to keep the anti-war movement within respectable limits. In fact, the CPA's position on Vietnam was to the right of sizeable sections of the Labor Party, who began to demand immediate withdrawal of the troops – while the CPA's slogan was still 'Stop the bombing, negotiate!'[4]

The best activists, therefore, went not to the CPA, but often to the new left groups. It did not seem to matter what the specific theoretical stance of those groups was. In Melbourne, and especially at Monash, the attraction was mainly to Maoism, which could claim links to the Chinese Cultural Revolution and an association with the general third world charisma of both China and Vietnam. In Sydney, the strongest pole was the Trotskyists, who could point to the important role played by their comrades in the radical wing of the student and anti-war movements overseas. In Brisbane, it was the anarchists and libertarians, who could appeal to the anti-authoritarian impulse which was so strong in the youth revolt.

Wherever you looked, the CPA was being outflanked. As the party leadership began to grasp the fact, it realised that it faced something of a crisis. Its cadres had survived the Cold War partly by sticking to the hope of an eventual new left upsurge; it had also begun to liberalise and break with Moscow and – naturally – expected this to pay off in recruitment among the newly radicalising forces. Now, it appeared that the party would miss the boat.

The CPA National Committee, meeting in November 1968, decided that, if the party was to have a future, it would have to enter the 'hurly-burly of the left'. It decided to do so by initiating a conference 'where by far the most significant element present would be the "new left"'.[5] The Left Action conference, held in April 1969, attracted some 790 people.

Engaging with the 'hurly-burly of the left': Left Action Conference, Sydney, 1969. Individual speakers, clockwise from top left: Jack Mundey, Laurie Carmichael, Bob Gould, Denis Freney, Dave Nadel, Audrey Blake and Jack Baker (podium).

LEFT ACTION CONFERENCE

A Conference for Left Action, will be held in Sydney in April of this year.

The Conference aims to provide a forum of all left and radical viewpoints to advance: criticisms and appraisals of Australian society, the policies of its governments and bureaucracies and their internal role and outlook; methods of action against the policies of the present controllers of Australian society and strategies of action for a radical change in Australian society.

The organisers also hope to provide an opportunity for discussion between students, intellectuals and industrial and white collar workers and "those with particular problems (eg. Aborigines, immigrants, pensioners and so on.) They aim to develop cooperation between these various groups.

Topics to be considered include: "Australia 1969: Myth and Reality"; "Whatever happened to democracy?" and "Where do we go from here?"

Participation in the conference is open to all who consider themselves to be left, radical, anti-establishment or anti-imperialist. It will be held on April 4, 5, 6 and 7 at the Teachers' Federation Auditorium.

For the CPA, the conference was a major breakthrough. To be sure, it adopted policies the CPA had formerly considered over-extreme, such as support for the Vietnamese National Liberation Front. It did not bring the party any significant organisational gains, but it achieved its immediate objective, which was to re-legitimise the CPA in the eyes of radical youth. Laurie Aarons commented that there had been 'not a shift to the Communist Party as such but to a wider acceptance that the Communist Party is sincere'.[6] A Trotskyist current around Denis Freney was drawn towards the party, and the CPA increased its collaboration with Brisbane new leftists organised in the Revolutionary Socialist Alliance. The party's concern to appeal to the youth was made abundantly clear by a *Tribune* front page headline that announced: '*It's Mayday, Man*'.[7]

In the case of the student movement, it was quite obviously a case of the CPA responding to, indeed tailing after, the struggles of the youth, rather than taking a lead. This was also very obviously true in the case of the CPA's reaction to the *women's liberation movement* that developed after 1971.

The growing equal pay struggles in industry had been resisted for a time by the Arbitration Commission. In 1969, its refusal to grant equal pay to

Tribune, 30 April, 1960.

Australian Left Review, No. 35, 1972.

all but a tiny minority led Zelda D'Aprano and her friends to chain themselves to public buildings and form the Women's Action Committee – the first modern style women's liberation group in Australia. The initiators of the Committee were members of the CPA, but neither the party nor the UAW was prepared to associate itself with what they saw as an extremist splinter group. Yet, within a few years, militant feminism of this sort became one of the strongest forces on the left.

The CPA responded, grudgingly at first. *Tribune* began to feature 'women's rights' articles more and more; and, if its consciousness was still low enough to permit an uncritical report about the 'Miss Equality Contest' on International Women's Day 1969,[8] by 1972, it had gone to the other extreme and published an interview labelled 'Germaine Greer as Revolutionary'.[9] The NSW BLF accepted women in the industry and campaigned for their right to work there. In 1973, CPA women were among those who stormed the Sydney May Day Platform in protest against the more sexist of the day's activities.

The changes in the outside world also began to have an impact on the party's internal life and debate. Daphne Gollan has described the impact of the new women's movement on some of the established CPA activists:

> For a very long time the women resented that they always had to do the typing and stencilling, and dreary work, as well as often having a lot of decision making. They were so competent! They could do every task in the office, and they always *had* to do them, the men were incapable. I think they sometimes bitterly resented the helplessness of the men ... After an initial rejection of what the women's movement had to say – 'bourgeois feminism once again' – nevertheless, the explosive quality of Germaine Greer, and Betty Friedan, and then all the stuff just pouring out of America! After 1968 it wasn't possible any longer in the party to tell people not to read it. And the party women read it. They could reject an enormous amount and still keep enough to be highly explosive.[10]

No wonder that, by 1973, Mavis Robertson was telling the National Committee in no uncertain terms:

> We want an end to situations ... where an action of importance to women was called trivial by some men, and worse, where men, including some communists, appointed themselves to take over the action ... We don't want party branches rejecting some women speakers on the grounds that they are too 'forceful' ... We do need a heightened awareness that the feminist movement and its theories bring to the revolutionary struggle a new dimension, that without it, the revolution will be incomplete.[11]

Similarly, the youth rebellion began to have its internal fall-out. A Youth and Students Working Group in Sydney complained of a 'condescending and paternalistic attitude towards youth in many branches' and a lack of activism in sections of the organisation which put young people off, as well as an over-centralism in the party's youth organisations.[12] And the party began to lecture those among its trade union officials who were slow to recognise the radical potential of the new militancy on the job. In 1970, Laurie Aarons attacked the 'narrowness of vision' of many of the trade unionists, including a 'conservative attitude to arbitration' and an 'even balancing of conservative passivity and "adventurism" as problems in unionism today when, in reality, the former is the main one'. He also deplored their hostility to criticism:

> When youth are solemnly warned not to criticise union officials lest this be destructive, then revolutionary spirit has been lost, and our own movement's experiences forgotten.[13]

The party's continuous leftward motion eventually found its expression in official documents. There was an important policy statement called 'Modern Unionism and the Workers' Movement' which called for workers' control actions to encroach on the rights of employers. A document entitled 'Women and Social Liberation', adopted in 1974, incorporated all the basic demands that had emerged from women's liberation. Above all, there were the main Congress documents of 1974, which were so radical in their phraseology that John Sendy was moved to comment wryly:

> In the 1970 Statement of Aims the CPA was described as an *independent Australian socialist party.* The political document adopted at the 1972 Party Congress spoke of the CPA as being an

independent revolutionary party of the Australian working class. But the political document of the 1974 Congress described the CPA as *an independent revolutionary party working for socialist revolution.* Furthermore the 1974 document used the words *revolution* and *revolutionary* (in the singular and plural) 54 times in nine pages![14]

Yet, within a few years, all the radical rhetoric was being disavowed, and the party was on its way to a new right-wing consensus. If we are to determine why, we must begin by analysing the *limitations* of the left lurch of the early 1970s, especially the underlying reformist methodology that permeated even the most radical features.

The limitations of the left turn

The first indications that the left turn was not as deeply rooted as it might appear lay in the impressionistic and eclectic nature of many of the new ideas. The party that prided itself on a new-found independence and critical awareness was, in reality, all too often simply following in the wake of every trend in the world around it. Having broken with Stalinism, it was seeking its place in the social mainstream; and, for a time, society was moving to the left. The danger, however, was that once society began to shift back to the right, the party would do likewise.

Even in the short term, there were obvious weaknesses. The party was prey to fads of every description. If Germaine Greer was a revolutionary one year, the centre of the revolution had shifted to Nimbin by the next year. And when Jerry Rubin of the American Yippies published a book whose (admittedly amusing) voluntarist nonsense was summed up in the title *Do It!*, *Tribune* published a rave review, prompting one contributor to the letters page to retort: 'Boy, I can hardly wait, when does Hugh Hefner take over as editor?'[15] There was even a tolerance of the anti-working class prejudices of the new left, as when *Tribune* opened its pages to a report on the Nimbin counterculture by a young man who wrote:

> A revolution is taking place but Communists and most Left-wing working class bogged down in their booze-oriented suburban life are unaware and not in touch with it.[16]

No wonder working-class cadres were lost to the CPA! Far more serious than such episodic lapses was the fact that the talk of revolution concealed an underlying method that remained within a framework of reformism and class collaboration.

This can even be demonstrated in that apparently radical area: workers' control. Here, too, there was a faddishness – the party simply ignored the serious weaknesses in the work-in tactic, for example, in its enthusiasm at seeing workers try new methods. The work-in at Harco, during which the employees worked for nothing in defiance of the sack, was hailed as a milestone. The fact that the objectives of the work-in were not achieved, and that only nine of the 17 participants felt that the action was a success, was played down.[17]

But the deeper problem was analytical. For Marxists, there are two quite central problems in an analysis of the capitalist system and to any strategy for overthrowing or transforming it. One is the *mode of production*: the systematic manner in which people interact with each other and with the means of production to produce wealth. The other is the *state*: the apparatus of both physical and (less directly) social and ideological repression which defends that mode of production. The fact that workers are located at the heart of the productive process is rather central to their role in socialist transformation. What distinguishes workers' control struggles from ordinary trade unionism is precisely that they point to a reorganisation of the mode of production. By contrast, ordinary trade unionism typically concentrates on the battle over the terms under which workers will participate in the existing system (and especially on the price of labour power, that is, on an issue concerning more the realm of exchange than production itself).

Given that capitalists will resist attempts to transform the mode of production and will, presumably, make use of their repressive institutions, workers' control struggles must ultimately raise the question of the state. How shall we confront it – by attempting to smash it, as Lenin believed, or by some more gradual kind of subversion?

The CPA conception of workers' control consistently fudged both questions, as becomes quite clear in a major article written by Denis Freney just before the 1973 Workers' Control Conference at Newcastle. He begins by blurring the qualitative distinction between workers' control and traditional trade unionism, presenting the former merely as an extension of the latter:

Workers' control, in general terms, is something as old as the labour movement itself. The right to strike and to form unions are forms of workers' control, limiting the bosses' power.[18]

What, then, is new about it? According to Freney, the new feature is that it can be extended beyond the workplace and people's:

> ability to manage their own working and, indeed, whole life without bosses or bureaucrats ... Workers' control and self-management in both France and Czechoslovakia were the major part of the movement ... for the *general social self-management* of all aspects of economic, social, political and cultural life[19]

What is conspicuously avoided is any consideration of the distinctive quality of workers' control as an intervention in the productive process itself. On the one hand, Freney blurs the distinction between workers' control and conventional trade unionism; on the other, he merges workers' control into a rather vague and romanticised conception of social liberation in general. From here, it is not far to divorcing workers' control from the workplace altogether. Freney begins by defining 'Green Bans' as workers' control, which is perhaps still legitimate, but then slips over rapidly to including any and all political action involving unions or workers:

> The different bans placed by the NSW Building and Construction Workers' Union on developers' plans for environmental destruction readily come to mind in this regard ... In other cases, unions have, in using normal strike tactics, taken over decision-making in certain spheres previously reserved for the boss or the bureaucrats ... Even the unions' participation in the Vietnam Moratoriums and the anti-apartheid campaign, despite its limitations, represented an intervention in directly political matters formerly the province of government ... Workers' control then is a concept which has spread beyond the workplace to the whole of society. It means basically that workers seek to take control of their own working and waking lives, and all aspects of social decision-making that affects them.[20]

Freney's whole analysis of workers' control has skirted carefully around the need to challenge the existing relations of production. Even so, the perspective is radical. One question arises immediately, however: how will the repressive forces in society react to these challenges? That is, what about the state? We recall that Freney saw the struggles in France in 1968 as examples of workers' control in action. He was quite expansive in enumerating the strengths of these struggles:

> workers' control and self-management were not only goals, models and visions to be fought for (even unconsciously) by the mass of workers and students and their newly forming leaderships, but also provided a tactic and a strategy to build in the here-and-now a new society of socialist democracy based on self-management.[21]

How one can fight unconsciously for goals, models and visions is not clear; but, at any rate, the movement apparently combined vision, tactics and strategy with great success. Why did it fail? Only because it did not spread far enough, it seems:

> In some places, these occupations changed to rudimentary practice of self-management, where workers operated factories and the circulation and distribution of goods was undertaken by strike committees. Perhaps if this system had been generalised in all the occupied factories and cities, if the workers had begun to produce the goods and services and organise their distribution themselves, then the outcome may have been different in France.[22]

Perhaps; but there was the small matter of the army and police, and also of the more indirect mechanisms of social control, ranging from the church to the French CP hierarchy itself, which helped to stifle the movement. These were some of the *reasons* why the movement did not spread beyond a certain point. Revolutionaries have traditionally called for the construction of a disciplined, revolutionary party to combat such institutions. If the 'Trotskyist' Freney could dodge this issue, it is no wonder that the party as a whole did the same.

So far, I have only indicted Denis Freney for vagueness rather than explicit reformism; but the point is that, by remaining vague, he allowed the established

CPA cadre to fill his categories with their own content. How easily this could occur becomes clear from a discussion document written by Brian Carey in 1968, in a much less radical tone but with some astonishing similarities of formulation all the same:

> From the trade unions, where the most sectarian attitudes of Stalinism never worked, the concepts of *peaceful transition*, sharing the leadership, and co-operation with religious workers developed ...
>
> The *mass trade union campaigns already spontaneously involve* the demand for worker control over management, over prices and wage policy, over computerisation, over national development and foreign policy.
>
> The CPA has correctly been giving a special stress to this slogan, which has long been in the centre of socialist thinking, but whose full implications have not yet been fully explored ... *Unconsciously*, workers are seeking such control over monopoly. Objectively, our guerrilla fights against the effects of capitalism cannot achieve permanent victories without worker control. But, in the era of transition to socialism, the struggles inside capitalism *flow on* into struggles to change the social system.[23] [Emphasis added.]

Here, the idea that ordinary trade unionism flows over naturally into workers' control, which in turn flows into anti-capitalist struggle, is explicitly linked to a peaceful transition to socialism as well as to 'sharing the leadership' (i.e., pluralism). Whatever Freney's own intentions, the ambiguities in his article meant that the reformist notions of Carey and others like him remained, at bottom, unchallenged.

Freney's article does have one great merit that should be mentioned: he distinguishes clearly between workers' *participation*, which 'seeks to integrate workers into the system', and workers' *control*, which 'seeks to mobilise them against it'.[24] Unfortunately, the CPA's propaganda frequently blurred this distinction too, calling all too often for such things as a 'voice in the management of industrial undertakings'.[25]

If workers' control, the most radical concept put forward by the party, was ambiguous at best, the underlying reform orientation came through much more clearly in the electoral propaganda. A major election broadsheet produced in 1972 provided an excellent survey of the CPA's policies, taking up various issues in turn. Class issues got one mention out of 26, under 'U' for unionism, while under 'Z', the party embraced the 'Zero Population Growth' fad. The central thrust was a classless conception of 'people's action', while inequality received the following treatment:

> The rich have become still richer; the really poor have increased and become poorer still; *the majority in between find it harder to keep abreast of rising prices, higher taxes and charges for essential services.* [Emphasis in original.]

If, in the discussion of living standards, the working class had disappeared into something called 'the majority in between', it was no more present when it came to allocating preferences. The ALP was supported because it favoured reform, but no more than the Australia Party, which 'also stands for reforms within the system'.[26] The fact that the Labor Party was the mass party of the working class, based on the trade unions, was obviously not a major consideration. And, at various times through 1974, Communist election candidates continued to give preferences to the Australia Party; so, in some ways, the CPA's general propaganda had a more classless quality during the left turn of the early 1970s than it did after 1975 – when Malcolm Fraser forcibly reminded the party of the centrality of class politics.

In the practical world of the unions, class politics could hardly be ignored; but they could certainly be compromised, especially in the metal trades, where some of the most conservative practices remained. To be sure, Laurie Carmichael lent his signature to a statement on the anti-war movement calling for 'more militant positions'[27] and called for stronger rank-and-file organisation, pointing to the 'Strike Committee organisation of Ford workers' as a particularly fine example.[28] But, in this regard, he was simply drifting with an overwhelmingly militant tide, in a situation where gains came easily. Carmichael's real understanding of the rank and file was soon tested by the very Ford rank and file he praised so highly. In 1973, a riot took place at Ford in Melbourne, when an elaborate plan developed by the union officials proved to be totally out of step with

LEFT TURN, RIGHT TURN: THE PARTY IN THE 1970S

23rd Congress of the CPA, Minto, Sydney, 1972.

the real aspirations of the workforce. In a stormy meeting, Carmichael's coat was torn, and he was soon kicked upstairs and moved to Sydney by his union.

The Ford events are well known; but, shortly before that, he had clashed with Communist boilermakers in Brisbane. Three metal trades unions were being amalgamated and were to adopt the AEU branch structure, with its locality branches. The Brisbane boilermakers, preferring the workplace branches they were used to and considered more democratic, protested. Carmichael came up to lay down the law, with the result that a number of militants left the party, and the Brisbane metal fraction was effectively wrecked.

The underlying weaknesses in CPA union work came to the fore with the federal intervention into the NSW BLF in 1975, when federal secretary Norm Gallagher, backed by the employers, carried out a massive operation to smash the state branch and ultimately succeeded after prolonged resistance.

The BLF's own weaknesses were revealed under the onslaught. While few will perhaps take seriously the notion that it was a 'revolutionary union' whose demands 'could not be contained within capitalism' and the mass of whose members had a revolutionary consciousness,[29] it was still one of the best unions ever seen in Australia. For that very reason, its weaknesses as well as its strengths deserve mention.

Looking back on the period leading up to the federal intervention, Jack Mundey has himself remarked that he 'did feel at the time that the union was travelling too quickly'[30] and that 'we made an error in taking up too many social issues at the final stages ... we took on too much, I think we failed to consolidate at a certain period'.[31] There had been a prolonged boom, and workers were prepared to take all sorts of advanced (and sometimes outrageous) actions, secure in the knowledge that labour was tight. It was possible for members and leaders to get a bit giddy – and to find themselves suddenly vulnerable when the boom came to an end in 1974.

One signal failure in this union, which otherwise stressed the role of the rank and file, was the absence of strong job organisation on most building sites. The comparatively conservative leaders of most tradesmen's unions in the building industry were no friends of the BLF, so it was crucial that links be forged directly with the rank and file of these unions through site committees. And, when the official structure of the BLF came under attack, job organisation was essential to hold things together at the local level. Where it *did* exist, as at Qantas or Bondi Plaza, the anti-Gallagher forces still had effective control as late as 1978. But, as Builder's labourer David Shaw commented:

> only two or three jobs in Sydney had site committees, linking BLs to the other unions. If more jobs had had them, we'd have had a better show of beating Gallagher.[32]

Nevertheless, far more of the blame for the defeat lies with the leaderships of other unions, including those led by CPA members. Bearing in mind that this was a case of an all-out and exceptionally blatant union-busting operation, it is obvious that left union leaders had certain responsibilities to show solidarity with the BLF. Except for the Federated Engine Drivers, they did little. The Amalgamated Metal Workers and Shipwrights Union (AMWSU), for example, which had members in the industry, did nothing to support Mundey and Co. despite a powerful CPA presence that included figures such as Carmichael and John Halfpenny. Mundey later alluded to this fact rather pointedly:

> Yes, mistakes, but always keep in mind that had other unions displayed working class solidarity with the democratically elected NSW leadership ... the 'invasion' would have certainly failed.[33]

Prominent CPA member Aileen Beaver, May, 1961.

Since the late 1960s, discipline within the party had grown continually slacker. This was partly a product of rank-and-file revolt against the old authoritarianism and partly a product of centrifugal tendencies unleashed by the period of political turmoil that began after 1963. The CPA generally claimed that this indiscipline was more democratic and thus desirable. It now became clear that the lack of discipline also meant that whole sections of the party could refuse to defend other sections they disliked; nor did they have to implement policies they disapproved of. Not only in the unions, but everywhere else, this meant that whole sections of the organisation could hold aloof from all the radical innovations of the time, remaining ghettoised in certain places and areas of work. The NSW BLF experienced a minor revolution; the Victorian AMWSU changed little. Similarly, the Adelaide branches were packed with leftists, but the left had little impact in Melbourne.

The resistance of the whole Victorian organisation to the left turn proved to be very important. *Tribune* was simply not widely sold in Melbourne, because it was considered too radical, and it was even suspected in Sydney that the Taft leadership in Victoria was prepared to split over the issues in dispute. Because the central leadership was not prepared to contemplate such a thing, Victoria had considerable bargaining power and provided a base for a mobilisation of the right wing. The Victorians could gradually begin to appeal to the 'silent majority' of members, who were dubious about the new radicalism but remained silent in the face of the energy and determination of the radicals.

In 1970, as the pro-Soviet minority made preparations to depart, Joyce Slater wrote in a letter to *Tribune*:

> The extreme Right-wing Stalinists have taken a beating, but what of the stay-putters, don't-rock-the-boat elements in the middle? We have only just begun the fight for radical change in the party.[34]

Slater had identified a real problem, although a few years were to pass before it really began to make itself felt.

The Left Tendency

One group of people who aroused the special hostility of the CPA's right wing were the Left Tendency, which represented the extreme edge of the radical turn. Its rise and fall provides an interesting counterpoint to the main trends in the party.

While the CPA had chased after the youth rebellion from 1969, it had not achieved immediate results in recruitment. The 1972 Congress documents commented sadly that 'the CPA has failed to win large numbers of youth to become active members' even though:

> scores of thousands of young people are revolting against the policies and values of the capitalist system and thousands are entering political activity of a radical or revolutionary kind.[35]

In fact, the party continued to find recruitment of young people difficult until the latter years of the decade. But there were some exceptions. Some elements of the 'new left' did begin to move into the CPA after 1972, bringing their ideas with them.

The anti-war movement had begun to decline at about the same time as Whitlam came to power. Some of the activists began to realise that the new left was going to dissipate as a movement and that the small revolutionary groups that had emerged from it had little chance of establishing a permanent mass presence. The CPA, with its roots in the labour movement and its links to rank-and-file workers, appeared to some as the logical place to begin a long-term revolutionary practice.

Those who joined the party, says Terry O'Shaughnessy:

> had a strong commitment both to the renewal of Marxism as a theoretical tool for the analysis of society and to Leninism as a guide to developing the sorts of instruments that would be necessary for radical transformation.[36]

One of their leading spokespersons, Winton Higgins, wrote in the *Socialist Register* that the CPA could be won to genuine Marxism and that it was 'demonstrating the potential to lead a viable communist movement in Australia'.[37] The young recruits aimed to turn this potential into reality.

O'Shaughnessy emphasises four points around which the tentative program of the Left Tendency cohered: firstly, 'a call for a materialist analysis' to replace the idealist and eclectic theory of the post-1967 period; secondly, a call for an analysis of the Whitlam government that went beyond noting individual strengths and weaknesses and focused on the structural role of Labor under capitalism; thirdly, an analysis of the USSR derived from Ernest Mandel;[38] and fourthly, a concentration on rank-and-file organisation in industry. This last deserves some comment.

The Tendency was, of course, critical of the old-style trade union bureaucrats in the party. At the same time, it was dissatisfied with the ideas contained in 'Modern Unionism and the Workers' Movement' and even with the practice of the NSW BLF:

> We believed that the key notion ... was independent organisations which could become the nucleus of a revolutionary society. We believed that the trade unions were not capable of being transformed in this way and that it was necessary instead to build organisations in the working class that could play this role. We believed that in the shop committee we could see the nucleus of such a way in which society could be both transformed and administered in a post-revolutionary situation.[39]

The model most looked to was ECCUDO in the power industry. From the undeniable strengths of this organisation, there was a slippage to the idea of soviets. The notion that shop committees could be the embryos of soviets was a common one to young Australian Marxists in the early 1970s, who were deeply influenced by Antonio Gramsci and the experience of the Turin factory councils. Tendency members attempted to translate elements of this theory into practice through involvement with the 'Link' groups in the metal trades and through an industry bulletin produced in Melbourne by the Carlton branch and the metal branch of the party.

Because the idea took on a certain importance on the Australian left at the time, it is worth a slight digression to suggest its limitations. No doubt, shop committees can, in certain circumstances, become the beginnings of soviets. On the other hand, they have never actually done so. Even the Turin factory councils were not really soviets in the sense of posing an alternative political power. In Russia, the classic case, a shop committee movement existed alongside the soviets but was not their origin. More recently, in the Portuguese upheaval of 1975, revolutionaries tried in vain to move the shop committees there in the direction of soviets.

Moreover, the actual ECCUDO was far from being a centre of radical politics, as we will see.

The Tendency was most successful in Adelaide, where some 30 or 40 young radicals poured into a party organisation that had been hard hit by the SPA split. It was more of a fusion than a recruitment process, and the Tendency soon found itself running the Adelaide CPA. It was vastly less successful in Melbourne, where it was ghettoised in the Carlton branch. In Sydney, its influence was somewhere in between. Sydney thus became something of a testing ground for the left's strategy for transforming the party.

At the 1974 Congress, the Aarons leadership accommodated the Left Tendency to a considerable degree, because they needed its support in a struggle with the Victorian leadership (which was beginning to demand a retreat from the party's most radical positions). The Tendency members felt that they had hit the big time, as O'Shaughnessy explains in a passage that is perhaps more self-revelatory than he intended:

> Those of you who've had a background in either the student movement or the sects will know that there's a constant feeling that one's not engaging in grown up politics ... and our work in the party at this period and particularly this important struggle ... gave us first of all a taste of what could and did go on in an organization like the Communist Party which had a significant presence in proper politics.[40]

Alas, the Tendency comrades were only temporarily tolerated among the grown-ups. Between the 1974 and 1976 Congresses, their fortunes faded drastically – partly because of tactical errors, but mainly because the party began its shift to the right.

The Left Tendency made the mistake, firstly, of publishing a document characterising the CPA's internal life and identifying what they considered to be three tendencies: the Victorian right wing, the 'centre', led by the Aarons group, and themselves. This aroused disquiet among wide sections of the membership, who had been somewhat traumatised by past splits and did not like the spectre of further division being raised so explicitly. The left responded by waging a struggle around the right of tendency; but, whatever the merits of their case in principle, this only made the hostility to them more intense, and their isolation grew.

More important than tactical errors were changes in the world outside. The new left radicals who had joined the party did so with the expectation that, as they changed the party, other activists from the same background would also join. But the radical movement born in the late 1960s was beginning to fade away, and the CPA felt less need to accommodate to it or to its representatives in the Left Tendency. By contrast, the Aarons group felt a growing need to heal the breach with the Victorians.

Many of the distinctive concerns of the Tendency were made peripheral or harder to argue for by the constitutional crisis of 1975. Debates over the nature of Labor governments were hardly germane after November 11. As the labour movement as a whole moved into a defensive phase, the left's insistence on the right of tendency could be portrayed as dangerously divisive. The Aarons' desire to conciliate the Victorians was also enhanced, and old differences between them could be declared outlived in the new situation.

The left, which regarded Sydney as a test of its strength, suffered a major defeat at the Sydney district conference held in 1976 in the run-up to the 25th Congress. A motion was carried by a substantial majority rejecting the right of tendency. To add insult to injury, the motion was moved by Jock Syme, secretary of the very ECCUDO organisation that the left had looked to as a model of radicalism. The left were given another lesson in 'grown up politics' when, despite their command of a sizeable minority at the district conference, they were permitted only one delegate from Sydney at the Congress.

At the Congress, the Tendency wasn't even in the hunt. The 'centre' and the Victorians were conciliated with a great show of unity, and three national secretaries were elected to represent different views – but not those of the left. The leaders of the Tendency now collapsed into the CPA mainstream. Rob Durbridge became politically indistinguishable from the Aaronsites, while Winton Higgins, who once hoped to pull the CPA to the left, was now so far to its right that he looked to Swedish Social Democracy as a model for social change.[41]

Farewell to radicalism

The CPA's move back to the right, which took place from about 1976, had been prepared in ideological terms by elements in the Victorian leadership during the early part of the decade.

The Victorians' lack of enthusiasm for the more radical trends in the party went back to the SPA split, which was insignificant in Victoria partly because, as John Sendy wrote:

> the Victorian leadership, while acting firmly in the ideological fracas, did not stalk the opposing comrades. We adopted a milder stance, deliberately setting out to maintain good relations with the opposition wherever possible.[42]

Members soon to join the SPA were elected to the State Committee in 1971, and Ralph Gibson was chosen as state representative on the National Committee despite his reservations about aspects even of Victorian policy. In 1972, Sendy and Taft defended a more pro-Soviet line within the party. In late 1973, Sendy produced a circular letter that represented a major document of the Victorian right wing.

The letter attacked the CPA central leadership for 'standing aloof from the problems of the ALP government' and for thinking that many of the more conservative party members were 'not much good'. It called for a conciliatory approach to internal political struggle:

> Now the whole concept of polarisation is a first class ticket to a scrap. We polarised the differences with Hill and then we polarised the differences with Brown and Clancy. Are we going to polarise the differences again? Well I'm not too bloody keen about being polarised.

Finally, it appealed to a sense of pride in the party's Stalinist traditions, which had come under continual criticism for several years:

> For example it is fashionable today to deride the whole history of the Party. To hear many comrades speak, even at National Committee meetings, one would think that the Party had always

been wrong in the past and that its history was rather laughable. This is sheer nonsense. No matter what the mistakes of the past the Party has always been the most relevant revolutionary organisation in Australia.[43]

Around the same time, the Victorian State Committee began to sound the alarm about the Left Tendency. A statement from the Committee appeared in *Tribune* expressing:

> grave concern at some of the extraordinary views voiced by a small minority of NC members and others invited to attend the meeting. We refer to such views expressed as that the USSR is not a socialist country at all or even socialist based, and that the international Communist movement is not a revolutionary force. We urge the National Executive and National Committee to wage a vigorous ideological campaign against such irresponsible stances.[44]

There followed a lively debate in the letters pages on the Left Tendency's ideas. It is not hard to imagine the appeal of such arguments to many members – especially those of long standing, who had been deeply upset by the splits of the previous decade, who saw the new radical ideas in the party as half-baked and divisive and who felt that criticism of the CPA's past was a rejection of their own many years of dedicated effort and struggle. But if Taft and Sendy could appeal to a widespread desire for unity, their increasing combativeness also appeared to contain a thinly veiled warning: if yet another split *were* to occur, it would be the fault of the central leadership for not moderating their policies and for not containing the left.

In 1974, the central leadership had fought the Victorians. By 1976, they were no

Pamphlet by John Sendy, 1971.

longer prepared to do so, and the Congress of that year brought a reconciliation of the contending forces. The key intervening event, I have suggested, was the sacking of Whitlam on 11 November 1975. It inaugurated a new era of defensive struggle and created a strong desire in the left and labour movement to close ranks against the new enemy in Canberra. This provided a strong boost to the Victorians' appeal for an end to internal factionalism, as well as an opportunity for the Aarons group to retreat from their previous policies without losing face – because the old policies could now be simply *dropped* as outlived. At the 1976 Congress, there was much emphasis on the need for a broad united front, and Laurie Aarons defended himself tartly against those on the left who called this a 'collapse' and a 'retreat'.[45]

Above all, the crisis of 1975 proved a turning point because it was the beginning of a period of defeat in the class struggle. The economy had begun to move into recession from 1974, and the employers had no confidence in the ability of the Labor government to discipline the working class and impose upon it the cost of the economic downturn. Hence, the rise of Fraser. Fraser took the offensive against the unions at a time when rapidly worsening unemployment and falling consumer demand was undermining workers' bargaining power, and he was able to win a series of victories.

There was, firstly, his electoral triumph in the 1975 elections. Then followed, within less than a year, the destruction of Medibank – despite a major trade union mobilisation. These political defeats for the organised labour movement were complemented by several years of defeat on the wages front, where the most important test was the struggle of the Latrobe Valley power workers in Victoria in 1977. The power workers, a group with considerable industrial muscle, made a heroic 11-week attempt to break through the government's wage indexation guidelines, only to finally return to work with virtually no gains. This setback ensured the triumph of the government's wage-cutting policies for several years and seriously demoralised Victorian workers in particular. The overall trend in industry is suggested by the strike figures in the table opposite.

The figures for 1975 and 1976 are somewhat 'inflated' by the political strikes over the Kerr coup and Medibank, so the general picture for the more conventional sort of industrial struggle is obviously depressed for the mid-1970s, compared with the massive push of the first part of the decade. Moreover, many of the strikes that did occur were defensive struggles aimed merely at holding one's ground against a ruling-class onslaught which succeeded generally in reducing real wages und worsening conditions for a time.

Strike Days Lost (thousands)[46]

Year	Days Lost	Year	Days Lost
1974	6,292	1977	1,654
1975	3,509	1978	2,130
1976	3,799		

The CPA reacted to the defeats by blending increasingly into the broad left of the ALP and trade union officialdom, which was moving rapidly to the right. In response to the constitutional crisis itself, the ALP moved rapidly to contain mass mobilisation, with Bob Hawke especially important in convincing workers and labour supporters to 'cool it'. The CPA did not disagree. In its own *Daily Tribune* issued during the crisis period, criticism of the ALP was almost non-existent until the last couple of issues, while statements by Labor leaders were given extensive verbatim coverage. At the very last, the *Daily Tribune* did stir itself to mention that Labor in office had 'retreated under pressure from Australian and foreign big business' and had:

> ... compounded the error by appealing to [supporters] to leave it to the government, not to rock the boat, not to organise or act on their own behalf.[47]

Well said; but, when the masses did mobilise in Melbourne on a massive scale in the wake of the constitutional crisis, what was the role of the CPA?

At least 50,000 rallied in Melbourne's City Square, looking for some sort of action. On the platform, however, the CPA's representatives were not distinguishable from those of the ALP. John Halfpenny, with Bernie Taft at his elbow, offered only commonplaces about the perfidy of Fraser, and the angry crowd was led *away* from the centre of town, where Halfpenny joined with Clyde Holding to appeal to them to disperse. At this point, the initiative was stolen from them by a small group of revolutionaries, who led at least 10,000 people on to the Stock Exchange, chanting 'General Strike!' This was the first time for several years that the CPA was very obviously to the *right* of a mass movement. It was not to be the last.

In June 1976, some 1,500 job delegates met in Melbourne's Dallas Brooks Hall to consider action over Medibank. Communist and other left officials met beforehand with the Trades Hall right wing and agreed on a proposal for a four-hour protest stoppage. When this proposal was put to the meeting, it was thrown out by an overwhelming vote in favour of a 24-hour stoppage proposed by a member of a small revolutionary group.

Again, during the Latrobe Valley strike, the CPA began organising for a return to work from the seventh week, succeeding only after several weeks' careful work designed to demoralise the strikers. Because the CPA has since argued that the strike, which was run by a committee of shop stewards, could for that reason not possibly have been sold out by the officials,[48] it is important to detail the methods used by John Halfpenny and supported by the CPA.

There was indeed a strong shop stewards' organisation, which was suspicious of interference by Halfpenny or anyone else from 'outside'. This was the strikers' great strength; but, to the extent that it was tied to parochialism, it also contained weaknesses. The power workers did not understand the state-wide and national implications of their struggle; nor did they, until quite late, understand the importance of mobilising outside support. Halfpenny was able to manipulate the resulting isolation.

Halfpenny first raised the idea of a return to work after about seven weeks out, at a stewards' meeting. He got no support. By the following stewards' meeting, he had made a small but significant breakthrough, gaining the support of stewards' secretary Sam Armstrong – a CPA member. He then went to work demoralising the rest, using the strikers' isolation from the rest of Victorian workers in two ways.

One way was to tie them up in arbitration. This meant repeatedly inducing them to make the exhausting drive to Melbourne, not to talk to fellow workers but to attend hearings that consisted of hours of tedium and stonewalling from the Electricity Commission. The other was to actively create the feeling that there was no outside support. Halfpenny told the strikers that a prolonged dispute would isolate them from other workers, and that they would become the centre of a political confrontation – with a federal election looming. Bernie Taft backed him up in *Tribune*, warning the power workers against 'playing right into Fraser's election plans'.[49]

Such a pessimistic outlook was quite unnecessary. Three shop stewards who *did* get involved in speaking to worker and student meetings in Melbourne saw the considerable public sympathy that the strike enjoyed, and these three opposed a return to work at all times. Two others toured Newcastle and Wollongong, including one who had previously voted to go back to work, and both sent a telegram to the final mass meeting saying that support was excellent and that the strike should continue. Had all the stewards been offered such experiences, things might have turned out differently. As for the danger of 'playing right into Fraser's election plans', this theory was soon tested in the Greensborough by-election, which produced a result suggesting that the strike was an electoral *plus* for Labor.

When the discouraged stewards finally recommended a return to work, *Tribune* applauded them for doing so. The paper suggested that arbitration might yield gains that militancy had failed to deliver and was scathing about anyone who suggested otherwise:

> Some commentators see the return to work in Victoria's power dispute as a total defeat for the workers. Some suggest that arbitration as the final umpire is the kiss of defeat.[50]

Unfortunately, the 'commentators' (*Tribune* had in mind the newspapers of the revolutionary left) were proved entirely correct. Four months later, the power workers were given pitiful rises of around $2 to $5 when they had fought for $40, with some 30 percent of the workers receiving no rise at all. Nor was this really any surprise; it is a commonplace of industrial relations known even to the editors of *Tribune* that, in the absence of effective action, 'arbitration as the final umpire' is indeed 'the kiss of defeat'.

The increasingly conservative industrial practice of the CPA was, however, covered for a time by a series of propaganda initiatives, launched through the Metal Workers' union and backed heavily by the CPA. These were the 'People's Budget' and the 'People's Economic Program'. The former was something of a trial balloon, launched with some fanfare at a press conference by Halfpenny. After it seemed to get a good response, it was superseded by a much more ambitious pamphlet entitled *Australia Uprooted*. The pamphlet called for a 'People's

Economic Program' and advanced some proposals for what such a program might contain. Both appeared to draw their inspiration from similar initiatives in Britain which have come to be associated with the term 'alternative economic strategy'.

There were two clear themes to the argument in *Australia Uprooted*. The first was that the economic crisis in this country was caused deliberately as part of a conspiracy by the multinationals: 'Australia plunged into its biggest economic crisis since the 1930s. All because of the decisions of a few owners of companies.'[51] The second was that investment was systematically being drawn away from manufacturing: 'Australia is becoming a vast quarry, supplying minerals for overseas manufacturing industries.'[52] The roots of the crisis were not located in the mode of production and its contradictions, as Marxist analysis attempts to do, but in the machinations of a few foreign boards of directors and their Australian puppets.

The analysis advanced in *Australia Uprooted*, whose crudity was all too apparent, has since given way to more sophisticated versions, but the general thrust remains: Australia is being 'deindustrialised' by foreigners, and a nationalist response is required to save domestic manufacturing.[53] The economics need not concern us here, but the *politics* of *Australia Uprooted* have been of considerable importance for the left ever since.

The *nationalism* became increasingly hegemonic as the 1970s drew to a close. The CPA had, in principle, accepted Australian nationalism as legitimate since the mid-1930s, but this aspect of its politics had been relatively unimportant in its left phase in the early 1970s. In fact, Laurie Aarons in 1973 attacked as a 'retreat' the Maoists' 'old concept of the "national bourgeoisie" with whom workers can supposedly unite against foreign capital'.[54] Now, however, the trade union left moved back towards just such ideas. The Metal Workers held joint seminars with the employers, and prominent CPA member Jim Baird launched the union's 'Buy Australian' campaign. And, while the Maoists had raised the Eureka flag as a nationalist symbol, the CPA now went one better: the conventional Australian flag appeared on the party's 1980 Queensland state conference booklet.

The programmatic proposals had a radical sound to them. On closer inspection, they proved to be set firmly within the context of the existing system of government. There was to be a 'Department of Economic Planning' which was to 'give advice to and carry out instructions from the elected government'. And this government was not even called upon to carry out full-scale nationalisation. Rather, it would:

> seek to effect changes in the constitution necessary to bring about the public ownership of as many of the largest Australian and Overseas owned corporations operating in Australia as it is necessary to control the direction and functioning of the Australian economy. Where full public ownership is unnecessary shares sufficient for control will be obtained.[55]

Nevertheless, whatever the limitations of the program, it was radical enough to be unacceptable to the Australian bourgeoisie. Had the Metal Trades officials been prepared to actually fight around it, that would have been a significant step forward for the labour movement. Unfortunately, only one clause in the program was ever given any practical application, and that was the one calling for tariff protection.

The rest of the program performed two functions: firstly, it provided a left-sounding smokescreen for protectionism. Secondly, it gave the AMWSU leaders something to talk at length about at delegates' meetings, to avoid embarrassing discussion of why the union hadn't waged a real award campaign for several years and showed no signs of doing so in the foreseeable future. In other words, it was a masterful left cover for a drift to the right in practice.

It was not only the labour movement that was moving to the right under the impact of defeats; the social movements and the 'middle-class left' did too. Consider, for example, the development of the women's movement.

Women's liberation had been an explosive force in the early 1970s and, during the Whitlam years, it had still probably been the healthiest aspect of the left. However, during the years of Labor government, some of the seeds of decline were sown. The movement was drawn heavily into self-help projects dependent on government funds. This created a certain orientation to piecemeal reform and governmental assistance. Because money came easily, a series of advances were achieved, and a certain overconfidence resulted; the essential vulnerability of the projects was overlooked.

There was also a growth of separatist notions, according to which a distinct women's struggle against 'patriarchy' was more and more separated out from the struggle for social liberation in general. Given that the women's movement was stronger and more radical during the first part of the decade than some other parts of the left, this tendency for women to strike out on their own had a certain plausibility and logic.

However, after 1975 and the constitutional crisis, it became much more problematic. Society was suddenly polarised very sharply in *class* terms. While the new government was – among other things – extremely anti-feminist, the focus of resistance to it shifted far away from any independent women's struggle to the trade unions. For a considerable period, the women's movement found itself tailing behind the organised labour movement.

Both the orientation to piecemeal reform and to separatism now grew in strength, but much more clearly as part of a *retreat* away from the original radicalism and also the socialist tendencies of women's liberation. Many women were drawn towards traditional electoral, legal and lobbying action of the sort associated with the ALP and Women's Electoral Lobby. Simultaneously, and sometimes overlapping with this, there was a trend to the fragmentation of the movement and an increasing sectarianism towards the socialist left. The original idea of an independent women's movement, in which women met separately in order to make their own decisions and develop confidence, now gave way to a rather different concept of *autonomy*. The term was used in many different ways but, increasingly, it meant a hostility to Marxism and socialism and to the 'male revolution'. Unfortunately, because the alternative concept of 'feminist revolution' has remained fuzzy in the extreme, even the most extreme 'radical feminism' tends to leave a theoretical void which, in the end, reformism fills.

Other independent left activists also began to move away from Marxism and Leninism and from the aggressive radicalism of the early 1970s. They became aware that the new left had faded as a mass movement; that they were isolated and impotent as individuals in the face of the crisis-torn economy and growing class conflict; and that the explicitly revolutionary groups were too small to really fill the gap. They began to question their own radicalism and were less willing to make major personal commitments. To some of them, the increasingly moderate CPA offered a home: one where not too much was expected of them – and certainly not any conformity to a coherent party line; where the dominant notions of social change were increasingly modest; but where there was some collective support and security. For those with nostalgic ties to a more radical past, there was also the comforting thought that they were 'Communists' – and had a party card to prove it.

An intake of rightward-moving people could only increase the rightward momentum of the party itself. This was certainly noticeable in Brisbane, where some of the new recruits – such as Lee Bermingham – moved into leading positions.

Consolidation on a new course

If the CPA has experienced a rightward *motion* since 1975, the years after about 1978 also saw a *consolidation*, a hardening up of the new conservative politics. Four important experiences served to make this quite clear: the adoption of a new program; a mass struggle in Queensland; a rather impressive public conference; and the crisis in Poland.

Although the party's Congress documents of 1974 had been full of revolutionary phraseology, they had nevertheless remained vague on the details of the proposed 'revolution' and, as we have seen, concealed an underlying method that was less radical than the rhetoric. In 1976, as the main factions began to be reconciled, the language was toned down, while the ambiguities remained. But the new program adopted in 1980, entitled 'Towards Socialism in Australia', made it quite clear that the party had left its revolutionary pretensions far behind.

It declared that 'capitalist power has to be challenged and the *exclusive* grip of the ruling class on the institutions involved broken' and called for 'expansion, through mass action and extended democratic rights, of popular control over the government and economic machinery' [emphasis added].[56] Clearly, there was to be a period of power sharing with the bourgeoisie, during which the people (not the working class) would extend its control gradually. Finally, at some later stage, we would see 'the remaining power and influence of the ruling class, sexism and racism tackled in the process of building socialism'.[57]

If these formulations were not clear enough, their implications were spelt out very sharply by John Boyd, a miner who had led the party's Mt. Isa branch for eight years before resigning in the wake of the 1980 Congress. He pointed out that the document was designed to breed illusions about the possibility of a peaceful transition to socialism and that it marked the final abandonment of the concept of the dictatorship of the proletariat:

I also stated at congress that I believed the programme had moved away from the principle of the dictatorship of the proletariat ... Several comrades argued that the principle was not lost and one quoted a particular passage to back the argument. All I can say is, that if I require the services of a lawyer to interpret the jargon in which it's disguised, then we've moved far enough away from that principle for it to become meaningless.[58]

One experience that influenced John Boyd's decision to leave the CPA was its role in the struggle in Queensland over civil liberties and the right to hold street marches. Premier Joh Bjelke-Petersen had announced in September 1977 that street marches were effectively banned. Resistance began quickly among students and spread gradually to broader layers of the population. A considerable movement came into being; within it, there was an ongoing debate over tactics – a debate that was to continue, in one form or another, for several years.

One strategy, argued for among others by the CPA, was for a very cautious response, concentrating on indoor meetings, petitions and the like. It was claimed that militant action would alienate the 'middle ground'. Associated with this argument was the thesis that there were important forces that could be won to some form of action against the march ban, but which would not be prepared to directly defy it, in particular sections of the Liberal Party and the churches.

The other strategy, put forward most consistently by the revolutionary left, was to defy the ban and march in the streets. This strategy, which consistently won the argument and the votes at meetings of up to 600, argued that most Queenslanders, particularly working-class Queenslanders, were already passively opposed to the march law. The task was to provide a focus for *mobilising* that opposition.

The latter view was soon vindicated, as thousands rallied and hundreds marched in defiance of the law. The movement grew so powerful that even senior Labor politicians were prepared to face arrest to be part of it – not only left figures such as Tom Uren, but also such a right-winger as John Ducker of the NSW Trades and Labor Council. Most importantly, Senator George Georges mobilised the left of the Queensland ALP. Meanwhile, there was growing trade union support, most notably from the Seamen's Union.

Belatedly, the CPA accepted the necessity of marching. Here was the first time since the early 1970s that the party confronted a new layer of activists moving dramatically leftward and beyond its influence: the question was, would it react as it had in 1969 and move to the left? In essence, the answer was no. Certainly, the party was prepared to march in the streets as long as Senator Georges was there. When the immediate mobilisation subsided, the party moved swiftly back to the right. When a second major explosion occurred in 1978, the whole debate was repeated.

Bjelke-Petersen announced his support for a particularly fierce attack on abortion rights in the form of a new bill, and a protest movement developed to fight it. Again, the revolutionary left argued for mass action; again, the CPA called for a moderate approach and an appeal to progressive elements in the Liberal Party. The CPA was particularly enthusiastic about Liberal MLA Rosemary Kyburz, who opposed the bill but was also on record as saying strikers should be shot.[59] This did not stop leading CPA member Eva Bacon from sending her flowers, nor keep the party from building her up as a heroine of the abortion struggle.

The CPA claimed that its moderate tactics were responsible for the defeat of the abortion bill; the revolutionary left attributed it to the militant actions they had led. There is probably no way to decide the issue conclusively, although it is interesting that Bjelke-Petersen himself said publicly that the militant marches to parliament were the major factor. What matters here is not so much who was right or wrong; the very obvious fact is that the party was not prepared to move to the left in any systematic way, despite considerable pressure from large numbers of radicalising activists.

If the hardening of the new conservative course was tested in practice in Queensland, it found its expression in the propaganda sphere at a major event in Melbourne in 1980: the public Communists and the Labour Movement conference, which was jointly sponsored by the CPA and others. There were two very obvious and important features of this conference, which drew hundreds of people from all areas of the left and labour movements. One was the confidence the party displayed, as a group that felt that it knew where it was going at last; the other was the consistent and systematic reformism of the politics.

Despite occasional interventions by critics from the floor, the CPA was able to dominate all the sessions and impose a reformist consensus on the discussions.

Bernie Taft writing on Poland in *Tribune*, 24 September, 1980.

One speaker after another sneered at 'super-militants'. The party that had once seriously discussed Trotskyism now put up the ex-Trotskyist Denis Freney to spend half an hour ridiculing it. Ted Hill was invited to speak on the 1963 split and was displayed more like a captured wild animal than as an enemy to be taken seriously. With a few exceptions, the party that Sendy had accused in 1973 of treating its history as 'laughable' now expressed a pride in its 'sixty years of struggle' – *all* of them. No one disagreed except the organised revolutionaries.

The final session on 'Socialism in the Eighties' provided a fitting consummation. Here was John Halfpenny, recently resigned from the CPA and moving closer to the Labor Party; here was Ian Mill of the ALP, who spoke of 'multi-class progressive action', including a 'pluralist parliamentary development' and an 'attempt to democratise the capitalist state'. To be fair, however, Mill actually sounded the most left-wing note of the session when he commented: 'I am not going to say that a gradualist policy commands my complete respect.'

John Halfpenny, 1979.

No such reservations were expressed by CPA speakers. Mark Taft spoke vaguely of a 'commitment to a genuine pluralism' in pursuit of 'better social relations'. He did mention the experience of Chile – indeed, he hinted that there were lessons to be learned – but he drew no lessons. Instead, he turned to the economic crisis at home, where there 'must be developed a whole range of programs which come to terms with our economic realities'. He did not elaborate even one.

Finally, there was Judy Mundey, to declare: 'We shouldn't all be in the one organisation' and to make the astonishing admission that she, the national president of the CPA, felt much more secure as a woman in the party with the women's movement to protect her.[60] The message was clearly that the CPA intended to blend into the labour mainstream as one group among many, with no distinctive communist program for which it sought to win majority support. By default, therefore, the day went to Ian Mill and his parliamentary road – the only strategy for socialism actually argued for in the whole session.

The Polish events at the end of 1981 provided a fitting counterpoint to the CPA's Australian approach. Just as the Prague Spring of 1968 had once inspired Australian Communists, who saw it as a model for their own notions of socialism with a human face, so the party's response to events in Poland reflected the political consequences of its now well-developed pluralism and reformism.

Throughout the previous year or so, the CPA had shown a great interest in Poland, with some of its prominent personalities visiting there and expressing support for the Solidarity trade union movement. Yet, when the army moved into the streets of Polish cities, strikes were crushed by armed force, and thousands were interned, the CPA reacted very cautiously indeed.

When the Soviet Union invaded Czechoslovakia, the party had *campaigned* against the action, calling a public meeting in the Sydney Town Hall and issuing a special edition of *Tribune*. Its response to the Polish crisis was markedly different. In Sydney, the party had to hold a major internal debate to decide whether to participate in demonstrations supporting Solidarity (it finally elected to do so). In Melbourne, it refused to support them. While Denis Freney wrote an article in *Tribune* supporting Solidarity, Steve Brook was also permitted to publish a piece assigning blame to 'radicals' and 'hardliners' on *both* sides of the confrontation.[61]

The party's national officers issued a public statement that was little different. To be sure, the statement blamed the crisis on the Polish state bureaucracy. The bureaucracy, it said, had been guilty of 'corruption, transparently false official propaganda, broken promises and a resort to force'. This had given rise to a 'deep cynicism', and the whole problem was 'compounded by Soviet pressures'. At the same time, it attacked 'inappropriate and misplaced ... tactics from strands within Solidarity' and expressed the pious hope that General Jaruzelski 'may be a sincere man'. The statement called for 'a return to dialogue between the forces involved'.[62]

If, at a time when strikers were being shot in Poland, the Communist Party of Australia was calling for *dialogue*, it did not take too much imagination to work out what the party would be saying, and doing, should Australia itself enter a period of crisis and confrontation.

8
Into the Mainstream

The latter part of the 1970s had been a time of working class defeat, beginning with the fall of Whitlam and continuing through the destruction of Medibank and the failure of the 11-week Latrobe Valley power strike. As we entered the 1980s, it appeared that this grim situation might be about to change.

Starting at the end of 1978 with a hard-fought dispute at Telecom which ended in something like a draw, Australian trade unionists began to regain confidence. This partly reflected a mild recovery in the economy, which improved workers' bargaining position. It was also partly due to psychological factors, as the Fraser government began, for electoral purposes, to talk up the emerging 'resources boom'. Having been told by the government that big money was about to be made, workers felt that they could, and should, get in for their chop.

In the three-year period 1979–81, strike levels revived dramatically. They even compared fairly well to the historic high point of 1974–76, as shown in the table overleaf.

The consequence was that, while the 'resources boom' was much overrated from the point of view of profits, the unions did succeed for the first time since the fall of Whitlam in shifting economic equations in their favour. The main information paper at the 1983 Economic Summit offered:

> All measures show a downward trend in the wages share from 1974–75 until 1978–80. Over this period the measures ... show only a partial recovery in gross operating surplus shares ... All measures show that the wages share increased again in 1981–82 and the half-yearly data ... suggest that this continued into the

first half of 1982–83. All the measures of gross operating surplus show falls over this period[1]

Workers were clawing back what had been taken from them in the early Fraser years. An alarmed Malcolm Fraser spoke of a 'wages explosion'.[2] Industrial Relations Minister Ian McPhee warned that 'the relative share of GDP for wages and profits is now at the same unhealthy proportion which prevailed in the notorious years of 1974–75'.[3] McPhee's comment, while perhaps exaggerated, nevertheless came perilously close to a confession of bankruptcy. If the union-bashing Fraser regime could not maximise profits as against wages, why should the ruling class continue to pay the high price of confrontation in terms of social polarisation?

Strike Days Lost (thousands)[4]

Year	Days Lost	Year	Days Lost
1974	6,292	1979	3,694
1975	3,509	1980	3,320
1976	3,799	1981	4,192
1977	1,654	1982	2,158
1978	2,130	1983	1,641

The working-class offensive at the start of the 1980s also contained underlying weaknesses, however. Unlike the period of historic militancy a decade or so earlier, it was not accompanied by significant signs of political radicalisation. There were no green bans or workers' control struggles. In very few cases did rank-and-file unionists adopt views and strategies that challenged the established union leaderships. The 'wages push' was just that, nothing more: a flexing of union muscle for limited demands within the system.

Nor did it last long. The metal trades unions, which had been relatively sluggish even at the height of the industrial offensive, made a lasting peace with their employers by the end of 1981. By this time, militancy was declining generally, as the 'resources boom' began to ebb. Towards the end of 1982, unemployment rose with startling rapidity as the boom gave way to recession. The unions were largely cowed. The government was able to impose a wage freeze in December 1982, and it appeared that Fraser had weathered the storm.

However, that appearance was misleading. The more farsighted employers had reflected upon the events of 1979–81 and drawn some lessons. Fraser-style confrontation with the unions had proved effective enough in forcing concessions in times of recession, but the unions had retained their basic organised strength and were able to redress the balance when the economic cycle turned upwards. Because any strategy for pulling Australian capitalism out of its long-term economic difficulties depends on permanently improving capital's position *vis-à-vis* labour, the Fraser methods had failed.

The prospect of arriving at some sort of 'social contract' with the union officials began to appear more attractive. During the wages offensive, the union officials had proved able to control their rank and file, and this was an important development. The Whitlam government's promise to contain wage demands had proved hollow, because the union rank and file was too militant and sometimes too radical, and even the union officials had often been willing to sanction relatively militant actions. By 1981, both workers and officials had experienced long years of economic instability and significant defeats. They were more cautious and more open to the idea of a government-sponsored wages policy, and the attractions of such a policy grew considerably with the emerging recession.

The ALP had been attempting to formulate some sort of 'social contract' for many months. Negotiations with the ACTU had reached the point of agreement in principle, and it seemed clear that large sections of employers were open to the idea. Labor had some difficulty putting the finishing touches on the deal, because leader Bill Hayden alienated the ACTU by his confused response to the Fraser wage freeze (firstly opposing it, then appearing to endorse it, before finally coming out in opposition). However, at this point, Bob Hawke emerged to articulate a coherent alternative to Fraserism. On 30 January 1983, he made an important speech to the Australian Institute of Political Science, in which the logic of Labor's approach to industrial relations was spelt out. The speech, which was reprinted in the press, flayed the Fraser government for combining union-bashing with a *laissez-faire* approach to wage fixation:

> In the pre-election period at the end of 1980, against the expert advice available to them, Ministers ceaselessly talked up the coming 'resources boom' ... And if [Fraser] brought the unions up to the starting blocks for the wages scramble by such statements he really fired the starting gun on 30 April [when he] argued the merits of deregulation ... It doesn't need the genius of an Einstein to understand that with the Government saying that those with power should use it and let prices be determined accordingly, the trade unions would embrace that philosophy ...
>
> And does the final irony escape your notice? The great deregulator of April 1981, the great unleasher of market forces in November 1982 became the greatest interventionist of them all – the architect of the wage freeze.
>
> Fundamental to everything Labor does will be the attempt to create an understanding between parties of the present and foreseeable economic environment.[5]

This, said Hawke, would lay the basis for a return to centralised wage fixing.

The message was pitched at the employers: Fraser had stumbled from letting market forces determine wages (and thus ensuring that strong unions would win gains) to crude methods of compulsion. Labor, by contrast, would cook up a deal with the union leaders to hold down wages over time by more subtle methods. Within days of this speech, as an early election loomed, a combination of pressure from establishment forces and panic on the part of the Labor caucus at Hayden's blunders led to Hawke's installation as leader. Just as swiftly, a complete wages policy was put together in the form of the Prices and Incomes Accord, which was agreed to at the highest levels by ALP leaders and ACTU officials and imposed bureaucratically on Australian trade unionists.

Labor swept to a dramatic election victory, whereupon the new government revealed that the previous Liberal regime had lied about the projected size of the budget deficit. The budget blow-out provided Hawke with an impeccable excuse to dump most of his election promises. The Hawke government would now, inevitably, be judged overwhelmingly on the success of its deal with the unions.

The CPA and the Labor government

Consistent with its new reformist program, the CPA began to consider one or another type of 'social contract' from the late 1970s. In 1982, the party published a policy statement calling for a 'comprehensive working class incomes policy'. The CPA made no pretence that such a policy was a radical, let alone socialist, measure:

> The ideas advanced here could well be adopted by left and centre forces in the unions if they hold a genuine commitment to improve living standards.

At the time, the party was toying with something it called 'centralised direct bargaining'. With its usual impressionism, the CPA was overly impressed with the temporary gains the unions had made in 1981 after the collapse of wage indexation. Not realising that these would be reversed in the following recession, the party imagined that direct bargaining had some inherent virtue of its own. These notions were soon to be abandoned. However, other features of the 1982 document were of lasting importance and prefigured the CPA's response to the ALP–ACTU Accord. One was the concept of the 'social wage': instead of simply trying to force up wages for their members and ignoring problems of welfare, inflation and the like, the unions were urged to develop a strategy to raise the overall living standards of the working class:

> The central concern of an incomes policy is how the national income is distributed. Present distribution accounts for social inequality, poverty and discrimination, and affects economic growth and creation of jobs ... concern about income distribution should be the entry point into economic policy in general.

In the abstract, this argument made a certain amount of sense. Taking the class struggle beyond immediate sectional economic demands has been an objective of the communist movement since its inception. It can be an essential part of encouraging workers to seek control over society as a whole.

Whether any 'working class incomes policy' actually *has* such a radical cutting edge, however, depends on two things. Firstly, it depends on whether the policy is implemented through *struggle* at the grass roots, rather than collaboration between union officials, employers and government. Secondly, it depends on whether the policy aims to present a revolutionary alternative to capitalist society, or whether workers are to be drawn into taking responsibility for making the *existing* capitalist society work.

Where did the CPA stand on these issues? The document did make a rhetorical gesture or two in the direction of radical alternatives, suggesting that 'a challenge to the ruling class in Australia can develop', but the rest of the text made it clear that these gestures were not to be taken too seriously. It spoke of 'intervention into government economic policy to encourage industrial expansion' and also of 'union cooperation in labour-market planning'. There was no mention of industrial action.[6]

The pattern became clearer in an interview with Laurie Carmichael on 'Social Agreements', published around the same time. Carmichael spoke of 'working class intervention in macro-economic policies' and then said: 'For example, we have proposed tripartite conferences between employer organisations, government and the ACTU'. He made it clear that the working class was to take responsibility for making capitalism work:

> In developing this idea in the working class movement, we also must bear in mind that we live in a real world, and that you cannot ask for everything without also finding the means of paying for it.[7]

It was thus hardly surprising that, when the ALP–ACTU Accord was announced, the CPA fell in behind it. In fact, Carmichael had played a role in its formulation. The ideas being floated in *Tribune* from 1982 also helped to provide the left and centre ALP union officials with a set of radical-sounding rationalisations for this exercise in class collaboration. When Labor assumed office in March 1983, the CPA immediately took up a political stance similar to that of the softer sections of the Labor left.

The CPA had reproached itself during the 1970s with having been 'sectarian' towards the Whitlam government, and it was determined not to repeat this supposed error. Shortly after Hawke came into office, dumping election promises right and left, and well before the Accord could be implemented, *Tribune* produced a banner headline: 'Defend and Extend Labor's Reforms'.[8] The reforms, of course, existed only in the imagination of the sub-editors, but the headline was meant primarily as a declaration of intent. The CPA would be ready and willing to apologise for the Hawke government at key junctures.

The party did criticise the Economic Summit for excluding women, the poor and others (because it wished to include these people in the process of class collaboration) but was also willing to praise aspects of it enthusiastically. Brian Aarons and Rob Durbridge wrote that the Summit had 'widened the concept of democracy'. And, while *Tribune* disliked the three economic 'scenarios' offered by the Treasury, it had much more sympathy with the 'clear alternative model' put forward by Victorian Premier John Cain, although the latter was simply somewhat more Keynesian in its approach.[9]

The CPA had originally declared that the ALP–ACTU Accord offered important opportunities for the working class, but it soon became clear that the Accord's main consequence would be to rein in wages. Labor was prepared to support very moderate wage rises during the recession, but without allowing the unions to do anything about their claim to recoup the 9.1 percent in wages they had lost under Fraser's wage freeze. As the economy moved into recovery, and inflation fell, the full import of the Accord became clear. The unions, having been thrown a few crumbs during the recession, were to exercise extreme 'restraint' during the recovery. The benefits of recovery were to go entirely to the employers.

Finally, at the start of 1985, the Arbitration Commission removed any remaining doubts. Poorly paid Commonwealth public servants were denied any wage rise at all, although they had fallen well behind their equivalents in the state services – despite a government proposal to give them a derisory two percent rise. The government immediately fell into line with the Commission.

The unions argued that their claim was within the Accord, pointing to a clause that called for maintenance of real wages over time and another that promised to maintain relativities with state public servants. The government and media promptly replied that the Accord also included a commitment to centralised wage fixing, and thus to accepting the decisions of the Arbitration Commission. It was a classic Catch-22. The Accord meant precisely what the government, employers and Arbitration Commission chose it to mean.

Yet, throughout 1984 and into 1985, the CPA continued to cling to it. In a resolution passed at its 1984 Congress, the party condemned the 'sectarian-dogmatic left who claim the Accord is "class collaborationist"'. The resolution went on to indicate just what criteria, in the party's view, were appropriate for judging the Accord. It is instructive to consider these four criteria. On closer examination, they offer sufficient grounds for concluding that the 'sectarian-dogmatic left' is entirely correct:

- Maintenance and improvement of working class living standards in their broadest sense, involving both the industrial and social wages.
- Bargaining about total incomes – the industrial and social wages – and about redistribution of wealth through tax reforms.
- A positive intervention by unions in economic planning at all levels, particularly to stimulate employment through industrial development.
- Mobilisation and education of union members needed to achieve these goals.

The resolution itself goes on to say about the first criterion: 'real wages have been *partially* maintained against the CPI' [my emphasis]. If so, it is a poor result indeed, because there has been an economic recovery. Normally, in a recovery, workers make *gains*. To hold the line is no achievement, because they can expect to lose ground in the recession which follows. Meanwhile, as the resolution quickly adds:

> profits have risen spectacularly. In September 1982, profits were 11.8 percent of GDP, by December 1983 they were 15.5 percent, and EPAC forecasts 17 percent of GDP for 1984.

In other words, the Hawke government, through its Accord, had managed to do what Fraser could not: to improve the employers' share of the national product throughout a phase of economic upswing. The resolution states these facts without censure. But what they prove is that the Accord is a device to maximise the exploitation of the working class.

On the second point, there has no doubt been a great deal of 'bargaining about total incomes', and the Hawke government did eventually offer small tax cuts. But the CPA resolution admits that this was partly achieved 'at the expense of the social wage incomes of pensioners, other welfare beneficiaries and of other public sector services'.[10] It might have added that the value of the tax cuts was effectively nullified by previous tax *increases* imposed by Labor.

The third criterion, 'intervention by unions in economic planning', simply means that the union officials now sit on committees, where they collaborate in administering the exploitation of their rank and file. As for the fourth, 'mobilisation and education of union members', the education amounts to selling the Accord's dubious virtues to a somewhat reluctant membership, while the party's own union officials have been prepared to *attack* trade unionists who do mobilise to fight for higher wages.

In 1983, the Food Preservers' Union (FPU) waged a prolonged strike at Heinz in Dandenong, near Melbourne. The government declared the wage demands to be outside the Accord and demanded that the union be excluded from the national wage case. The FPU was threatened with fines and its officials were attacked by ACTU heavies at the ACTU Congress in September. Among those joining in the attack was Laurie Carmichael, who announced:

> Those who've got the idea that the road to socialism is made up of individual wage struggles in half a dozen companies without mobilising all the workers combined in the strength of all the workers have no bloody idea what it's all about.[11]

One doubts that the FPU imagined their little strike represented the 'road to socialism'. Nevertheless, they were at least mobilising a small number of workers in a real struggle. Carmichael and the CPA, on the other hand, were clearly in the business of *demobilising* 'all of the workers combined'. No wonder an *Age* correspondent remarked that Carmichael's statement probably made the ACTU leaders' day.[12]

The CPA was not, to be sure, entirely uncritical of the Labor government. In July 1983, Peter Ormonde wrote in *Tribune* that 'Keating's obsession with deficits, interest rates and inflation has almost completely overshadowed Labor's commitment to stimulate the economy and create new jobs'.[13] One year later, another correspondent had this to say about the government's second budget:

> A few minimal handouts have been given to placate the unions and welfare recipients in the lead up to the election while

business has been given the scope for further increased profits. But none of the underlying economic or social questions have been addressed.[14]

Tribune was scathing about the Hawke government's policy on nuclear issues. But the criticisms were characterised by important limitations. Firstly, with regard to economic questions, the CPA consistently argued within the framework of the Accord. The Accord had great potential, said the CPA, if only it were implemented properly. A struggle was needed to ensure that the progressive character of the Accord was not subverted by the government:

> The Accord is as yet far from an effective instrument because of insufficient support inside the union movement and from the disadvantaged outside unions including pensioners.[15]

The means of struggle which the party proposed to rank-and-file workers and pensioners were hardly such as to excite enthusiasm. Real class struggle was out of the question, because it would have threatened the whole machinery of class collaboration. Instead, *Tribune* praised bureaucratic devices such as a 'Jobs and Social Needs Inquiry' and 'moves for a tripartite council (government, employers, unions) for the manufacturing industry'.[16] The CPA's criticisms appeared rather lame, while it was unwilling to advocate serious struggle.

The party's stance on the anti-nuclear movement was more militant. *Tribune* was full of abuse for the government's stance on uranium mining and disarmament. Party members were often quite active in the peace campaigns, which mobilised large numbers in the streets (although they usually represented a conservative pole within them). But this was only possible because, in taking such a stand, the party blended in with the Labor left and sections of the centre. Even John Cain was prepared to address anti-nuclear rallies, and a great many ALP rank-and-file members were involved in the peace movement. Battles went on repeatedly over the issue inside the Labor Party.

In both cases, the CPA was simply keeping in step with the left – and sometimes the centre – of the mainstream labour movement. Various union officials grumbled from time to time about government wages policy but were not prepared to do much about it; and the CPA response was much the same. The ALP left wanted to fight over uranium, and so did the CPA.

At no time did the party represent an *alternative* to Laborism. At best, it occasionally played the role of providing theoretical rationalisations for sections of the ALP.

Feminism versus class politics

The CP's accommodation to the ALP was, of course, entirely consistent with its rightward drift since 1975. The party's move to drop the last vestiges of Marxism also manifested itself in other ways. One that deserves separate treatment is its accommodation to feminism.

We have seen that the women's liberation movement had a major impact on the CPA in the early 1970s, an impact that was largely healthy, given the militant and often socialist direction of the movement. From about 1974, however, women's liberation gave way gradually to a 'feminism' that was increasingly hostile to socialist ideas, advocated an 'autonomy' for women's struggles (which began to imply hostility to the 'male left') and was increasingly reformist in its political strategies (concentrating on reforms which most benefited professional women and on piecemeal welfare projects that depended on government funding). These later trends in the women's movement (the term 'liberation' was gradually, but significantly, dropped) also affected the CPA. CPA women began particularly to take up the increasing feminist hostility to Marxism and class politics.

A major statement on the latter issues, written by Joyce Stevens, appeared in 1983 as the party discussed the centenary of Marx's death.[17] This statement merits some discussion. Stevens began with some rather unoriginal criticisms of Marxism and the socialist left, arguing that 'Marx's views on the class struggle were often sketchy and incomplete'. There had, it was true, been 'subsequent debates' which had clarified some matters, but 'all forms of this debate have one shared characteristic – sex blindness'. Moreover, 'most men ... persist in speaking about the working class as though it were a male monolith'.

These charges were neither very profound nor very accurate; one suspects that they were not very honest either. Had Stevens never encountered Frederick Engels' *Origin of the Family*, or the writings of Alexandra Kollontai or Wilhelm Reich? Had she never visited the CPA's own International Bookshop, which stocked various writings by modern Marxists (some of them male) on women and the class struggle? Whatever one might think of the quality of this work, the suggestion that it is all 'sex-blind' is preposterous. Joyce Stevens would also be aware of the instrumental role played by socialists in launching the women's liberation movement in the first place. Her charges did not reflect a considered argument but were simply a recital of dogmatic radical feminist clichés aimed at laying the basis for an all-out attack on Marxism.

Joyce Stevens, 1975.

Stevens proceeded to argue for removing the class struggle as the central strategic concept for socialists and feminists both. She was scathing about those who assumed 'that the working class is *or can be* a unified group' [my emphasis] and who thought in class terms:

> Efforts to accommodate women's oppression within theories of class struggle stem, at least partly, from the fact that Marxists still accept working class struggle as the motor force for social change. Yet there has not yet been a successful 'socialist' revolution as the result of such class struggle, nor has the numerical growth of the working class in industrially developed countries produced revolutionary consciousness on a mass scale.

History has actually known both a socialist revolution based on working-class struggle (Russia in 1917) and mass consciousness in the industrialised West (in Germany and Italy after World War I, where very large numbers of workers followed the Communist International, built factory councils, staged insurrections and so on). And these are rather more impressive achievements than anything feminism can claim. However, it is true that classical Marxism has no massive accomplishments to its credit in recent decades, so it would be wrong to dismiss a proposed theoretical revision out of hand. The question is: where does the revision lead? We shall see that, in the case of Stevens, it does not lead anywhere very constructive.

Certainly, she intended a major challenge to Marxism:

> Such a suggestion requires not a small revising of Marxism, but rather a questioning or jettisoning of really basic notions of Marxist theory, starting with the idea that Marxism, or for that matter any other 'ism', can provide a total, unified and integrated world view.

This is the pluralism first introduced into the CPA by Eric Aarons, which is now leading to drastic conclusions. Writing about the whole complex of gender, race and class conflict, Stevens argued:

> These various contradictions and struggles cannot be reconciled in any simple way, though they share some common enemies and aspirations. Though they may not be understood theoretically or politically in isolation from one another, neither can they be accommodated *within any single practice* or theoretical development. [My emphasis.]

On this reasoning, women's struggle for liberation or even for reforms not only could, but *must*, be waged separately from the class struggle. The argument was reinforced in practice by the party's support for separate women's actions over disarmament, women-only actions against the RSL's Anzac Day parades and the like. It was also reinforced by the star treatment afforded to visiting writer Beatrix Campbell, who preached hostility to male trade unionists ('the men's movement which has highjacked the labour movement').[18] Such stances were tailor made to make Stevens and her allies in the CPA popular with feminists, both of the reformist sort and those in Sydney's separatist ghetto.

However, there were problems. Stevens offered no strategy for socialist (or other radical) transformation of society that would replace the allegedly bankrupt Marxist orientation to the class struggle. And that is no surprise; the only practical proposal that can arise from a pluralist argument is a *non*-strategy: everyone will do their own thing. This inability of feminism to formulate any coherent strategy apart from revolutionary Marxism and reformism also ultimately reflects social realities. It reflects the fact that only capital and labour are really powerful forces in Australian society. Those who reject a strategy of class struggle against capitalism will usually be impelled, quickly or slowly, towards a reformist capitulation to it.[19]

Further, Stevens' argument offered no reason whatsoever why feminists – or indeed anyone involved in social movements – should join the CPA. If anything, it suggested the reverse: that there was no role for a coherent socialist party organisation of any kind. So it was no accident that those who thought like Stevens were prominent in moves to liquidate the CPA which began to gain momentum from 1983.

Towards dissolution

From 1982 onwards, a discussion began inside the CPA about its future and its viability as a political party. The first development was a suggestion that the party's name be changed, on the grounds that the term 'Communist' no longer reflected the reality of the organisation's politics and was simply a factor in isolating it from a populace that associated 'Communism' with Russia. The discussion over the name soon blossomed into a debate about basic perspectives, and prominent members began to speak of a 'crisis' in the CPA. The party's numbers, notionally about 2,000, were claimed by some to have fallen to 1,500 or even 1,300. And the CPs in Europe, to whom the CPA had looked for inspiration in the 1970s, were not doing very well either.

For a time at the start of the 1980s, things had seemed rather more hopeful. In Brisbane, a nearly moribund organisation had been revived by an influx of young activists led by Lee Bermingham; in Sydney, an organising project in the western suburbs seemed to be going well; and in Melbourne, the party claimed that 'a greater number of sincere and devoted younger people who look for an effective alternative are joining the CPA'.[20]

But the temporary successes appear to have been simply the consequence of the party's rightward movement, which brought it into step with the motion of its environment. The party could recruit or win the sympathy of people whose response to the political climate was similar to its own. This situation could not last for long. For people moving rightwards, the name, history and traditions of the CPA were an obstacle to winning real influence in reformist politics, while its organisation was too weak to offer much support. If you were going to be a reformist, it made much more sense to join the Labor Party.

In the period from late 1982, the rightward drift of Australian society appears to have accelerated. Not only was the industrial struggle at low ebb, but the number and size of political demonstrations began to decline. The one exception appeared to be the disarmament movement, which was able to put many tens of thousands of people into the streets of the capital cities once a year. However, even this movement was politically limited. It lacked the militancy and also the working-class support that had characterised the earlier Movement Against Uranium Mining. It was unable to recruit ongoing activists out of the large marches on any significant scale. In fact, its ongoing organisations were little more than bureaucratic shells – except in Melbourne, where a sizeable layer of established (and ageing) left activists joined People for Nuclear Disarmament and gave it something of a (modest) 'mass' quality.

This was not the sort of climate in which socialists of whatever stripe could make major organisational gains. They could only hope to consolidate their organisations, clarify their ideas and recruit in small numbers. A holding operation was required until times changed.

For the CPA, which had so drastically watered down its politics precisely in order to win friends and influence people, such a situation was a bitter blow. A major internal debate began, whose logic was spelt out by Pete Cockcroft of the CPA's South Coast organisation:

> A new word came into vogue in our national discussions – 'mainstream'. How were we to get into the mainstream? Why were we not in the mainstream? If we said this or did that, would we become part of the mainstream?[21]

Various proposals were made to resolve this problem. On the right wing of the discussion stood, as usual, the Melbourne leadership, grouped around Bernie and Mark Taft.

The Melbourne organisation had the strongest links with the trade union officialdom and with the ALP. It also had within its ranks a number of important union officials, such as Roger Wilson of the Seamen's Union and Jim Frazer of the Railways Union. The Tafts had the connections to make some sort of regroupment with sections of the Labor Party and official union movement a serious proposition. They therefore became the strongest partisans of liquidating the existing CPA.

Of course, they did not put it in quite those terms. Rather, they harped on the CPA's 'crisis' and failure to progress and called on its members to abandon the party in favour of a new, broader 'socialist organisation' which was to be 'independent of political parties':

> Such an organisation will tap into a much broader activist base than the CPA is able to. Apart from being open to the ALP centre and left organised factions, it will be open to the vast majority of ALP members who are not members of any faction. Beyond that, and most importantly from our experience, it will be open to people who see themselves as broadly on the left, but who are not part of any political grouping.[22]

Given that a two-year waiting period is normally required by the ALP before ex-Communists can join, such a non-party formation would also offer a convenient way station on the way into the Labor Party.

The centre and majority view was that of the Aarons family in Sydney and their supporters, such as Rob Durbridge and Joyce Stevens. They accepted the Taft argument that the CPs had failed to make advances but argued that there was still room for some kind of broader, independent socialist party outside the ALP. Rob Durbridge pointed out the flaws in the Tafts' proposals:

> While the idea [of a new 'socialist organisation'] may be tolerated by the ALP right, centre and sections of the left as long as the SO was ineffective and confined itself to vague socialist discussions, I cannot believe that it would not be proscribed if it started to tread on toes. If it did not tread on toes it would hardly be worthwhile. If it was proscribed then where would we be ... having put all our eggs into a basket that the bottom fell out of![23]

Other critics pointed out that the CPA lacked the right connections outside Victoria to make the Taft project viable anywhere but in that state.

But what of the proposal for a 'new socialist party'? In one sense, it had an obvious logic. Certainly, the term 'Communist' appeared incongruous and anachronistic as applied to the contemporary politics of the CPA, and it was undoubtedly an obstacle for those who sought immersion in the political mainstream. It was equally true that the party's politics were now so similar to those of other (reformist-minded) leftists, feminists and trade unionists that the divisions between the Communists and the others sometimes seemed arbitrary. Moreover, the party was now so loosely organised, and contained within it so many currents of opinion, that broadening out further would not be terribly difficult.

In another sense, it was most unrealistic. The Aarons brothers and their supporters appeared to imagine that a regroupment of leftists around the existing CP, together with a further softening of politics, could lead to dramatically increased influence and growth. Merv Nixon and a number of other South Coast members claimed that 'in many ways it would be true to say that in Australia the Left is growing while the CPA is declining':

> The growing peace movement which protests the insanity of the arms race; the women's movement which challenges the hierarchical organisation of a society based on profit and not social need; the increasing autonomous organisation of blacks and other oppressed peoples; the environmental movement – all these autonomous organisations are raising sharp criticisms of the capitalist system. The problem is that at this stage, there is no organisation that can adequately fuse these disparate criticisms into a whole, offering a vision and a strategy to successfully challenge capitalism.[24]

A new socialist party, Nixon felt, might do the job. Yet, surely, the whole argument was illusory. The peace movement was a real force, but politically limited. The women's movement was no longer inclined towards socialism, the Black movement was in disarray, and the environmentalists represented an established cadre rather than a growing current. (The party was perhaps impressed by the mass support for struggles over the Franklin Dam but ignored the fact that this support was conditioned by the hostility of influential sections of the ruling class to the dam.)

It was possible, even likely, that some activists from the peace and environmental movements might be drawn into a revamped party, as might some trade unionists. It was unlikely that large numbers would be attracted. Most certainly, the established feminists had shown no interest. At the same time, it was likely that the regroupment process would lead to losses as well as gains.

It was possible, for example, that the grouping of ex-members of the Socialist Party led by Pat Clancy would join. It was equally possible that they would stay outside, hoping that the left wing of the CPA would be propelled out of the party by an influx of more right-wing elements and would then merge with the Clancy forces.

There was another danger. By opening up the party to a wider range of people, and watering down its political program in order to make itself more attractive to them, the CPA risked strengthening the centrifugal tendencies which were already strong within it. The party was already more a meeting place for different tendencies than a united organisation. A great many of its members saw their work in various external arenas as more important than the party itself. Within the organisation, there were little autonomous fiefdoms (the *Tribune* collective, the Sydney bookshop, various areas of union work). Holding a new party together might prove quite difficult.

But the success of the 'new party' proposal was ensured by the sudden departure of the Taft grouping. A statement by 23 members of the Victorian State Committee announced their resignation from the party, on the grounds that their proposals were meeting what they considered pig-headed resistance:

> To those who will question why we have not stayed on longer in order to fight for our position ... we say that it is no longer a serious or fruitful option ... it has become impossible to sustain the enthusiasm and will of those who support change in the face of such opposition.[25]

The new 'Socialist Forum' established by the Tafts attracted a substantial layer of people from the CPA, plus various academics and union officials (most notably in the public service). It also enjoyed some support in the ALP (not necessarily among the most left-wing sections), and it seemed likely that this was where the 'Socialist Forum' would eventually end up.

The split in Melbourne was a major blow to the Victorian organisation. While the remaining members rallied and showed some enthusiasm for maintaining the party, it was by no means clear whether morale could be sustained over time in what was now a fairly small organisation.

With the departure of the Taft grouping, the party could postpone a resolution of the debate no longer, scheduling a special Congress for November 1984.

Launch of the New Left Party, 1991.

Its result, of course, was a foregone conclusion. The only significant opposition to the Aaronsite perspective came from a rather fragmented and vague left wing, centred in Sydney and on the South Coast.

Revolutionary critics of the CPA were not invited to the special Congress. However, I was able to listen to tapes of the Sydney district conference held shortly beforehand, which offered a good impression of the various points of view. (The quotes that follow were all transcribed from these tapes.)

Introducing the majority resolution, Brian Aarons said that the proposals were aimed at creating a party with 'more clout'. Yet, he proceeded immediately to admit (indeed proclaim) that the CPA leadership had no clear way forward to offer: 'We can't keep on pretending we have all the answers.' In fact, the leaders had been unable to resolve the fundamental problem raised by the relations between the class struggle and the struggles of the oppressed. Between those like Joyce Stevens, who wished to separate the two (and, implicitly at least,

downgrade the former in favour of the latter) and those who wished to maintain an emphasis on the working class, the leadership had only arrived at an 'ambiguous compromise'. From the outset, therefore, the CPA's attempts to lay the basis for a new party rested on a blurring of fundamentals.

One CPAer argued for the new perspective on a feminist basis, stating that 'in many ways Marxism has been an inadequate method to understand women's oppression' and that it was better to think in terms of 'a contradiction not to do with class but one which is around how women perceive some of their struggles between men and women'. Explicitly anti-Marxist and idealist statements of this type were at no time challenged by the leaders of the majority, although some of them must have disliked the implications. They were too concerned with maintaining the momentum towards change – for fear, as one of their supporters put it, that the party was about to 'disappear up its own orifice' if the changes did not take place desperately soon.

The left made its main stand on an argument for class politics, and several of them made Marxist arguments. The most prominent figures arguing the left point of view were postal worker Brian Carey and trade union official Linda Carruthers. Carruthers challenged those feminists who wished to separate women's liberation from the class struggle:

> There is not a united working class ... But I don't think having said that, that you then proceed to organise as though that will always be the case, should be the case, and can be no other way ... Capital imposes those divisions ... I don't think we ought to be seen to be in a position where we're adding our little bit to that process.

But, while the left was prepared to challenge bits of the majority resolution, all but a handful nevertheless accepted the general framework. When Carey was attacked for 'fundamentalism', his supporters protested that he was in fundamental agreement with the NC resolution, but only wished to clarify it somewhat. While Carruthers opposed the separatist logic of some feminists' views, she nevertheless addressed other women present as 'sisters' rather than comrades. By and large, the left argued abstractions. They were not concerned to present alternative practical proposals. The idea of seeking to create a 'new socialist party' had effectively become hegemonic.

How was the new party to be created? The beginning would be a process of discussion. CPA members in NSW had been impressed by joint forums which had been held with other leftists, particularly with Clancy's grouping. The CPA proposed to hold more such 'socialist forums', which would 'involve all socialist groups and individuals sincerely seeking the movement's renewal'. It proposed to make attempts to 'develop a common program' and to establish local 'socialist alliances'.[26] One important focus, not too conspicuous in the final Congress resolution but prominent in discussions surrounding it, was electoral work, especially at the local level. Joint left tickets had achieved some success in this area, and it was hoped that these could be built on.

What was certain was that the events of 1984 signalled the end of Australian Communism as any sort of distinctive current. The former Communists would end up in that mainstream towards which they had been striving for so long. They were part of it because they had liquidated themselves into it politically.

The CPA that was launched in 1920 to lead the workers to power in revolutionary struggle is today a political corpse. Anyone who wants to wage a struggle for socialism in the tradition of Marx and Lenin must seek to build an alternative to it. Even the bogus revolutionary pretensions of Stalinism are gone, replaced in the end by nothing but liberal bourgeois politics. Dr Graeme Duncan of Melbourne University foresaw this logic of the party's development as early as 1968. He was allowed to publish his comments in *Tribune*. His predictions seemed misguided for a time in the early 1970s but now provide a fitting speech at the graveside:

> Certainly the Marxist teeth have been drawn, and the new model Australian Communist Party has moved explicitly into the mainstream of Western democratic theory. We are all bourgeois gentlemen now.[27]

Abbreviations and Acronyms

ACTU	Australian Council of Trade Unions
AEU	Amalgamated Engineering Union
AMWSU	Amalgamated Metal Workers and Shipwrights Union
ASP	Australian Socialist Party
AWU	Australian Workers' Union
BLF	Builders Labourers' Federation
CMUC	Coal Mining Unions' Council
Cominform	Communist Information Bureau
CP	Communist Party
CP(ML)	Communist Party (Marxist–Leninist)
CPA	Communist Party of Australia
CPGB	Communist Party of Great Britain
CPSU	Communist Party of the Soviet Union
ECCUDO	Electricity Commission Combined Union Delegates' Organisation
FIA	Federated Ironworkers Association
FPU	Food Preservers' Union
IWW	Industrial Workers of the World
MMM	Militant Minority Movement
MM	Minority Movement
NHA	New Housewives' Association
RSL	Returned and Services League of Australia
SLP	Socialist Labor Party
TLC	Trades and Labour Council
UAW	Union of Australian Women
WEB	Women's Employment Board

Endnotes

Foreword 2025 Edition

1. A more detailed critique of the Accord written at the time, to which O'Lincoln contributed, is L. Ross, T. O'Lincoln and G. Willett, *Labor's Accord: why it's a fraud*, Melbourne, Socialist Action, 1986. https://www.reasoninrevolt.net.au/bib/PR0001136.htm. For a more sustained analysis, see L. Ross, *Stuff the Accord. Pay Up*, Interventions, 2020.

2. G. Jericho and D. Richardson, 'The share of GDP going to workers is at record lows', News & Analysis, The Australia Institute, 7 September, 2022. https://australiainstitute.org.au/post/the-share-of-gdp-going-to-workers-hits-a-record-low/, accessed 15 August 2024.

3. Australian Bureau of Statistics, 'Trade Union Membership', https://www.abs.gov.au/statistics/labour/earnings-and-working-conditions/trade-union-membership/latest-release, accessed 15 August 2024.

4. See the political memoir, T. O'Lincoln, *The Highway is for Gamblers*, Melbourne, Interventions, 2017.

5. T. Cliff, *State Capitalism in Russia*, Haymarket, 2019.

6. See, for example, the special edition of *Labour History* dedicated to papers discussing histories of working-class anti-imperialism and anti-colonialism in Australia, no. 126, 2024.

7. P. Gibson, 'Communists and the 1933 campaign that ended frontier massacres in Australia', *Labour History*, no. 126, 2024,pp. 47–71.

Publisher's Preface

1. T. O'Lincoln, *'The Expropriators are Expropriated' and other writings on Marxism*, Melbourne, Interventions, 2015.

2. R. Kuhn, 'Introduction' in O'Lincoln, *'The Expropriators are Expropriated'*. At the time Rick wrote this comment, some of the standard works included A. Davidson, *The Communist Party of Australia: a short history*, Stanford, Hoover Institution Press, 1969; R. Gollan, *Revolutionaries and reformists: Communism and the Australian labour movement, 1920-1955*, Sydney, George

Allen & Unwin, 1985 [1975]; S. Macintyre, *The Reds: the Communist Party of Australia from origins to illegality*, St Leonards, Allen & Unwin, 1999.

Author's Preface

1   This version of the author's preface is an amalgamation of the prefaces that appeared in the first edition (1985) and the second edition (2009), except for the acknowledgements that were noted there, which are now incorporated into the publisher's preface.

CHAPTER 1 The Fate of a World Movement

1   L. Trotsky, *On Lenin*, London, 1971, p. 143.
2   Quoted in M. Shachtman, 'The Struggle for the New Course', Introduction to L. Trotsky, *The New Course*, Ann Arbor, 1965, p. 125.
3   V.I. Lenin, *Collected Works*, Moscow, 1962, vol. 29, p. 310.
4   V.I. Lenin, *Left Wing Communism, An Infantile Disorder*, Moscow. 1968, p. 506.
5   Lenin, *Collected Works*, Moscow 1962, vol. 33, pp. 430–2. In this section, I have greatly oversimplified the extent to which the seeds of the Stalinisation of the Comintern were sown in the early and mid-1920s. Cf. E.H. Carr, *The Bolshevik Revolution*, London, 1973, vol. 3, *passim*.
6   I. Birchall, *Workers Against the Monolith*, London, 1974, p. 11. Much of this chapter is influenced by Birchall's account.
7   Quoted in F. Claudin, 'The Split in the Spanish Communist Party', *New Left Review*, no. 70, p. 79.
8   Cf. F. Morrow, *Revolution and Counterrevolution in Spain*, London, 1963, *passim* for details.
9   Birchall, *Workers Against the Monolith*, p. 33.
10 Birchall, *Workers Against the Monolith*, p. 29.
11 Birchall, *Workers Against the Monolith*, p. 41.
12 J.P. Cannon, *The Struggle for a Proletarian Party*, New York, 1972, p. 145. The pronouns are antiquated but reflect the era.
13 A. Koestler in R. Crossman (ed.), *The God That Failed*, London, 1965, p. 58.
14 For details on Czechoslovakia, including the real role played by the workers in the Communist takeover, see C. Harman, *Bureaucracy and Revolution in Eastern Europe*, London, 1974, pp. 45–8.
15 Birchall, *Workers Against the Monolith*, p. 13.
16 *Basic Questions of Communist Theory*, Sydney, Current Book Distributors, 1957, p. 17.
17 Quoted in the *Guardian*, 23 February 1956.
18 Quoted in Birchall, *Workers Against the Monolith*, p. 116.
19 Quoted in Birchall, *Workers Against the Monolith*, p. 117.
20 *PCI Bulletin*, December 1974, p. 53.
21 S. Carrillo, quoted in *Tribune*, 6 October 1976.

ENDNOTES

CHAPTER 2 The rise of Australian Communism

1　J. Waten, *The Unbending*, Melbourne, Australasian Book Society, 1954, p. 298.
2　Quoted in H. McQueen, *A New Britannia*, Melbourne, 1978, p. 194.
3　Quoted in McQueen, *A New Britannia*, p. 200.
4　Quoted in P.J. O'Farrell, *Harry Holland, Militant Socialist*, Canberra, ANU, 1964, p. 12.
5　O'Farrell, *Harry Holland*.
6　'The Awakening of Labor', ASP leaflet, Sydney, n.d.
7　Quoted in *Communist Review*, August 1937, p. 56.
8　Australian Bureau of Statistics.
9　F. Farrell, *International Socialism and Australian Labour*, Sydney, 1981, p. 95.
10　Farrell, *International Socialism and Australian Labour*.
11　Quoted in N. Jefferey, *The Labour Movement in Australia and Overseas, 1911 to the End of the First World War*, Sydney, n.d., p. 12.
12　Quoted in N. Jefferey, *A Stormy Period in Australia, First World War to the Russian Revolution*, Sydney, n.d., p. 11.
13　'Manifesto of the Communist International to the Workers of the World', in L. Trotsky, *The First Five Years of the Communist International*, New York, 1972.
14　J.B. Miles, 'Who Are the Communists?' supplement to *International Communist*, 24 September 1921.
15　Quoted in M. Dixson, 'The First Communist "United Front" in Australia', *Labour History*, vol. 10, May 1966, pp. 27–8.
16　R. Dixon, 'Early Years in the Party', *Australian Left Review*, no. 48, September 1975, p. 49.
17　Letter from 'The Communist Party of Australia' (ASP) to the Garden group, Sydney, 4 January 1922. Photocopy in possession of the author.
18　Report from P. Lamb to ASP, from Moscow, n.d. Photocopy in possession of the author.
19　Farrell, *International Socialism and Australian Labour*, pp. 61–2.
20　Farrell, *International Socialism and Australian Labour*, p. 59.
21　Farrell, *International Socialism and Australian Labour*, p. 60.
22　Cited in Farrell, *International Socialism and Australian Labour*, p. 59.
23　*Workers' Weekly*, 27 July 1923 ('Did the Coal Vend Want a General Strike?').
24　*Workers' Weekly*, 6 May 1927.
25　Quoted in L.L. Sharkey, *An Outline History of the Australian Communist Party*, Sydney, 1944, p. 22.
26　Quoted in Sharkey, *An Outline History*.
27　Quoted in E. Campbell, *History of the Australian Labour Movement*, Sydney, 1945, pp. 132–3.
28　Quoted in Campbell, *History of the Australian Labour Movement*, p. 132.

29 *Workers' Voice*, 29 March 1935.
30 Quoted in P.J. Morrison, *The Communist Party of Australia, and the Australian Radical-Socialist Tradition, 1920–39*, Ph.D. thesis, University of Adelaide, 1975, p. 325.
31 D. Rose, 'The Movement Against War and Fascism, 1933–39', *Labour History*, no. 38, May 1980, p. 32.
32 *Workers' Weekly*, 13 December 1939.
33 *Workers' Voice*, 29 September 1933.
34 Quoted in Rose, 'The Movement Against War and Fascism', p. 86.
35 *Workers' Weekly*, 15 September 1936.
36 Quoted in J. White, 'The Port Kembla Pig Iron Strike of 1938', *Labour History*, no. 37, November 1979, p. 73.
37 White, 'The Port Kembla Pig Iron Strike of 1938', p. 66.
38 White, 'The Port Kembla Pig Iron Strike of 1938'.
39 Quoted in C. Johnston, 'The "Leading War Party": Communists and World War 2', *Labour History*, no. 39, November 1980, p. 70.
40 *Workers' Weekly*, 29 February 1924.
41 'Report of MMM Conference', in Plebs League Folio, Mitchell Library, Sydney.
42 L.L. Sharkey, *An Outline History*, p. 23.
43 J. Blake, 'The Australian Communist Party and the Comintern in the Early Thirties', *Labour History*, no. 23, November 1972, pp. 44–5.
44 *Red Leader*, 4 January 1933.
45 J. Devanny, *Sugar Heaven*, Vulgar Press, 2002.
46 *Red Leader*, 27 July 1932.
47 *Workers' Voice*, 1 November 1935.
48 L.L. Sharkey, *The Trade Unions*, Sydney 1961; and *An Outline History*.
49 Quoted in White, 'The Port Kembla Pig Iron Strike of 1938', p. 66.
50 White, 'The Port Kembla Pig Iron Strike of 1938', p. 11.
51 Morrison, 'The Communist Party of Australia', p. 63.
52 Quoted in Morrison, 'The Communist Party of Australia', p. 66.
53 Morrison, 'The Communist Party of Australia', p. 67.
54 Quoted in J. Stevens, '"Work Among Women" in the Communist Party, 1920–40', duplicated paper distributed at the Communists and the Labour Movement conference, Melbourne, 1980.
55 *Red Leader*, 6 July 1932.
56 *Red Leader*, 10 March 1932.
57 *Working Woman*, September 1930.
58 *Working Woman*, April 1931.

59 *Our Women* (Union of Australian Women, Sydney), anniversary issue, 1963, p. 17.
60 *Our Women* (Union of Australian Women, Sydney), anniversary issue 1963.
61 *Woman Today*, e.g., the March 1937 issue.
62 Quoted in D. Menghetti, 'North Queensland Women and the Popular Front of 1935–40', *Literature in North Queensland*, vol. 8, no. 3, 1980, p. 34.
63 Morrison, 'The Communist Party of Australia', p. 312 fn.
64 Cf. *Tribune*, 18 November 1970, for an account of CPA work in the armed forces during World War II.
65 *Guardian*, 18 November 1944.
66 *Guardian*, 22 September 1944.
67 'After waging a fierce battle against European chauvinism in the 1920s and 1930s, the Communist Party produced a pamphlet entitled *Smash Japan*, in which a Japanese officer is described as having a "physique ... in tune with his dwarfed, twisted soul ... Ridiculously small, bow-legged, repulsive to look at, his teeth stuck out at an angle of 45 degrees through thick lips which he never stopped licking". The pamphlet ends with plea for proletarian internationalism'. H. McQueen, 'Glory Without Power', in Playford and Kirsner (eds.), *Australian Capitalism*, Melbourne 1977, p. 353.
68 Johnston, 'The "Leading War Party": Communists and World War 2', p. 23.
69 Quoted in P. George, *Power Politics – A Study of Industrial Conflict in the NSW Power Industry*, BA (Hons) thesis, Sydney University, 1975, p. 11. George discusses the integration of power industry shop committees during the war on pp. 10–11.
70 N. Origlass, 'The Second Imperialist War and the CPA', *International*, Sydney, April 1971, p. 3.
71 Quoted in J. Stone, 'Women in the Metal Trades', *Front Line*, Melbourne, no. 5, December 1976, pp. 15–16.
72 This story is told in D. Gollan, 'The Balmain Ironworkers' Strike of 1945', Parts I and II, *Labour History*, nos. 22 and 23, May and November 1972.
73 A. Davidson, *The Communist Party of Australia*, Stanford, Hoover Institution Press, 1969, p. 83.
74 D. Menghetti, *The Red North: the Popular Front in North Queensland*, James Cook University of North Queensland, 1981, p. 165.
75 *Women In Our New World*, Sydney, 1947, p. 165.

CHAPTER 3 The Communists on the Offensive

1 Quoted in T. Sheridan, 'Labour v. Labor', in Iremonger, Merritt and Osborne (eds.), *Strikes, Studies in Twentieth Century Australian Social History*, Sydney, 1975, p. 181. Much of the account of the Victorian metal trades dispute is derived from this article.
2 *Tribune*, 17 September 1946.
3 Sheridan, 'Labour v. Labor', p. 177.
4 Sheridan, 'Labour v. Labor', pp. 214–15.

5 Most of the account of the Queensland rail strike follows M. Cribb, 'State in Emergency', in Iremonger, Merritt and Osborne (eds.), *Strikes, Studies*.
6 E.F. Hill, 'Defeat of the Essential Services Act', *Communist Review*, January 1949, p. 9. I have relied on Hill's article for much of this account.
7 J.D. Blake, 'Unite for Postwar Progress', in *Communists in Congress*, Sydney 1945, p. 9.
8 R. Gibson, *My Years in the Communist Party*, Melbourne, 1966, p. 150.
9 Quoted in P. Deery, *The 1949 Coal Strike*, unpublished Ph.D. thesis, La Trobe University, 1976, p. 80. Deery's thesis contains important material not included in his published work, Deery (ed.), *Labour in Conflict*, Sydney, 1978.
10 'The Report of L.L. Sharkey to the 15th Congress of the Australian Communist Party, May 1948', in *For Australia Prosperous and Independent*, Sydney, 1948, p. 12.
11 'Declaration of Information Conference', in *Communist Review*, April 1951, pp. 745–6.
12 Quoted in Deery, *The 1949 Coal Strike*, p. 70.
13 Deery, *The 1949 Coal Strike*, p. 96.
14 Deery, *The 1949 Coal Strike*, pp. 94 and 88.
15 Deery, *The 1949 Coal Strike*, p. 99.
16 Deery, *The 1949 Coal Strike*, p. 106.
17 *Communist Review*, July 1948, p. 198.
18 *Communist Review*, April 1949, p. 108.
19 L.L. Sharkey, 'Report', p. 25.
20 *Guardian*, 26 November 1948.
21 *Guardian*, 5 November 1948.
22 *Guardian*, 27 February 1948.
23 'Letter to the CPGB', *Communist Review*, September 1948, p. 272.
24 Davidson, *The Communist Party of Australia*, p. 120.
25 R. Gollan, *Revolutionaries and Reformists*, Canberra, ANU, 1975, p. 247.
26 *Communist Review*, April 1946, p. 114.
27 *Tribune*, 8 December 1949. On this, see also A. Barcan, *The Socialist Left in Australia 1949–59*, Australian Political Studies Association, Occasional Monographs, no. 2, Sydney, 1960, pp. 23–4.
28 *Tribune*, 17 November 1948.
29 *Tribune*, 9 June 1948.
30 *Communist Review*, March 1947, p. 147.
31 Gollan, *Revolutionaries and Reformists*, p. 247.
32 Davidson, *The Communist Party of Australia*, pp. 133–5.
33 Quoted in Gollan, *Revolutionaries and Reformists*, p. 247.
34 Gibson, *My Years in the Communist Party*, p. 149.

35 J. Blake, 'The 1949 Coal *Strike*', *Australian Left Review*, no. 70, August 1979, p. 13.
36 *Tribune*, 15 August 1979.
37 Gibson, *My Years in the Communist Party*, pp. 148–9.
38 Gibson, *My Years in the Communist Party*, p. 149.
39 Quoted in Deery, *The 1949 Coal Strike*, p. 209.
40 Deery, *The 1949 Coal Strike*, p. 209 fn.
41 Quoted in Deery, *The 1949 Coal Strike*, p. 175.
42 Deery, *The 1949 Coal Strike*, p. 263.
43 Deery, *The 1949 Coal Strike*, p. 108 fn.
44 Deery, *The 1949 Coal Strike*, pp. 217–8. Deery suggests that Williams himself may honestly have believed this line, but that other CPA officials, who also pushed it, certainly did not.
45 Deery, *The 1949 Coal Strike*, pp. 201–2.
46 Deery, *The 1949 Coal Strike*, p. 360.
47 Deery, *The 1949 Coal Strike*, p. 377.
48 Deery, *The 1949 Coal Strike*, p. 377 fn.

CHAPTER 4 A Party Besieged

1 Quoted on a CPA leaflet, *They Lie About Communists*, n.d.
2 B. Connell and T. Irving, 'The Making of the Australian Industrial Bourgeoisie: 1930–1975', *Intervention*, no. 10–11, August 1978, p. 22.
3 Quoted in Gollan, *Revolutionaries and Reformists*, p. 170.
4 Quoted in Gollan, *Revolutionaries and Reformists*, p. 175.
5 R. Kuhn, 'A Poor Start to Prosperity', *International Socialist*, no. 8, Autumn 1979, p. 9.
6 *Tribune*, 9 March 1949.
7 Quoted in Gibson, *My Years in the Communist Party*, p. 156. Some rather more critical memoirs are cited elsewhere in the present work.
8 *Tribune*, 9 March 1949.
9 Gibson, *My Years in the Communist Party*, p. 138.
10 Gibson, *My Years in the Communist Party*, p. 139.
11 *Tribune*, 1 August 1951.
12 *Tribune*, 26 September 1951.
13 Quoted in Gollan, *Revolutionaries and Reformists*, p. 268.
14 J. Sendy, *Comrades Come Rally*, Melbourne, 1978, p. 64.
15 V. Williams, interview with the author, 7 October 1981.
16 *Tribune*, 13 August 1949.

17 *Tribune*, 13 August 1949.
18 *Tribune*, 31 August 1949.
19 *Tribune*, 7 January 1950.
20 *Tribune*, 28 April 1951.
21 W.A. Wood, *The Life of L.L. Sharkey, Fighter for Freedom*, Sydney, 1950, p. 16.
22 F. Hardy, *The Hard Way*, Melbourne, 1961, p. 40.
23 Hardy, *The Hard Way*, p. 95.
24 L.L. Sharkey, 'CPSU 20th Congress an Epoch-Making Event', in *Basic Questions of Communist Theory*, Sydney, 1957, p. 23.
25 J. Morrison, *Black Cargo*, Melbourne, 1955, p. 224.
26 Z. D'Aprano, *Zelda, the Becoming of a Woman*, Melbourne, 1977, p. 75.
27 R. Marriot, untitled article in *Discussion*, no. 1, November 1967, p. 14. This was a CPA internal discussion journal.
28 *Communist Review*, September 1956, p. 302.
29 *Communist Review*, May 1952, p. 147.
30 D. Gollan, 'The Memoirs of "Cleopatra Sweatfigure"', Part II, in *Extra Papers*, Women and Labour Conference, May 1978, p. 102.
31 *Communist Review*, October 1951, p. 945.
32 *Communist Review*, November 1948, p. 339.
33 Williams, interview.
34 *Tribune*, 3 November 1954. The party has since declared that it was wrong to scapegoat Blake and Henry. See 'CPA NC Resolution', *Australian Left Review*, no. 76, June 1981.
35 J. Mundey, 'Towards New Union Militancy', interview in *Australian Left Review*, August–September 1970, p. 3.
36 Williams, interview.
37 *Communist Review*, September 1956, p. 302.
38 Untitled duplicated internal document, issued by 'Central Cadres and Education Committee', 4 June 1956, p. 11. In possession of the author.
39 *Communist Review*, September 1956, p. 302.
40 A. Gramsci, *Prison Notebooks*, New York, 1971, p. 336.
41 Gramsci, *Prison Notebooks*, p. 337.
42 J. Blake, 'Party and People', *Discussion Journal*, no. 1, March 1967, p. 30. This was an internal CPA discussion journal.
43 L.L. Sharkey, report to 18th Congress, Sydney, 1958, p. 18.
44 *Communist Review*, October 1951, p. 947.
45 Williams, interview.
46 D. Hewitt, *Bobbin Up*, Melbourne, 1959, p. 127.

ENDNOTES **241**

47 D. Mortimer, 'On Some Welcome Changes', *Discussion Journal*, no. 3, May 1967, p. 82.
48 Williams, interview.
49 Quoted in R. Gibson, *My Years in the Communist Party*, p. 160.
50 S. Goldbloom suggested this obliquely in a talk at the Communists and the Labour Movement conference, Melbourne 1980. Cf. S. Goldbloom *et al.*, 'The Peace Movement', tape in Latrobe Library, Melbourne.
51 G. Roberts, 'A Chance for Peace?', *Cold War International History Project*, Woodrow Wilson International Center for Scholars, Washington, December 2008, p. 4, https://www.wilsoncenter.org/sites/default/files/media/documents/publication/WP57_WebFinal.pdf.
52 Reference missing. See Publisher's preface.
53 V.I. Lenin, 'The Question of Peace', *Collected Works*, vol. 21, Moscow, 1974, p. 293.
54 Newsletter, Union of Australian Women, Victorian Section. Details unavailable.
55 'Elizabeth', personal interview, October 1979.
56 Cited in T. O'Lincoln, 'Against the Stream' in S. Bloodworth and T. O'Lincoln (eds), *Rebel Women in Australian Working Class History*, Interventions, 2022.

CHAPTER 5 The Monolith Cracks

1   J. Sendy, *Comrades Come Rally*, p. 49.
2   *Guardian*, 23 February 1956.
3   Sendy, *Comrades Come Rally*, p. 100.
4   *Basic Questions of Communist Theory*, Sydney 1957, p. 3.
5   *Basic Questions of Communist Theory*, p. 6.
6   *Basic Questions of Communist Theory*, p. 23.
7   *Basic Questions of Communist Theory*, p. 4.
8   *Basic Questions of Communist Theory*.
9   Quoted in A. Barcan, *The Socialist Left in Australia, 1949–59*, p. 15.
10 *Basic Questions of Communist Theory*, p. 71.
11 *Basic Questions of Communist Theory*, p. 68.
12 Davidson, *The Communist Party of Australia*, p. 121.
13 Sendy, *Comrades Come Rally*, p. 101.
14 *Communist Review*, August 1956, p. 27.
15 *Communist Review*, September 1956, p. 304.
16 *Communist Review*, October 1956, p. 345.
17 *Communist Review*, October 1956, p. 348.
18 *Communist Review*, December 1956, p. 398.
19 *Communist Review*, May 1957, pp. 160–2.

20 It is not correct, however, to conclude (as some writers have) that there is a direct link between the CPA members trained in China and the element that left the party in the early 1960s to form a new pro-China organisation. Most of the Chinese-trained cadres ended up supporting the liberal Aarons line after 1967. Cf. A. McIntyre, 'The Training of Australian Communist Cadres in China', *Studies in Comparative Communism*, vol. 11, no. 4, Winter 1978, pp. 419–23, and Chapter 6 of the present work.

21 *Foundations of Communist Unity*, Communist Party of New Zealand, Auckland, 1964, pp. 7–8.

22 Davidson, *The Communist Party of Australia*, p. 153.

23 Davidson, *The Communist Party of Australia*, pp. 151–3 provides a reasonably plausible exercise in Kremlinology on this question.

24 Quoted in *Differences in the Communist Movement*, CPA, Sydney, 1963, p. 30.

25 Sendy, *Comrades Come Rally*, p. 127.

26 L. Aarons, *Labor Movement at the Crossroads*, Sydney, 1964, p. 10.

27 Aarons, *Labor Movement*, p. 21.

28 V.I. Lenin, *Left Wing Communism, an Infantile Disorder*, Moscow, 1968, pp. 69–71.

29 Williams, interview.

30 D. Davies, 'One Minute Parking', *Tribune*, 24 August 1977.

31 L. Aarons, *Party of the Working Class*, Sydney, 1959, pp. 19–20.

32 'Towards a Coalition of the Left', in CPA 21st National Congress Documents, 1967, *passim*.

33 L. Churchward, 'Realism and the Document Perspectives', *Discussion Journal*, no. 1, CPA, Sydney, March 1967, p. 92.

34 'K', '"Towards a Coalition of the Left" – Some Comments', *Discussion Journal*, no. 2, April 1967, p. 7.

35 D. Beechy, 'On the Role of the Communist Party', *Discussion Journal*, no. 2, April 1967, p. 47.

36 L. Aarons, 'Report of the Central Committee', Sydney, 1967, pp. 14–15.

37 Quoted in J. Sendy, 'Democracy and Socialism', *Australian Left Review*, March 1968, p. 8.

38 Draft: 'Charter of Democratic Rights', first issue of Information Service of CPA, 1968, pp. 1, 3 and 8.

39 A. Miller, untitled contribution to *Discussion*, no. 2, January 1970, p. 27.

40 *Guardian*, 24 February 1966.

41 *Guardian*, 1 March 1966.

42 *Tribune*, 28 June 1968.

43 *Tribune*, 28 August 1968.

44 J.C. Henry, 'My Viewpoint on the Czechoslovakian Crisis', *Discussion*, no. 4, October 1968, p. 52.

45 *Tribune*, 11 September 1968.

46 Cf. *Lenin on the National and Colonial Questions*, Peking [Beijing] 1975, *passim*. For a discussion of the views of Marx and Lenin on the national question, including documentation of what is

asserted here, see T. O'Lincoln, 'An Imperialist Colony? An Analysis of Australian Nationalism', *International Socialist*, no. 10, Melbourne, August 1980, p. 40.

47 'E.W.', 'A Major Principle', *Australian Left Review*, December 1968, p. 25.
48 Quoted in J.B. Henderson, 'Self-Determination Qualified', *Australian Left Review*, December 1968, p. 21.
49 This passage was constructed by paraphrase and quotation from W.J. Brown, *What Happened to the Communist Party of Australia?* Sydney, 1971, pp. 5–8.
50 Quoted in *What's Happening in the CPA? – Will the Communist Party Split?* CPA, Sydney, 1970, p. 10.
51 Quoted in *What's Happening in the CPA?* p. 7.
52 Sendy, *Comrades Come Rally*, p. 187.

CHAPTER 6 A Revolution in Theory?

1   N. Harris, *India/China; Underdevelopment and Revolution*, Delhi, 1974, p. 228.
2   'Manifesto of the Communist International', p. 19.
3   Quoted in A. Barcan, *The Socialist Left in Australia, 1949–59*, Australian Political Studies Association, Occasional Monograph No.2, Sydney 1960, p. 15.
4   Cf. for example the articles reproduced in M. Kidron, *Capitalism and Theory*, London, 1974.
5   B. Taft, 'Changes in Modern Capitalism', *Australian Left Review*, no. 1, June–July 1966, pp. 4–5.
6   R. Hearn, 'Questions on the Mass Party Aim', *Discussion Journal*, March 1967, pp. 73–4.
7   N. Harris, *The Mandate of Heaven*, London, 1978, p. 287.
8   E. Aarons, 'As I Saw the Sixties', *Australian Left Review*, no. 27, October–November 1970, pp. 61–2.
9   A. McIntyre, 'The Training of Australian Communist Cadres in China', *Studies in Comparative Communism*, vol. 11, no.4, Winter 1978, pp. 412–3.
10 Quoted in McIntyre, 'The Training of Australian Communist Cadres in China', pp. 416–7.
11 R. Mortimer, 'The Benefits of a Liberal Education', *Meanjin*, June 1976.
12 E. Aarons, 'As I Saw the Sixties', p. 70.
13 E. Aarons, *Philosophy for an Exploding World*, Sydney, 1972, p. 8.
14 Aarons, *Philosophy for an Exploding World*, p. 11.
15 Aarons, *Philosophy for an Exploding World*, p. 128.
16 Aarons, *Philosophy for an Exploding World*, p. 152.
17 Trotsky's analysis is contained in *The Revolution Betrayed*, New York, 1965. The most straightforward statement of that aspect of Deutscher's analysis which I have paraphrased can be found in his *Stalin*, London, 1966, pp. 14 and 612–14.
18 Eric Aarons, Discussion Document, 1974.
19 *Statement of Aims*, CPA 22nd Congress, March 1970, pp. 9–10.

20 *Statement of Aims*.
21 *Tribune*, 11 August 1971.
22 Aarons, Discussion Document, p. 2.
23 Aarons, Discussion Document, pp. 3–4.
24 Aarons, Discussion Document, p. 13.
25 Quoted in Deutscher, *Stalin*, p. 328.
26 M. Haynes, 'The USSR and the Crisis', *International Socialism* (first series), London, May 1976, p. 36.
27 Aarons, Discussion Document, p. 9.
28 Aarons, Discussion Document.
29 Aarons, Discussion Document.
30 Quoted in T. Cliff, *Russia, a Marxist Analysis*, London, 1970, p. 59.
31 Aarons, Discussion Document, p. 11.
32 Aarons, Discussion Document, p. 17.
33 Aarons, Discussion Document.
34 V.I. Lenin, *State and Revolution*, Moscow, 1972, p. 36.
35 R. Gibson, 'Why a Left Coalition', *Discussion Journal*, no. 1, March 1967, p. 89.
36 *Guardian*, 23 February 1956.
37 R. Gibson, *My Years in the Communist Party*, Melbourne, 1966, p. 15.
38 J. Sendy, *The Communist Party; History, Thoughts and Questions*, Melbourne, 1978, p. 28.
39 *Tribune*, 4 April 1972.
40 E. Aarons, 'The Chilean Revolution', *Australian Left Review*, no. 42, December 1973, p. 4.
41 Aarons, 'The Chilean Revolution'.
42 Aarons, 'The Chilean Revolution', p. 7.
43 Aarons, 'The Chilean Revolution', p. 8.
44 E. Aarons, 'The State and Australian Socialism', *Australian Left Review*, no. 63, March 1978, p. 19.
45 Aarons, 'The State and Australian Socialism', p. 18.
46 V.I. Lenin, *State and Revolution*, pp. 8–9.
47 E. Aarons, 'The State and Australian Socialism', p. 20.

CHAPTER 7 Left Turn, Right Turn: the Party in the 1970s

1 Australian Bureau of Statistics.
2 See P. Thomas, *Taming the Concrete Jungle*, Sydney, 1973, pp. 40ff; and J. Mundey, *Green Bans and Beyond*, Melbourne, 1981, pp. 79–117.

ENDNOTES

3   P. Thomas, *Taming the Concrete Jungle*, p. 31. The spelling of the full name of the BLF is exactly as it appears in the original.
4   *CPA Public Statement*, 'De-escalation', April 1967.
5   M. Robertson, 'Conference for Left Action – Report to National Committee', *Discussion*, no. 2, July 1969, p. 34.
6   'National Committee Discussion of Left Action Conference by M. Robertson', *Discussion*, no. 2, July 1969, p. 39.
7   *Tribune*, 30 May 1969.
8   *Tribune*, 19 March 1969.
9   *Tribune*, 1 February 1972.
10   D. Gollan, interview with the author, January 1979.
11   Report by Comrade Mavis Robertson to the Meeting of the National Committee, CPA, held on 11–12 August 1973, duplicated.
12   *Tribune*, 15 January 1972.
13   *Tribune*, 14 January 1970.
14   Sendy, *The Communist Party*, pp. 27–8.
15   *Tribune*, 26 August 1970.
16   *Tribune*, 5–11 June 1973.
17   For example: 'The Harco workers did not win their jobs back, but that was through no fault of their own, nor of the tactic of the work-in. What they did, however, was to popularise the idea of the work-in, at least among militant workers, throughout the country.' D. Freney, 'Workers' Control Perspectives', *Australian Left Review*, no. 39, March 1973, p. 4.
18   Freney, 'Workers' Control Perspectives', p. 3.
19   Freney, 'Workers' Control Perspectives', pp. 3–4.
20   Freney, 'Workers' Control Perspectives', p. 5.
21   Freney, 'Workers' Control Perspectives', p. 4.
22   Freney, 'Workers' Control Perspectives'.
23   B.T. Carey, 'Communists and Other Marxists', *Discussion*, no. 2, June 1968, p. 41.
24   Freney, 'Workers' Control Perspectives', p. 5.
25   CPA Industrial Newsletter, Sydney, June 1971.
26   *The Elections and the Future*, CPA Sydney, 1972.
27   *Tribune*, 18 March 1970.
28   *Tribune*, 29 April 1970.
29   Meredith Burgmann, speaking at the Communists and the Labour Movement conference, Melbourne 1980. Jack Mundey spoke immediately afterwards and put Burgmann's contention neatly in perspective by noting that most NSW BLs were straightforward Labor voters. The tape of both talks is in the Latrobe Library, Melbourne, under the title 'NSW BLF'.

30 Mundey, *Green Bans and Beyond*, p. 120.
31 J. Mundey, 'NSW BLF' (see note 29).
32 *The Battler*, 15 December 1976.
33 *Praxis*, no. 8, March 1976, p. 28.
34 *Tribune*, 15 April 1970.
35 'The Left Challenge for the '70s', in *CPA Documents of the Seventies*, Sydney, n.d., p. 35.
36 T. O'Shaughnessy, 'Arguing About a Strategy for the Seventies; the Rise and Fall of the Left Tendency in the Communist Party of Australia, 1972-80'; a talk given at the Communists and the Labour Movement conference, Melbourne, 1980. Tape in Latrobe Library, Melbourne.
37 W. Higgins, *Reconstructing Australian Communism*, reprinted from the *Socialist Register* as a pamphlet by Queensland CPA, Brisbane, 1975, p. 1.
38 E. Mandel, *Marxist Economic Theory*, London, 1968, was very influential among younger Marxists in Australia in the early 1970s. Mandel's treatment of the USSR is to be found in Chapter 15.
39 O'Shaughnessy, 'Arguing About a Strategy'.
40 O'Shaughnessy, 'Arguing About a Strategy'.
41 W. Higgins, 'Working Class Socialism in Sweden', *Intervention*, no. 13, October 1979, *passim*.
42 Sendy, *Comrades Come Rally*, p. 188.
43 Sendy, *Comrades Come Rally*, pp. 233-4.
44 *Tribune*, 13-19 November 1973.
45 L. Aarons, 'National Secretary's Report to the 25th Congress', *CPA 25th Congress*, Sydney, 1976, p. 7.
46 Australian Bureau of Statistics.
47 *Tribune*, 12 December 1975.
48 Mostly, these have been verbal arguments, but see Max Ogden's comments in an interview entitled 'The La Trobe Valley Power Dispute', *Australian Left Review*, no. 64, May 1978, p. 12. My own account of the dispute, including this aspect, is based on discussions with Alec Kahn, who covered the strike in depth for *The Battler*.
49 *Tribune*, 2 November 1977.
50 *Tribune*, 2 November 1977.
51 *Australia Uprooted*, AMWSU, Sydney, n.d., p. 10.
52 *Australia Uprooted*, p. 11.
53 For an example of this general line of argument, see E. Crough, E.L. Wheelwright and E. Wilshire, *Australia and World Capitalism*, Melbourne, 1980. For a substantial critique of the left nationalist approach to the Australian economy, see R. Kuhn, 'Whose Boom?', *International Socialist*, no. 12, Summer 1981-82, pp. 22-9.
54 *Tribune*, 20-26 February 1973.
55 *Australia Uprooted*, p. 18.

56 *Towards Socialism in Australia.*

57 *Towards Socialism in Australia.*

58 John Boyd, resignation letter from CPA, 1979.

59 A. Anderson, 'The Abortion Struggle in Queensland', *Hecate*, vol. VI, no. ii, 1980, p. 11.

60 All comments from the 'Socialism in the Eighties' session of the Communists and the Labour Movement conference, Melbourne 1980, are on tape under the title 'Socialism in the Eighties' in the Latrobe Library, Melbourne.

61 *Tribune*, 16 December 1981.

62 *Poland: State of Emergency*, Statement by National Officers, Communist Party of Australia, Sydney, December 1981.

CHAPTER 8 Into the Mainstream

1 *Financial Review*, 11 April 1983.

2 *Age*, 28 January 1983.

3 *Age*, 2 February 1983.

4 Australian Bureau of Statistics.

5 *Age*, 1 February 1983.

6 *Tribune*, 27 October 1982.

7 *Tribune*, 13 October 1982.

8 *Tribune*, 4 May 1983.

9 *Tribune*, 20 April 1983.

10 *Socialist Perspectives on Issues for the '80s*, CPA 28th National Congress, 3–4 November 1984, Sydney, n.d.

11 *Financial Review*, 16 September 1983.

12 *Age*, 16 September 1983.

13 *Tribune*, 13 July 1983.

14 *Tribune*, 22 August 1984.

15 *Tribune*, 8 April 1984.

16 *Tribune*, 4 May 1983.

17 *Tribune*, 4 May 1983.

18 In *Marxism Today*, London, December 1984. Quoted in *Socialist Worker Review*, London, February 1985, p. 17.

19 I have discussed feminism's inability to provide a coherent strategic orientation at more length in my 'Behind the Fragments', *International Socialist*, Summer 1981–82; and 'What's Wrong with Disarmament Feminism', *Hecate*, vol. X, no. i, 1984. See also J. Stone, *Perspectives for Women's Liberation*, Redback Press, Melbourne, 1981.

20 *Tribune*, 23 January 1980.

21 *Praxis*, no. 25, April 1982, p. 12.
22 *The Prospects Discussion; Views and Proposals*, CPA, Sydney, 1983, p. 3.
23 *Praxis*, no. 33, p. 38 (my bootlegged photocopy does not have a date).
24 *The Prospects Discussion*, p. 34.
25 *Tribune*, 24 April 1984.
26 *Australian Socialism; a proposal for renewal*, CPA, Sydney, n.d.
27 *Tribune*, 3 July 1968.

Image Credits

NOTE: Every effort has been made to identify the copyright holder of the images published in this book. Should there be any queries or concerns, please contact the publisher.

Acronyms

NLA National Library of Australia
SLNSW State Library of New South Wales
SLQ State Library of Queensland
SLV State Library of Victoria

Front cover, clockwise from upper left:

    Jean Thompson, Belmore Park 1927. ANU Archives

    Vladimir Tatlin's model for Monument to the Third International, known as Tatlin's Tower. Wikimedia Commons

    Lenin speaking with Trotsky at foot of podium 1920. Wikimedia Commons

    Laurie Carmichael addressing a demonstration in support of Clarrie O'Shea, Hyde Park, Sydney, May 1969. SLNSW and Search Foundation

    Robert Menzies at Port Kembla 1938. Australian Trade Union Institute

    Newcastle Waterside Workers' Federation Women's Strike Committee 1956. Still image from Hewers of Coal (WWFFU 1957), courtesy National Film and Sound Archive and Maritime Union of Australia

    Jack Mundey 1972. SLNSW and Search Foundation

    New Left Party launch 1989. SLNSW and Search Foundation

250 INTO THE MAINSTREAM

	Ted Hill meeting with Mao Zedong 1968, China. E. F. Hill website: https://www.efhill.com/photos
Back cover, clockwise from upper left:	
	CPA National Congress 1943. SLNSW and Search Foundation
	CPA headquarters Sydney, c.1950. Jacobin website
	Jock Garden 1920s. Wikimedia Commons
	Abortion march, Sydney, 1974. SLNSW and Search Foundation
	UAW Equal Pay march, early 1960s. Photograph Zillah Lee (courtesy Anne Sgro)
pp. xvi–xvii	Sydney Wharfies Mural from WWF headquarters Sydney, now at the Australian National Maritime Museum, Sydney. More information at: https://www.sea.museum/en/whats-on/exhibitions/wharfies-mural. Reproduced with the kind permission of the ANU Open research repository.
p, 2	Wikimedia Commons
p. 3	Wikimedia Commons
p. 4	Communist International, vol. 1, no. 1, May 1919 at Revolution's Newsstand website
p. 7	SLNSW and Search Foundation
p. 18	Photograph Nikolai Punin 1921. Wikimedia Commons
p, 27, left	Tweed Daily (Murwillumbah) 2 November 1920, p. 3. Trove/NLA
p. 27, right	NLA
p. 31	Photographer unknown. Papers of Marjorie Pizer, SLNSW, MSS7428/1/6
p. 32	State Library of Western Australia
p. 36	NLA
p. 37	Photograph Sam Hood. Sam Hood Photographic Collection, SLNSW
p. 38	Reproduced with the kind permission of the ANU Open research repository.
p. 39	SLV
p. 45, upper	Australian Trade Union Institute
p. 45, lower	Australian Trade Union Institute
p. 47, left	Reason in Revolt website
p. 47, right	ANU Archives Library Exhibition: Reds Under the Bed: 100 Years of Communism in Australia
p. 50	SLNSW and Search Foundation
p. 52	The Daily Telegraph (Sydney) 28 February 1943. Trove/NLA
p. 54	Reason in Revolt website. Reproduced with kind permission of Anne Sgro.
p. 60	Seated left to right: 'Red' Ted Englart, Secretary Brisbane Branch WWF; Max Julius, Barrister and CPA member; Mick Healy, Secretary, Queensland TLC. SLQ
p. 64	SLQ

IMAGE CREDITS   **251**

p. 66, left	ANU Archives Library Exhibition: Reds Under the Bed: 100 Years of Communism in Australia
p. 66, right	Photographer unknown. Collection Anne Sgro, reproduced with her kind permission
p. 70	SLNSW
p. 75, Clockwise from upper left:	
	Miners at Wonthaggi, Victoria, receive strike pay. Reproduced with the kind permission of the ANU Open Research Repository.
	Prime Minister Chifley confronted by miners. Chifley Research Centre
	Striking miners at a meeting organised by the ALP. ANU Archives Library
	Pamphlet by J. D. Blake, Newcastle Morning Herald and Miners' Advocate 1, 1949. Trove/NLA
p. 79	Reproduced with the kind permission of the ANU Open Research Repository.
p. 85	Communist Party of Australia (Collection of election and propaganda leaflets issued by the Communist Party of Australia). Trove/NLA
p. 88	SLNSW and Search Foundation
p. 89	Tribune 26 September 1951, p. 2. Trove/NLA
p. 90	SLNSW and Search Foundation
p. 93	Tribune 7 January 1950, p. 1. Trove/NLA
p. 97	Search Foundation
p. 98	The Canberra Times 25 August 1961, p. 1. Trove/NLA
p. 103	Jacobin website
p. 104	ANU Archives Library
p. 111, upper	Noel Butlin Archives Centre, Australian National University: Australasian Coal and Shale Employees' Federation, Edgar Ross collection, E165-56-10
p. 111, lower	Photographer Zillah Lee. Courtesy of Anne Sgro
p. 112	Still image from Waterside Workers' Federation Film, News No.1 (WWWFFU, 1956). Images courtesy of National Film and Sound Archive and Maritime Union of Australia
p. 115	Tribune 31 October 1956, p. 1. Trove/NLA
p. 121	The Australian Women's Weekly, Front Cover. Trove/NLA
p. 122	Search Foundation Website
p. 131	Collection of Phillip Whitefield
p. 132	Collection of Phillip Whitefield
p. 134	Tribune 28 August 1968, p. 1. Trove/NLA
p. 137	SLNSW and Search Foundation
p. 138	SLNSW and Search Foundation
p. 140	Collection of Phillip Whitefield

p. 151	E. F. Hill website: https://www.efhill.com/photos
p. 154	Collection of Phillip Whitefield
p. 159	SLNSW and Search Foundation
p. 164, left	Reason in Revolt website
p. 164, right	Reason in Revolt website
p. 166	SLNSW and Search Foundation
pp. 170–1	SLNSW and Search Foundation
p. 172	SLNSW and Search Foundation
p. 173	SLNSW and Search Foundation
pp. 176–7	SLNSW and Search Foundation
p. 178, upper	Tribune 30 April 1969, page 1. Trove/NLA
p. 178, lower	Australian Left Review, no. 35, 1972, University of Wollongong Archives Online and Search Foundation
p. 187	SLNSW and Search Foundation
p. 189	SLNSW and Search Foundation
p. 195	Collection of Phillip Whitefield
p. 206	Tribune 16 December 1981, p. 1. Trove/NLA
p. 206	Tribune 24 September 1980, p. 6. Trove/NLA
p. 207	SLNSW and Search Foundation
p. 211	ANU Archives Library
p. 220	SLNSW and Search Foundation
p. 227	SLNSW and Search Foundation
p. 228	Collection of Phillip Whitefield
p. 263	Photograph Janey Stone
p. 265	Photograph Janey Stone
p. 267	Supplied by Padraic Gibson

Further Reading

Works marked with an asterisk (*) are informed by a perspective similar to that of this book.

General

Aarons, Eric, *What's Left? Memoirs of an Australian Communist*, Penguin, 1993.

Birchall, Ian, *Workers Against the Monolith*,* Pluto, 1974. International Communism in the postwar period.

Davidson, Alistair, *The Communist Party of Australia*, Stanford Institution Press, 1969. The closest thing to a standard history, covering 1920–66. Aaronsite politics.

Gibson, Ralph, *My Years in the Communist Party*, International Bookshop, 1966. Memoirs covering 1931–65. Reflects politics of the late Sharkey regime. An enjoyable way to get an overview is to read this and the work by John Sendy.

Humphrys, Elizabeth, *How Labour Built Neoliberalism: the Labour Movement and the Neoliberal Project*,* Brill, 2019.

Sendy, John, *Comrades Come Rally!* Thomas Nelson, 1978. Memoirs covering 1941–74. Taftite politics.

Early history

O'Lincoln, Tom, 'Australia's "Militant Minority Movement"', in T. O'Lincoln, *'The Expropriators are Expropriated' and other writings on Marxism*,*

Interventions, Melbourne, 2016.

Stone, Janey, 'Brazen Hussies and God's police: Fighting back in the Depression Years, in S. Bloodworth and T. O'Lincoln (eds), *Rebel women in Australian Working Class History*,* Interventions, Melbourne, 2022.

Stone, Janey, 'Class struggle on the home front: Women, unions and militancy in the Second World War, in S. Bloodworth and T. O'Lincoln (eds), *Rebel Women in Australian Working Class History*,* Interventions, Melbourne, 2022.

Macintyre, Stuart. *The Reds: The Communist Party of Australia from Origins to Illegality*, Allen & Unwin, 1998.

Postwar history

Aarons, Eric, *Philosophy for an Exploding World*, Brolga Books, 1972. Important theoretical document for the changes in CPA politics after 1966.

Deery, Phillip (ed.), *Labour in Conflict: The 1949 coal strike*, Hale & Iremonger, 1978. Useful information about the 1949 coal strike.

Douglas, Jordon, *Conflict in the unions: The Communist Party of Australia, Politics & the Trade Union Movement, 1945–60*, Resistance, 2013.

Macintyre, Stuart. *The Party: The Communist Party of Australia from Heyday to Reckoning*, Allen & Unwin, 2022.

O'Lincoln, Tom, 'Against the Stream: Women and the Left 1945–1968', in S. Bloodworth and T. O'Lincoln (eds), *Rebel women in Australian working class history*,* Interventions, Melbourne, 2022.

Thomas, Pete, *Taming the Concrete Jungle*, New South Wales Branch of the Australian Building Construction Employees & Builders Laborers' Federation, 1973. The story of the NSW BLF, written at the height of their power.

Culture

Beasley, Jack, *Red Letter Days*, Australasian Book Society, 1979. Studies of Communist and 'progressive' writers.

Devanny, Jean, *Sugar Heaven*, Redback Press, 1982. Novel based on strikes in the North Queensland cane fields in the 1930s.

Ferrier, Carole, *Jean Devanny: Romantic Revolutionary*, Melbourne University Press, 1999.

Lisa Milner (ed.), *The New Theatre: The people, plays and politics behind Australia's radical theatre*, Interventions, 2022.

Theory

Callinicos, Alex, *The revolutionary ideas of Karl Marx*,* Bookmarks, 2010.

Cliff, Tony, *State Capitalism in Russia*,* Haymarket, 2019.

O'Lincoln, Tom, *State Capitalism and Marxist Theory*,* International Socialists, 1985. A short survey.

Index

Aarons, Brian   215, 227
Aarons, Eric   68, 139, 146, 149, 150, 152–8, 160–2, 165–8, 192–3, 196, 221, 224–5, 227
Aarons, Laurie   74, 76, 78, 120–1, 124, 128–30, 136, 138–40, 156, 158, 159, 162, 165, 178, 180, 192-3, 196, 200, 224, 225, 227
Allende, Salvador   165
Amalgamated Engineering Union (AEU)   58–9, 80, 187
Amalgamated Metal Workers and Shipwrights Union (AMWSU)   188–9, 201
Anglo–Soviet Trade Union Committee   7
Arbitration Commission   170, 178, 215
Arbitration Court   42, 62, 65
Arena   127, 131, 132, 140
Armstrong, Sam   198
AUKUS   vi
Austral Bronze   52
Australia Party   186
Australia Uprooted   199, 200
Australian Council of Trade Unions (ACTU)   i, ii, 39, 42, 58, 69, 76, 77, 91, 124, 211, 212, 214, 217
Australian Institute of Political Science   211
Australian Labor Party (ALP)   i, ii, iv, v, vi, vii, xiv, 15, 23–31, 33–5, 41, 43, 58–9, 62, 63, 65, 68, 71–2, 76–8, 83, 84, 87, 90, 92, 98, 99, 106, 108, 116, 122–4, 139, 145, 149, 165, 174-5, 186, 191, 193, 196, 197, 199, 201-2, 204, 206, 211-15, 217–19, 222–4, 226
Australian League for Peace and Democracy   39
Australian Left Review   128, 148, 178

Australian Railways Union   43, 223
Australian Security Intelligence Organisation (ASIO)   132
The Australian Socialist   140
Australian Socialist Party (ASP)   24, 26, 28–9
Australian Workers' Union (AWU)   29, 31, 42, 105

Bacon, Eva   205
Baird, Jim   200
Baker, Jack   176
Ballarat Trades Hall   43
Balmain Trotskyists (*see also* Origlass, Nick)   53, 90
Baracchi, Guido   31
Basic Questions of Communist Theory (Gollan)   115
Beaver, Aileen   189
Beechy, D.   129
Bermingham, Lee   203, 222
BHP   39, 40
Bjelke-Petersen, Joh   204, 205
Black Cargo (Morrison)   94
Blake, Audrey   176
Blake, Jack   42, 62, 72, 75, 78, 97, 100, 104, 105
Bobbin Up (Hewitt)   105
Bordiga, Amadeo   5
Bowling, Peter   xvii
Boyd, John   203, 204
Brook, Steve   208
Brown, J. J.   43
Brown, W. J.   95, 117, 194

Builders Labourers' Federation (BLF)   ii, 126–7, 139, 171, 173, 179, 183, 187–9, 191
Building and Construction Workers' Union   *see* Builders Labourers' Federation

Cain, John   84, 215, 218
Calwell, Arthur   124
Campbell, Beatrix   221
Cannon, James   12
Carey, Brian   185, 229
Carmichael, Laurie   100, 177, 186–8, 214, 217
Carruthers, Linda   229
Casey, R. G.   83
Central Council of Railway Shop Committees   87
Charter of Democratic Rights   132–3, 139
Chiang Kai-shek   6
Chifley, Ben   71, 73, 75, 77, 84, 92, 124
Chile   13, 165, 166, 207
China   6, 15, 20, 21, 40, 113, 119, 121, 124, 139, 149, 150, 152, 175
Churchill, Winston   9, 125
Churchward, Lloyd   129, 135
Clancy, Pat   136, 194, 226, 230
Coal Industry Tribunal   73, 78
Coal Mining Unions' Council (CMUC)   73, 80
Coates, Ken   174
Cockcroft, Pete   223
Cold War   14, 15, 19, 54, 62, 71, 83, 102, 108, 117, 147, 175
Collings, Vi   xvii
Committee for the Defence of Labor Principles and Platform   77
Commonwealth Council   58
The Communist   7
Communist Information Bureau (Cominform)   14, 63
Communist International (Comintern)   v, 2, 4, 5, 8, 11, 14, 27, 28, 29, 34, 35, 36, 41, 90
Communist Party (Marxist–Leninist) (CP(ML))   126
Communist Party of Great Britain (CPGB)   7, 67
Communist Review   90, 118, 128
Conciliation and Arbitration Act   84
Congress for International Cooperation and Disarmament   108
Congress of the Communist Party of the Soviet Union   113, 120
Conlin, Megan   xi
Counihan, Noel   35
Country Party   61
Cranwell, Joe   58
Czechoslovakia   14, 19, 21, 134, 135, 136, 137, 138, 139, 183, 207

D'Aprano, Zelda   94, 176, 179
Daniel, Yuli   135
Danton, Georges   157
Davidson, Alistair   53, 68, 69, 117, 121
Davies, Dave   127
Davis, Lulla   136, 137
De Leon, Daniel   24
Deery, Phillip   78, 80
Democratic Rights Committee   91
Deutscher, Isaac   140, 156, 157, 159
Devanny, Jean   43
Dimitrov, Georgii   8, 36, 38, 129
Dixon, Richard   29, 62, 63, 64, 96, 97, 120, 137
Dixson, Miriam   28
Dubček, Alexander   21, 137
Ducker, John   204
Duncan, Graeme   230
Durbridge, Rob   193, 215, 224

Eastern Bloc   139, 157, 158
Eastern Europe (*see also names of individual countries*)   113, 132, 133, 138, 144, 163
Electricity Commission Combined Union Delegates' Organisation (ECCUDO)   173, 191, 192, 193
Engels, Frederick   162, 167, 219
Engine Drivers and Firemen   61, 188
Essential Services Act   61
Eureka stockade   39
Eureka Youth League   107
Evatt, H. V.   90

Farrell, Frank   29, 30
Federal Arbitration Court   62
Federated Clerks Union   85
Federated Ironworkers Association (FIA)   53, 58, 60, 65, 78, 84, 85, 95
Foenander, Orwell   51
Food Preservers' Union (FPU)   217
France   v, 9, 13, 14, 15, 19, 183, 184
Franco, Francisco   9

INDEX

Franklin Dam   225
Fraser, Malcolm   126, 186, 196, 197, 199, 209, 210, 211, 212, 216
Frazer, Jim   223
Freedom   84
Freney, Denis   140, 177, 183, 184, 185, 206, 208
Friedan, Betty   179
Fryer, Peter   19

Gallagher, F.   73, 78, 80
Gallagher, Norm   187, 188
Garden, Jock   24, 26, 27, 28, 29, 30, 31
Georges, George   204, 205
Germany   v, 2, 4, 5, 8, 11, 19, 36, 40, 49, 50, 220
Gibson, Ralph   38, 62, 71, 72, 76, 77, 87, 126, 164, 194
Glynn, Sonny   xvii
Gollan, Daphne   66, 69, 70, 179
Gollan, Robin   68
Goode, W.T.   26
Gorbachev, Mikhail   xiv
Gould, Bob   177
Graham, Pat   xvii
Gramsci, Antonio   102, 103, 191
Great Britain   v, 6, 9, 13, 49, 67
Greer, Germaine   179, 181
The Guardian   50

Halfpenny, John   188, 197, 198, 206, 207
Hanlon, Ned   71, 84
Harco Steel   174
The Hard Way (Hardy)   93, 102
Hardy, Frank   93, 94, 102
Harris, Nigel   150
Hawke, Bob   i, ii, 197, 212, 213, 214, 215, 216, 218
Hayden, Bill   211, 212
Heagney, Muriel   48
Healy, Evelyn   xvii
Healy, Jim   xvii, 40, 45, 76, 94
Hearn, Ron   148
Hefner, Hugh   181
Heinz   217
Henderson, J. B.   125
Henry Lawson Press   90
Henry, Jack   63, 72, 91, 92, 97, 136
Hewitt, Dorothy   105
Higgins, Winton   190, 193

Hill, Ted   61, 93, 95, 118, 120-2, 124, 126-8, 139, 151, 194, 206
Hitler, Adolf   8, 9, 11, 36, 49
Holding, Clyde   197
Holland, Harry   24
Holloway, E.J.   26
Hollway, Thomas (Premier)   61, 66
Housewives' Association   65
Hughes, Billy   25, 40
Hungary   14, 19, 114, 116, 117

Indochina   9, 15
Industrial Groups/Groupers   69, 70, 77, 85, 95, 108
Industrial Workers of the World (IWW)   23, 28, 29, 39
Institute of Workers' Control   174
International Monetary Fund (IMF)   14
Isaacs, Sir Isaac   40
Italy   13, 14, 15, 19, 20, 127, 220

Jackson, G.E.   120
Japan   2, 39, 40, 51
Jaruzelski, Wojciech   208
Jeffery, Norman   31, 33
Johnson, Frank   126
Johnson, Hewlett   107
Johnston, Craig   51
Jones, Claude   152

Kavanagh, Jack   31-4, 42
Keating, Paul   ii, 217
Kerr, John   196
Khrushchev, Nikita   16, 17, 19, 21, 113, 116, 117, 119, 156, 163
Kisch, Egon   37
Koestler, Arthur   12
Kollontai, Alexandra   219
Korea   15, 107, 113
Kyburz, Rosemary   205

Labor Movement at the Crossroads (Aarons)   124
Labour Party (UK)   9
Lane, William   23
Lang, Dunmore   39
Lang, Jack   35, 71
Lawson, Henry   xvii
League of Nations Unions   37
Left Action Conference   175, 176, 178

Left Tendency   190, 191, 192, 193, 195
Left Wing Communism (Lenin)   124
Left Wing Movement   41
Leichhardt Boy Scouts' Band   57
Lenin, V.I.   1–2, 3, 4–6, 8, 22, 26, 40, 64, 93, 109, 124, 137, 138, 145, 155, 163, 166, 167, 230
Liberal Party   61, 83, 85, 204, 205
Liebknecht, Karl   11
Little, Vic   126
Lowe, Justice   86
Luxemburg, Rosa   11

Macdonald, Alex   60
Malaysia   15
Mandel, Ernest   191
Mann, Tom   24
Manning, Frank   80
Mannix, Daniel   26
Manson, J.   120
Mao Zedong   120, 150, 151, 156
Marat, Jean-Paul   157
'The Marseillaise'   8
Marshall Plan   13
'Marx House'   103
Marx, Karl   1, 2, 12, 24, 64, 137, 144, 145, 155, 162, 219, 230
Masons   107
McConnan, L. J.   83
McPhee, Ian   210
McPhillips, L. J.   78
Medibank   196, 198, 209
Melbourne Chamber of Commerce   64
Melbourne Union Congress   27
Menghetti, Diane   54
Menzies, 'Pig Iron' Bob   45, 83, 84, 85, 87, 88, 91, 92, 107, 108
metal workers   52, 52, 58–60, 70, 71, 186, 187, 191
Metal Workers (unions) (*see also names of individual unions*)   72, 84, 188, 199, 200–1, 210
Miles, J. B.   28, 34, 93, 118
Miles-Sharkey group   34, 36, 38, 42
Militant Minority Movement (MMM)   iv, vii, ix, 41, 42, 43, 44, 46, 47
Militant Women's Groups   46–7
Mill, Ian   206, 207
Miller, Ken   86

Millward, Clem   xvii
miners   30, 42, 43, 72–5, 76–8, 80
Miners' Federation   42, 44, 73, 76, 78, 81, 85
Miners' Women's Auxiliaries   111, 112
Minority Movement (MM)   *see* Militant Minority Movement
Moore, Herbert   34
Moran, Cardinal   23
Morris, William   135
Morrison, John   94
Mortimer, Dulcie   106
Mortimer, Rex   121, 127, 152
Morton, Alma   66
Moss, Jim   114
Movement Against Uranium Mining   223
Movement Against War and Fascism   37
Mundey, Jack   99, 155, 171, 173, 176, 188
Mundey, Judy   207
Murray-Smith, Stephen   116
Myles, Bob   64

Nadel, Dave   177
National Bank   83
New Guard   35
New Housewife   66
New Housewives' Association (NHA)   65, 66, 110
New Left Party   xiv, 227
New Left Party Bulletin   228
New Zealand   28, 120
New Zealand Labor Party   28
Nixon, Merv   225
North Atlantic Treaty Organisation (NATO)   20
North Australian Workers' Union   vi
NSW Trades and Labor Council   42, 204

O'Shaughnessy, Terry   190–2
O'Shea, Clarrie   85, 126, 170–2
Origin of the Family (Engels)   219
Origlass, Nick (*see also* Balmain Trotskyists)   53, 90
Ormonde, Peter   217
Orr, Bill   43, 44

Pablo, Michel   140
Palmer, Helen   116
Pankhurst, Adela   46
Pankhurst, Sylvia   5
Pannekoek, Anton   5

INDEX

Paris Commune   162
Parkes, Henry   39
Parkinson, Bill   78
Party of the Working Class (Aarons)   128
Pastoral Workers' Union   42
Paterson, Fred   60, 83
People for Nuclear Disarmament   223
Philosophy for an Exploding World
   (Aarons)   153, 154
Poland   14, 19, 158, 203, 207, 208
Popular Front   vii, 8, 11, 36, 37, 44, 48, 123,
   163
Portugal   192
Power Without Glory (Hardy)   102
Prices and Incomes Accord (ALP–ACTU
   Accord)   i, ii, iii, vi, 211, 212–16, 218

Qantas   188

Rakosi–Gero regime   116
Ransome, Arthur   26
Red International of Labor Unions   42
Red Leader   42–4
Reed, John   26
Reich, Wilhelm   219
Returned and Services League of Australia
   (RSL)   87
Revolutionary Socialist Alliance   178
Robertson, Eddie   121
Robertson, George   113
Robertson, Mavis   179
Robins, Colonel   26
Rodgers, John   87
Romania   14, 19, 21
Rosmer, Alfred   8
Ross, Edgar   78
Ross, W. J.   109
Rowe, 'Red' Ted   43, 58, 60, 96
Russia (*see also* USSR)   iii, iv, 4, 5, 6, 7, 10, 14,
   16, 22, 41, 49, 54, 62, 110, 124, 137, 143,
   144, 150, 167, 175, 192, 220
Ryan, Jack   33

Salmon, Malcolm   136
Santamaria, B.A.   84, 85
Sawyer, Ralph   xvii
Scullin, James   71
seamen   60, 112
Seamen's Union   30, 61, 101, 204, 223

Sendy, John   91, 114, 117, 122, 126, 127, 128,
   131, 164, 180, 194, 195, 206
Seventh Congress (Comintern 1935)   36
Shannan, Mick   105
Sharkey, Lance   34, 36, 50, 63, 65, 86, 93, 94,
   97, 104, 117, 120, 121, 125, 127, 128, 139,
   147
Sharpley, Cecil   86
Shaw, David   188
Shaw, Rod   xvii
Sino–Soviet split   108, 128, 144
Sinyavski, Andrei   135
Slater, Joyce   189
Snowden, Philip   125
Socialist Forum   xiv, 226
Socialist Labor Party (SLP)   24, 26, 46
Socialist League   24
Socialist Party of Australia (SPA)   139, 192,
   225
Socialist Register   190
The Socialist Sixth of the World (Johnson)   107
Solidarity (Poland)   207, 208
Soviet Union   *see* Russia *and* USSR
Spain   xvii, 9, 165
Stalin, Joseph   v, 6, 7, 9, 10, 14, 17, 21–2, 33,
   40, 62, 94, 113–17, 119, 121, 143, 144, 149,
   156–8, 160
Stalin–Hitler pact   37, 49
Staples, Jim   116
The State and Australian Socialism
   (Aarons)   166
State and Revolution (Lenin)   26, 164, 168
State Electricity Commission (SEC)   99, 198
Stevens, Joyce   219, 220, 221, 222, 224, 227
Street, Jessie   52
Sugar Heaven (Devanny)   43
Syme, Jock   193
Syson, Ian   xi

Taft, Bernie   121, 127, 137, 138, 148, 159, 194,
   195, 197, 198, 206, 223, 224, 226
Taft, Mark   207, 223
Tatlin, Vladimir   18
Telecom   209
Ten Days that Shook the World (Reed)   26
Third Period   34, 36, 43, 46, 119
Thorez, Maurice   8, 13
Thornton, Ernie   58, 65, 94
Throssel, Hugo   26

Tito, Josip Broz   14, 15, 159
Togliatti, Palmiro   13, 15, 19
Topham, Tony   174
Trade Union News   61
Trades and Labour Council (TLC)   24, 31
Trades Union Congress (UK) (TUC)   7
Tramways Union   126
Transport Workers' Act   39, 45
Tribune   x, 57, 66, 69, 89, 90, 92, 93, 115, 134, 135, 136, 178, 179, 181, 189, 195, 197, 199, 206, 208, 215, 217, 218, 226, 230
Trotsky, Leon   xiii, 1, 3, 6, 12, 20, 40, 156, 157, 159
Truman, Harry S.   13
Turner, Ian   116

The Unbending (Waten)   23
Union of Australian Women (UAW)   109, 110, 111, 112
United Communist Party of Australia   29
United Front Against Fascism   8, 36
United Kingdom   *see* Great Britain
United Nations (UN)   54, 108
Uren, Tom   204
USA   v, vi, 13, 19, 49, 54
USSR (*see also* Russia)   v, xiv, 9, 13, 21, 40, 49, 51, 121, 123, 132, 136, 138, 156, 161, 162, 191, 195, 207

Varga, Eugen   64
Victorian Socialist Party   24, 46
Vienna Peace Appeal   109
Vietnam   15, 108, 113, 140, 169, 174, 175
Vietnam Moratoriums   183
Vietnamese National Liberation Front   175, 178
Vyshinskii, Andrei   108

War – What For?   39
Waten, Judah   23
waterside workers   xvii, 32, 39, 40, 42, 45, 60, 64, 76, 79, 94, 112
Waterside Workers' Federation (WWF)   xvii, 39, 85, 112, 112
Watt, Alf   135
Wells, H.G.   135
Werth, Alexander   161
wharfies   *see* waterside workers
Whitlam, Gough   190, 191, 196, 209, 211, 214
Wicks, Harry   34

Wilcox, V.G.   120
Williams, Idris   76, 78
Williams, Rhys   26
Williams, Vic   iii, xi, xiv, 91, 96, 99, 105, 106, 125, 126
Willis, A.C.   30
Wilson, Roger   223
Woman Today   48
The Woman Worker   46, 47
Woman's Road to Freedom   47
Women in Australia, From Factory, Farm and Kitchen   47
Women In Our New World   54, 55
Women's Action Committee   179
Women's Electoral Lobby   202
Women's Employment Board (WEB)   52, 53
Women's Progress Club of Townsville   48
Workers' Control Conference   182
Workers' Weekly   30, 38
The Working Woman   46, 47, 48
World Peace   39
World Peace Council   107
World War I   xvii, 3, 11, 23, 25, 46, 220
World War II   xvii, ix, 9, 40, 41, 49, 51, 57, 114, 146, 163
Wright, Tom   70

Youth and Students Working Group   180
Yugoslavia   14, 21, 114

Tom O'Lincoln Legacy Project

Tom O'Lincoln, 1980s.

Tom O'Lincoln was born in California in 1947. He grew up in Walnut Creek, east of San Francisco, and attended the University of California, Berkeley. His experiences as an exchange student at the University of Göttingen in Germany in 1967–68 had a major impact on the direction of his life. Tom was radicalised and became an activist and a Marxist. In late 1969, he joined the Berkeley branch of the International Socialists (I.S.). In 1971, together with Janey Stone, he came to Australia. In 1972, he became involved in revolutionary politics in this country, a commitment that lasted all his life.

Starting with the small grouping, the Marxist Workers Group, which became Socialist Workers' Action Group at the end of 1972, Tom was a leader and member of various formations which carried through the I.S. tradition, finally joining Socialist Alternative in 2003. Tom was an activist in many political movements and an active trade unionist as a teacher and in the public service.

Always a keen traveller, Tom witnessed major struggles in Germany, Portugal and Indonesia; he engaged with socialists and activists in countries as far apart as Nicaragua, Peru, Lebanon, Poland, South Korea and the Philippines. He corresponded with, and met, leading socialists in the UK, the USA, Germany and elsewhere. His language skills enhanced this experience – Tom could conduct political discussions in German, Russian, Spanish (with some excursions into Portuguese, French and Croation) and, later in life, Indonesian.

Tom was a prolific writer. He wrote extensively for left-wing newspapers, magazines and websites, including his own website, which he managed for many years. Tom also translated political material into Indonesian and helped to run an Indonesian language website for 10 years.

Tom's political interests were always very wide. Having settled here, he made Australia his focus. He published books on Australian history, Australian imperialism, the Communist Party of Australia, the left and social struggles. He contributed works on many international topics, with Indonesia being a special interest during the 1990s. He also wrote on Marxist theory and economics, Stalinism and other theoretical subjects. A list of all Tom's longer works is included in his book *'The Expropriators are Expropriated'* (Interventions 2016).

Unfortunately, following a diagnosis of Parkinson's disease in 2012, Tom found it increasingly difficult to continue the creative process. He published the last two of his books with help from others. Subsequently, Tom lived in an aged care facility for several years, where he continued his interest in current events and the development of politics in the world. He died on 13 October 2023.

Tom's long-time comrades have written moving obituaries about him and his contribution:

Mick Armstrong	redflag.org.au/article/tom-olincoln-political-life
Janey Stone	redflag.org.au/article/vale-tom-olincoln-life-worth-living
Ian Rintoul	solidarity.net.au/highlights/vale-tom-olincoln

Tom's writings are in the process of being uploaded to Marxist Internet Archives. The aim is to source and upload as much of his work as possible, so that it is available for all and free to access. This will include not only well-known pamphlets and articles, but also many items unavailable for a long time. See www.marxists.org/archive/olincoln/index.htm.

Some of Tom's books were published with the help of Vulgar Press. Generally, although various imprints were named, they were effectively self-published, mostly with funds from the Jeff Goldhar Project. When Interventions was set up in 2015 as an independent, not-for-profit radical publisher, we took over Tom's backlist.

All the books prior to 2015 were published conventionally, with print runs determined by finances at the time. This led to variable stock levels, not helped by the failure of the main distributor and the disappearance of some stock. As several titles became out of print, Interventions initiated a project of publishing new editions of all Tom's major works, with new design, illustrations and new contextual essays or prefaces. Importantly, these titles are added to print-on-demand services, ensuring that these political ideas will always be accessible. The content of Tom's books has stood the test of time. His is a literary legacy worth preserving and extending to new audiences.

Tom O'Lincoln at the launch of first edition of *United We Stand* in 2005.

The books that constitute this project are:

1985, 2009, 2025	*Into the Mainstream: The Decline of Australian Communism*
1993, 2023	*Years of Rage: Social Conflicts in the Fraser Era*
1998, 2008, 2022	*Rebel Women in Australian Working Class History* (co-edited with Sandra Bloodworth)
2005, 2024	*United We Stand: Class Struggle in Colonial Australia*
2011, 2025	*Australia's Pacific War: Challenging a National Myth*
2014, 2021	*The Neighbour from Hell: Two Centuries of Australian Imperialism*
2016	*'The Expropriators are Expropriated' and other writings on Marxism*
2017	*The Highway is for Gamblers: a Political Memoir*

The final work in this list, Tom's political biography, was brought unaltered into print on demand in 2023. With the present work, *Into the Mainstream*, and *Australia's Pacific War,* planned to be released later in 2025, the project will come to its conclusion.

There are no plans at present to re-issue *The Expropriators are Expropriated*, because it is an anthology, and the contents are expected to be available on Marxist Internet Archive.

Tom was an activist, a revolutionary socialist and a Marxist his whole adult life. In his political memoir, *The Highway is for Gamblers* (Interventions 2017), he writes:

> I have been a Marxist for half a century. In that time I have participated in and been witness to great struggles and momentous historical events. I've had the privilege of standing shoulder to shoulder with selfless fighters around the world. Those events and the people involved only confirmed in my mind that human liberation can be won through the mass struggles of the working class.

Tom then asks the question, 'Why be a revolutionary socialist today?' His answer? 'It's a life worth living'. We at Interventions want to keep this legacy alive.

Padraic Gibson

Padraic (Paddy) Gibson is a historian at the Jumbunna Institute for Indigenous Education and Research, University of Technology Sydney. Paddy is an active socialist and trade unionist. He co-edits Solidarity magazine and has organised protest movements in Sydney for two decades. In 2021, Paddy completed his PhD thesis on the Communist Party of Australia and struggles for Aboriginal rights from 1920-1934. He is currently working on a post-doctoral project continuing this research into the relationship between socialists, trade unionists and Aboriginal people and struggle in the 20th Century.

About Interventions

Interventions is an independent, not-for-profit, incorporated publisher. We publish left-wing, radical and socialist books by Australian authors. We welcome books which, for political or financial reasons, are unlikely to be accepted by commercial publishers. Our books cover a wide range of topics, including labour history, left-wing politics, radical cultural themes, socialism and Marxism, memoirs and works about resistance to racism, sexism and all other forms of oppression.

At Interventions, we believe that radical ideas matter. We want our books to be part of the development of a critical and engaged Australian left.

By highlighting alternative voices, especially those who have been pushed to the margins, we hope to contribute to a greater insight and awareness of the injustices that exist in society and the many efforts at the grassroots to right these wrongs.

We welcome publishing proposals. If you are interested in submitting a proposal, please check out the information for authors on our website, interventions.org.au/forauthors. If you think that your proposal fits our guidelines, please follow the submission process outlined there. Please note that we are not currently publishing poetry or fiction.

Interventions has no independent source of income and is committed to keeping prices affordable. As bookshops and warehouses close around the world, our future hangs in the balance. By supporting us, you will help us keep radical ideas alive and accessible to all. If you would like to support radical publishing in Australia, please consider supporting us with a donation. Visit our website for further information as to how to do this.

Website   interventions.org.au
Contact us   info@interventions.org.au or use the contact form on the website.

About this Book

Janey Stone was Interventions editor and production project manager for this book with assistance from Phillip Whitefield and Stephanie Grigg. Tess Lee Ack edited the text of the 2nd edition in preparation for this edition. Images were sourced and selected by Phillip Whitefield, Janey Stone and Stephanie Grigg. Janey Stone, Tess Lee Ack and Phillip Whitefield assisted with proof reading.

The cover and interior of this book was designed by Stephanie Grigg. Stephanie is a graphic designer based in Melbourne. She recently made the jump to book design after many years of magazine, website and event design.

This book was copy edited by Eris Harrison of Effective Editing.

OTHER BOOKS BY TOM O'LINCOLN

The Highway is for Gamblers: A political memoir
Introduction by Janey Stone

A moving political memoir that is a testament to a life worth living, in the ranks of those fighting for human liberation. It captures the rich political history of the past six decades, written with a pen that burns with indignation against oppression. This is not a nostalgic memoir of reminiscence, but an insight for the activists of tomorrow who hope to change the world.

The Neighbour from Hell: Two centuries of Australian imperialism

This book offers an original study of Australia's "boutique imperialism". Far from being servile and passive agents of the United States and Great Britain, Australia's rulers callously seek to extract maximum benefits from calculated interventions in the global capitalist system.

United We Stand: Class struggle in colonial Australia

Australian workers were organising well before the gold rushes, and later a mass labour movement confronted the employers across the continent, opening the way for bitter confrontations.
'A vivid and immensely readable account ... (and) an important contribution that shows how worker organisation and resistance shaped the country and one that incorporates race and gender dimensions in a nuanced way.'
– *Michael Quinlan Michael Quinlan, Emeritus Professor, University of New South Wales*

OTHER BOOKS BY TOM O'LINCOLN

Rebel Women in Australian Working Class History
Edited, with Sandra Bloodworth

Strikes and demonstrations throughout the 20th century shatter traditional images of women as passive victims. From the women of Broken Hill, who fought strike-breakers with axes and broom handles in the early part of the century through the 1930s Depression and World War II to the postwar period, women played an important role in working class action. These women fought their oppression alongside working men, as participants in - and leaders of - the class struggle.

'The Expropriators are Expropriated' and other writings on Marxism
Edited by Janey Stone, introduced by Rick Kuhn

This book is an anthology of nine short articles written over a 30 year period. It includes five popular presentations of basic Marxist theory and two articles on the topic of the nature of the system in Russia and state capitalism. The other two chapters are on trade unionism – one on the development of the Marxist theory of trade unions from Marx to the Communist International and the other outlines the history of the Communist-led Minority Movement in Australia during the early 1930s.

Years of Rage: Social conflicts in the Fraser era

The 1970s were indeed, years of rage. A furnace of social conflict forged a resistance to the Fraser regime, on multiple fronts. At times, the temperature was white hot. The actions of organized workers were pivotal, along with the social movements against oppression, war, and environmental ruin. Tom O'Lincoln's book, written in 1993, explains why neither capital nor labour were victors. The social temperature may have cooled since Fraser's time, but the outcomes of the stalemate are enduring.

www.ingramcontent.com/pod-product-compliance
Lightning Source LLC
Chambersburg PA
CBHW071956290426
44109CB00018B/2041